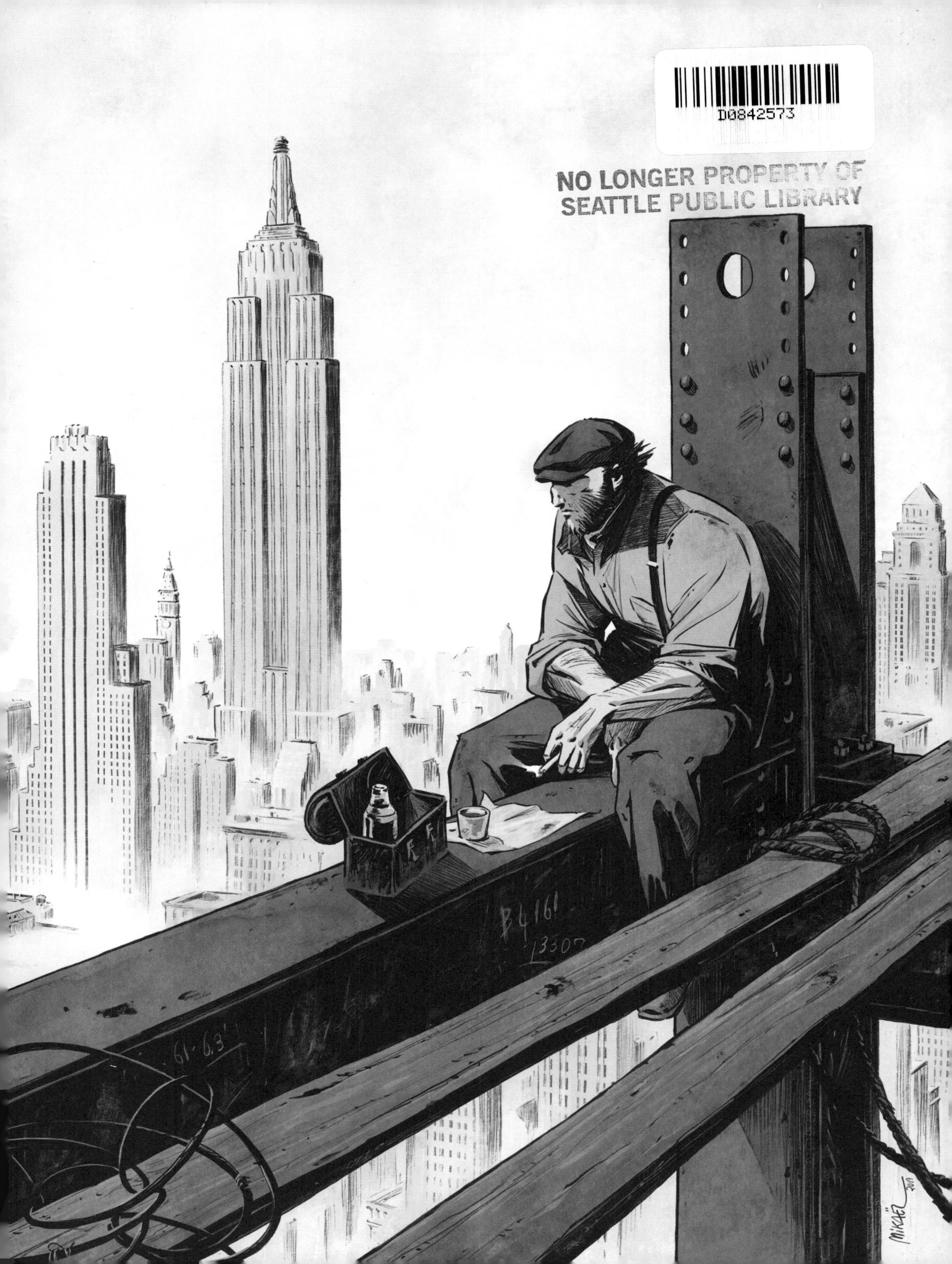

MIKAËL
GIANT

GRAPHIC NOVELS

Thanks to Yves Schlirf, Valérie Beniest, and the whole team at Dargaud.

Thanks to Jean-Louis Tripp, Michel Falardeau, Émilie Dilhac, Jean-Luc Cornette, Tristan Roulot, Thierry Lamy, Line Bélanger, Marco Duchêne, Christel Rober, and Francesca Carpentier.

Thanks to the guys at "La Shop à Bulles" studio in Quebec: Djief, Richard Vallerand, and Paul Bordeleau.

Thanks to Caroline Dufresne from the Quebec Government Office in New York and to Christine Roussel of the Rockefeller Archive Center.

Dedicated to my three favorite immigrants: Séverine, Thomas, and Salomé.

M.

ISBN 9781681122533
© 2018 Dargaud-Benelux
© 2020 NBM for the English translation
Originally published in French as Giant, vols. 1 & 2
Library of Congress Control Number 2020930239
Translation by Matt Maden
Lettering by Calix Ltd.
Printed in Malaysia

This graphic novel is also available as an e-book, ISBN 9781681122540

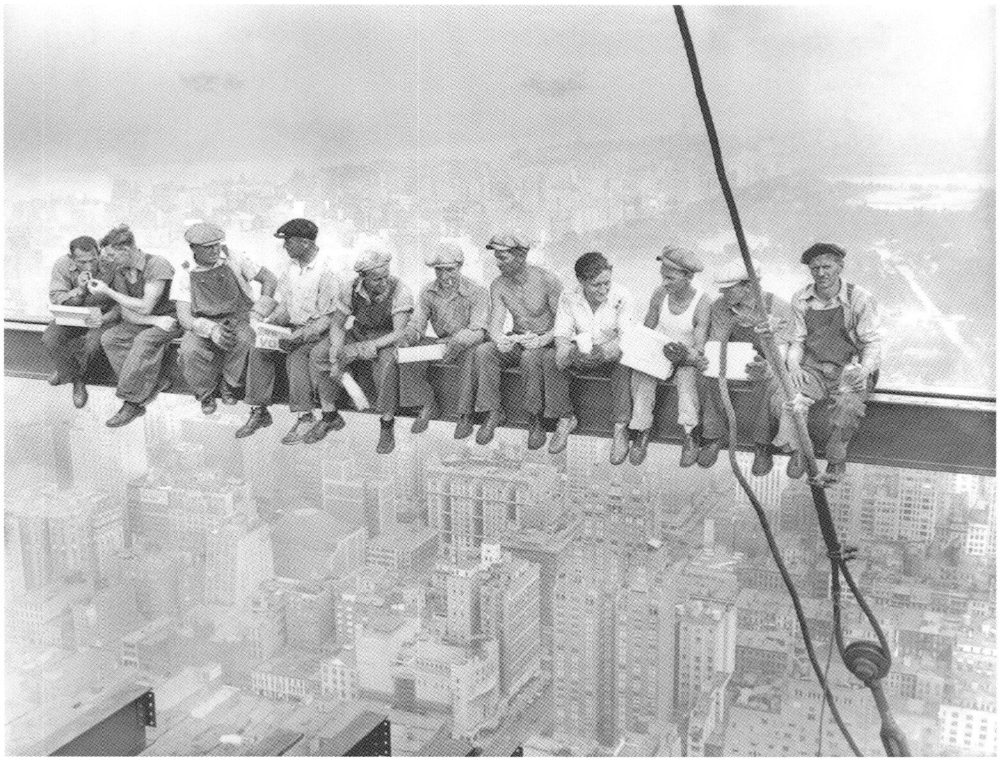
© Contributor/Bettmann/Getty Images

While Régis Loisel and I were working on the script for *Magasin Général* (General Store), we worked at a desk in a corner of our studio which overlooked Davaar street in Montreal. Above the desk was a poster of the incredibly famous photo showing a group of workers sitting on an I-beam hanging over the void. ● This photo was originally attributed to Charles Clyde Ebbets and later to Lewis Hine, but in the end no one is sure who took it. We also don't know who any of the workers on the I-beam are except for two of them: Joseph Eckner (third from the left) and Joe Curtis (third from the right).● Looking at this image, the imagination reels. Who are these guys? Where do they come from? Where did they find the courage to traipse about at such dizzying heights? What could their lives have been like? People often mention the Mohawk workers who supposedly don't have the vertigo chromosome, but the guys in the photo don't look like American Indians... Anyway. ● Around the same time (not of the photo; the time when Régis and I were writing under the photo), I met Mikaël at the Quebec Book Fair. In between gusts of wet snow, he gave me a comic for young children that he had just finished. I gave it a glance out of curiosity and, to my great surprise, I was immediately transported by the story (it was for little kids, honestly!). ● I really like being told a good story. And having it told well. And Mikaël knows how to do that. Well. From the first page of *Giant* we are immersed in the New York of the Great Depression with colorful but believable characters and spot-on dialogue. And we get to learn about the fascinating world of the men who built skyscrapers like the one in that anonymous photo, the one that sparked my imagination... Well, it's true that the photographer may have been anonymous, but not the person who commissioned the photograph. We know that it was a publicity assignment... for none other than the Rockefeller Center! Enjoy!

Jean-Louis Tripp

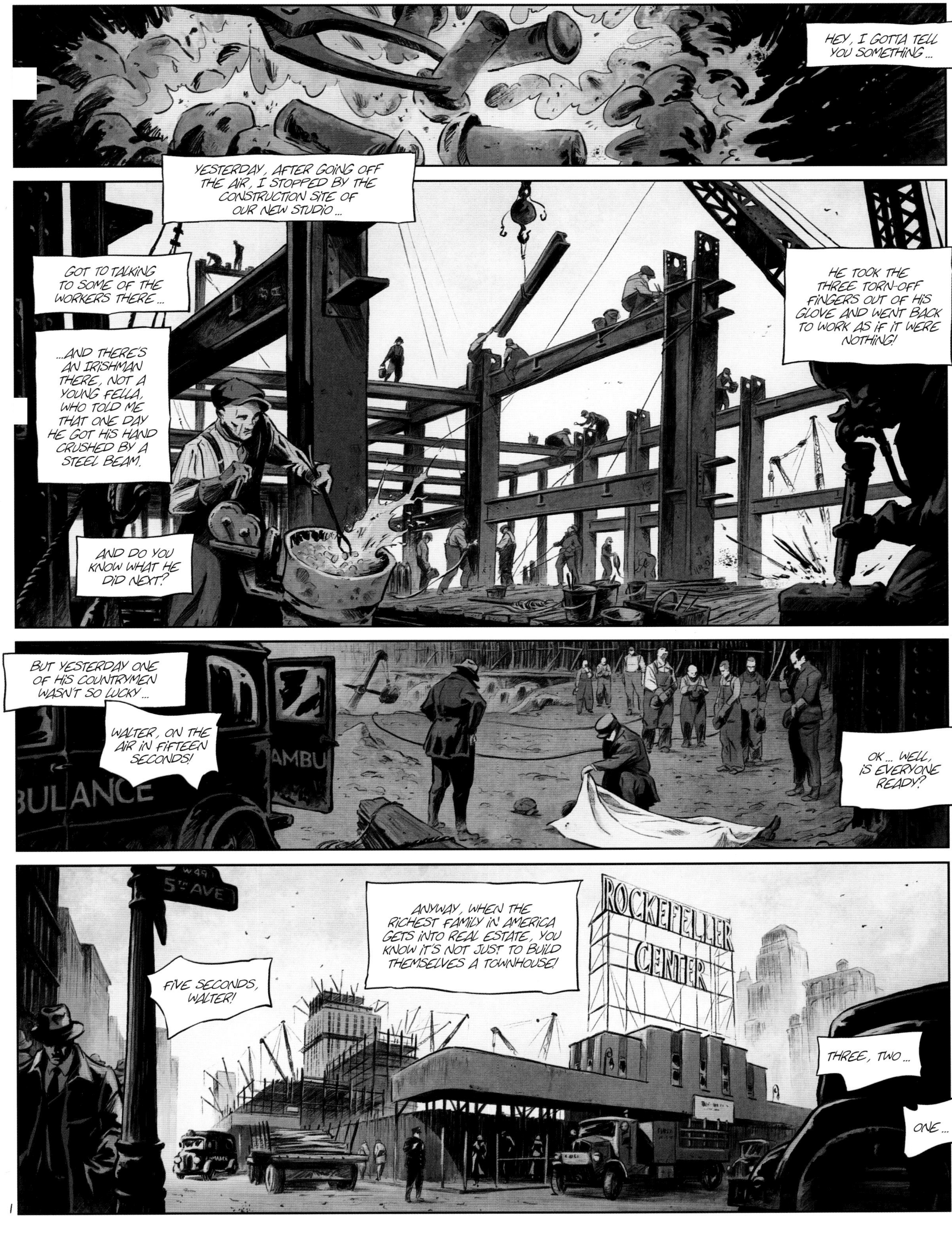
HEY, I GOTTA TELL YOU SOMETHING...
YESTERDAY, AFTER GOING OFF THE AIR, I STOPPED BY THE CONSTRUCTION SITE OF OUR NEW STUDIO...
GOT TO TALKING TO SOME OF THE WORKERS THERE...
...AND THERE'S AN IRISHMAN THERE, NOT A YOUNG FELLA, WHO TOLD ME THAT ONE DAY HE GOT HIS HAND CRUSHED BY A STEEL BEAM.
AND DO YOU KNOW WHAT HE DID NEXT?
HE TOOK THE THREE TORN-OFF FINGERS OUT OF HIS GLOVE AND WENT BACK TO WORK AS IF IT WERE NOTHING!
BUT YESTERDAY ONE OF HIS COUNTRYMEN WASN'T SO LUCKY...
WALTER, ON THE AIR IN FIFTEEN SECONDS!
AMBU
BULANCE
OK... WELL, IS EVERYONE READY?
5TH AVE
ANYWAY, WHEN THE RICHEST FAMILY IN AMERICA GETS INTO REAL ESTATE, YOU KNOW IT'S NOT JUST TO BUILD THEMSELVES A TOWNHOUSE!
ROCKEFELLER CENTER
FIVE SECONDS, WALTER!
THREE, TWO...
ONE...

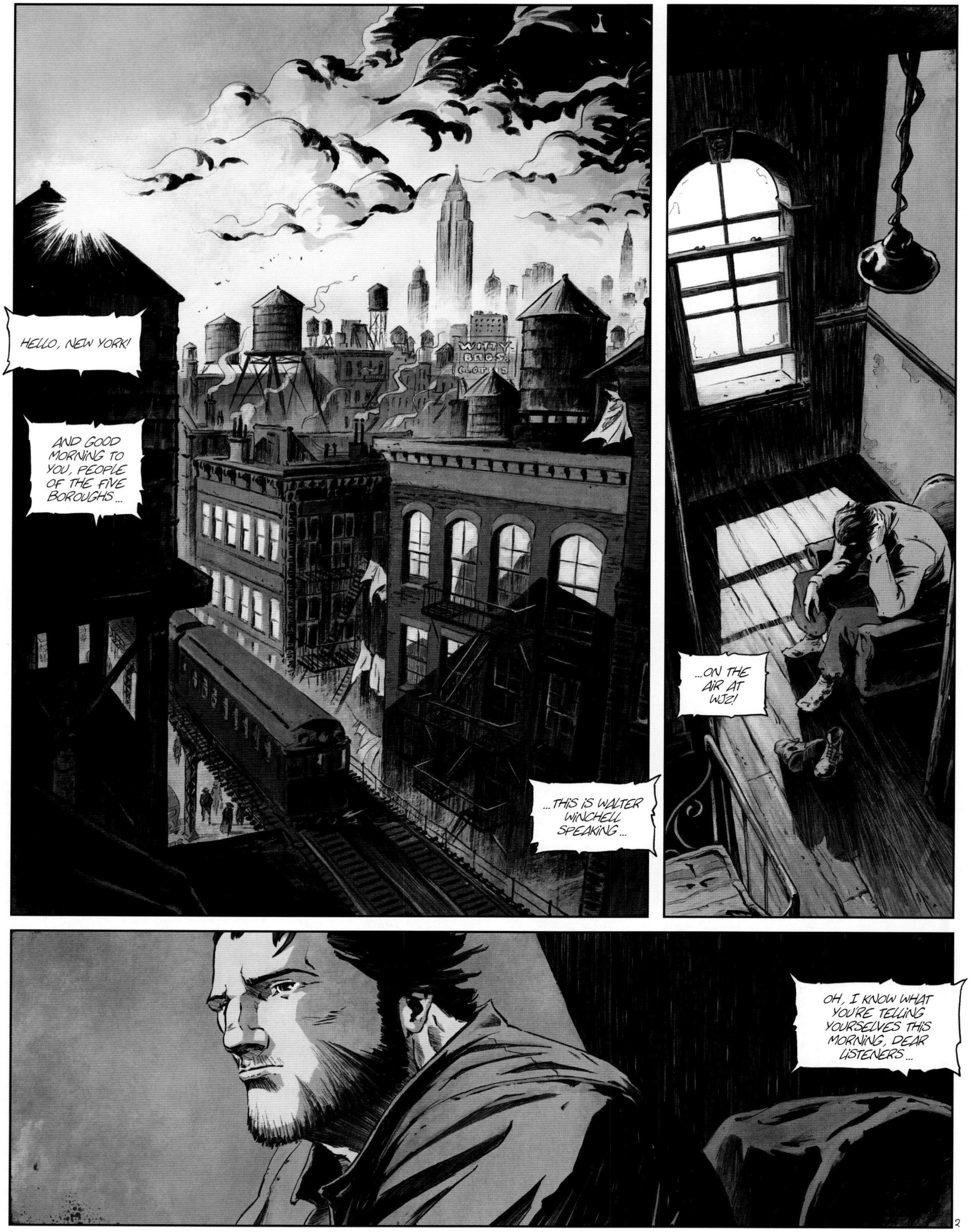
HELLO, NEW YORK!
AND GOOD MORNING TO YOU, PEOPLE OF THE FIVE BOROUGHS...
WITTY BROS. CLOTHS
...THIS IS WALTER WINCHELL SPEAKING...
...ON THE AIR AT WJZ!
OH, I KNOW WHAT YOU'RE TELLING YOURSELVES THIS MORNING, DEAR LISTENERS...

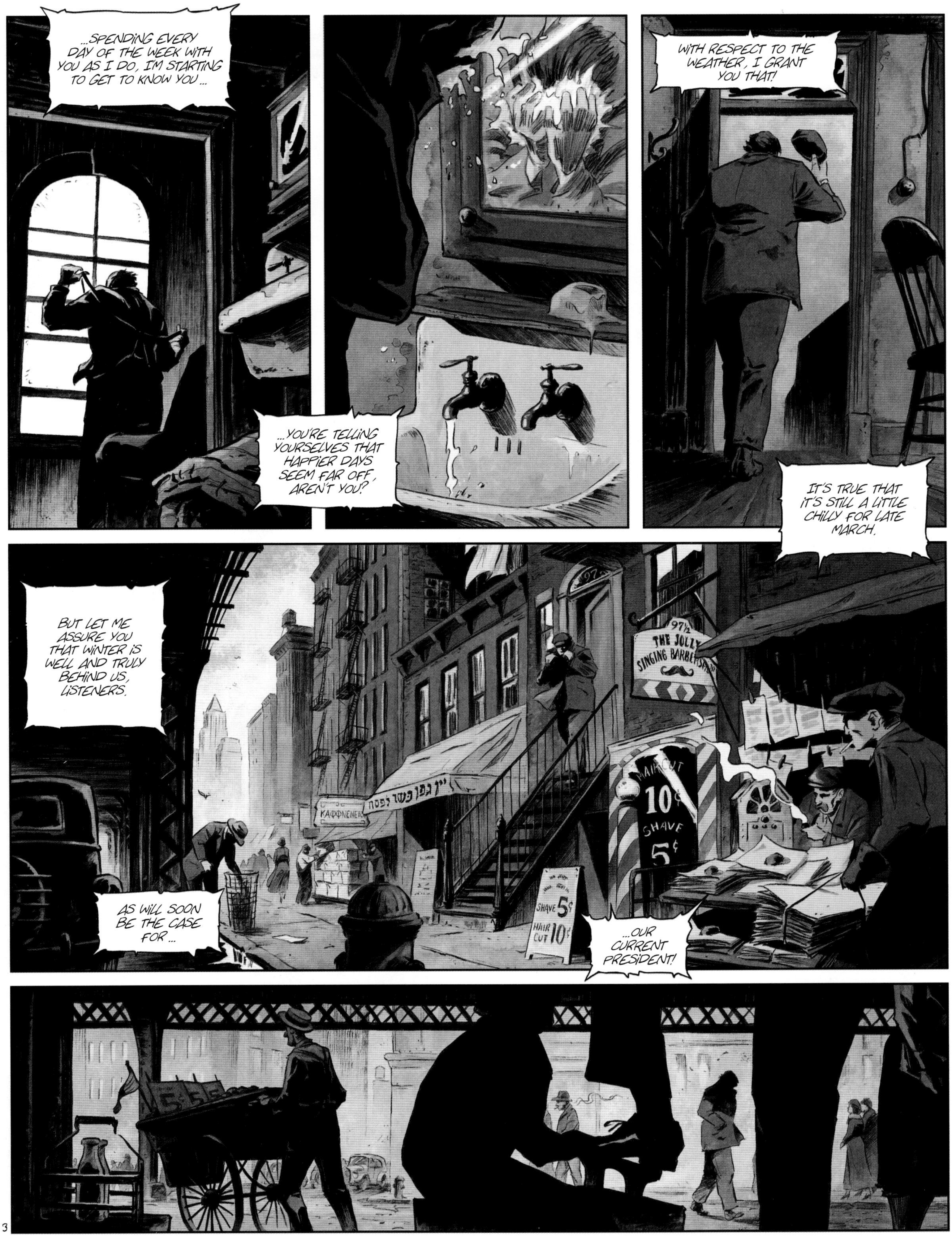
...SPENDING EVERY DAY OF THE WEEK WITH YOU AS I DO, I'M STARTING TO GET TO KNOW YOU ...
...YOU'RE TELLING YOURSELVES THAT HAPPIER DAYS SEEM FAR OFF, AREN'T YOU?
WITH RESPECT TO THE WEATHER, I GRANT YOU THAT!
IT'S TRUE THAT IT'S STILL A LITTLE CHILLY FOR LATE MARCH.
BUT LET ME ASSURE YOU THAT WINTER IS WELL AND TRULY BEHIND US, LISTENERS.
HAIRCUT 10¢ SHAVE 5¢
SHAVE 5¢ HAIR CUT 10¢
AS WILL SOON BE THE CASE FOR ...
...OUR CURRENT PRESIDENT!

3

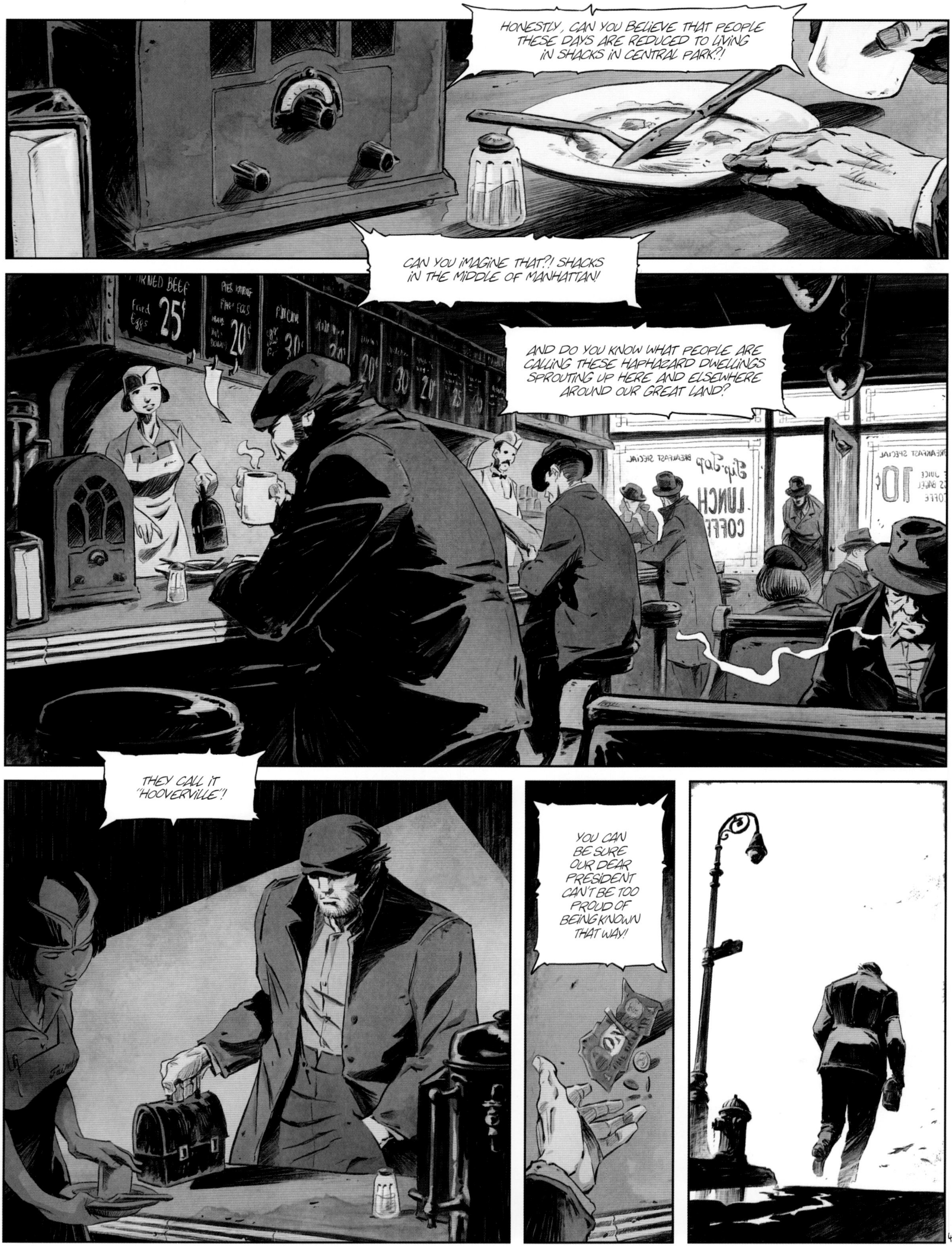
HONESTLY, CAN YOU BELIEVE THAT PEOPLE THESE DAYS ARE REDUCED TO LIVING IN SHACKS IN CENTRAL PARK?!
CAN YOU IMAGINE THAT?! SHACKS IN THE MIDDLE OF MANHATTAN!
AND DO YOU KNOW WHAT PEOPLE ARE CALLING THESE HAPHAZARD DWELLINGS SPROUTING UP HERE AND ELSEWHERE AROUND OUR GREAT LAND?
LUNCH
THEY CALL IT "HOOVERVILLE"!
YOU CAN BE SURE OUR DEAR PRESIDENT CAN'T BE TOO PROUD OF BEING KNOWN THAT WAY!

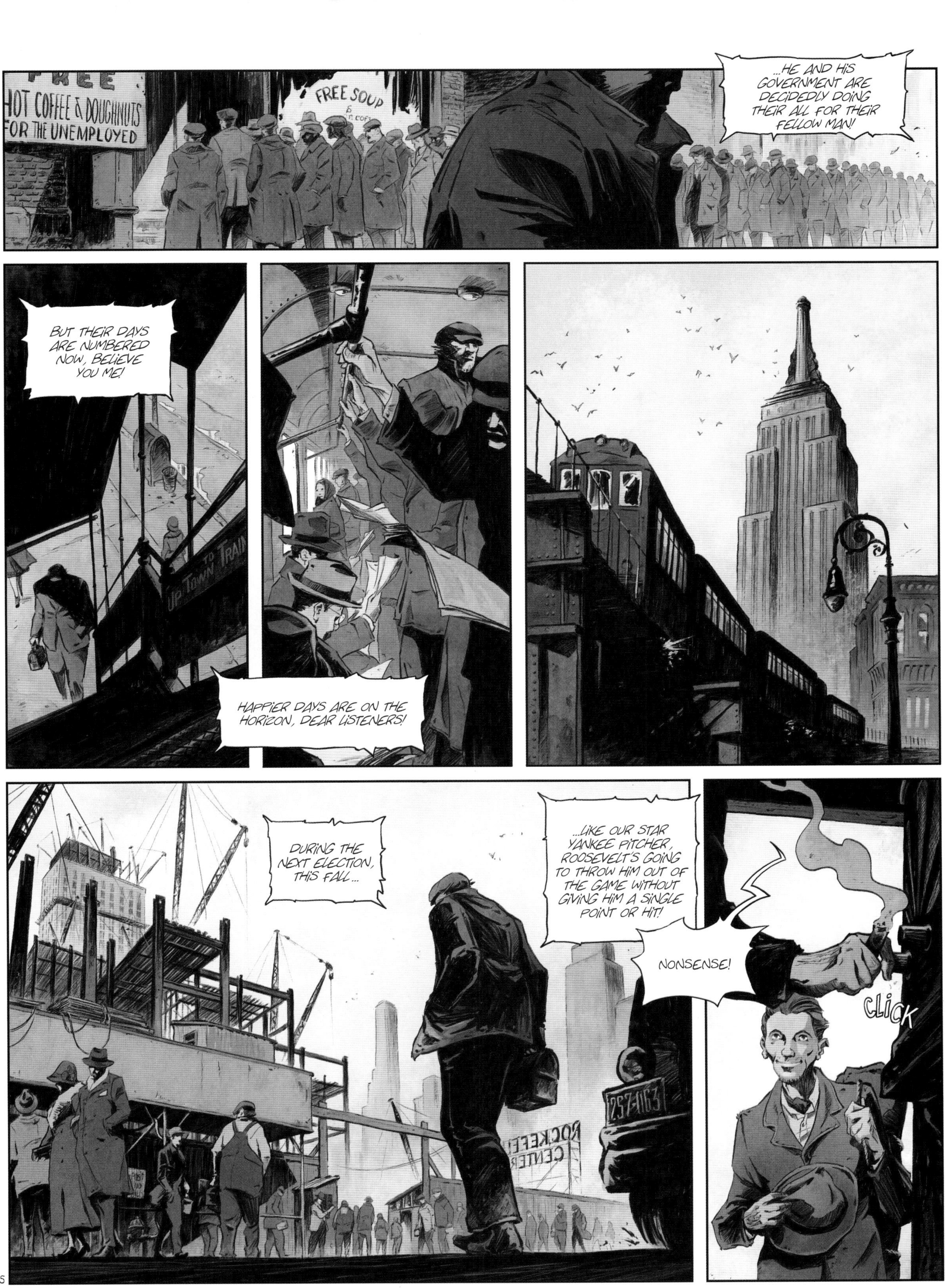

FREE
HOT COFFEE & DOUGHNUTS FOR THE UNEMPLOYED
FREE SOUP
...HE AND HIS GOVERNMENT ARE DECIDEDLY DOING THEIR ALL FOR THEIR FELLOW MAN!
BUT THEIR DAYS ARE NUMBERED NOW, BELIEVE YOU ME!
UP TOWN TRAIN
HAPPIER DAYS ARE ON THE HORIZON, DEAR LISTENERS!
DURING THE NEXT ELECTION, THIS FALL...
...LIKE OUR STAR YANKEE PITCHER, ROOSEVELT'S GOING TO THROW HIM OUT OF THE GAME WITHOUT GIVING HIM A SINGLE POINT OR HIT!
NONSENSE!
CLICK
257-1163

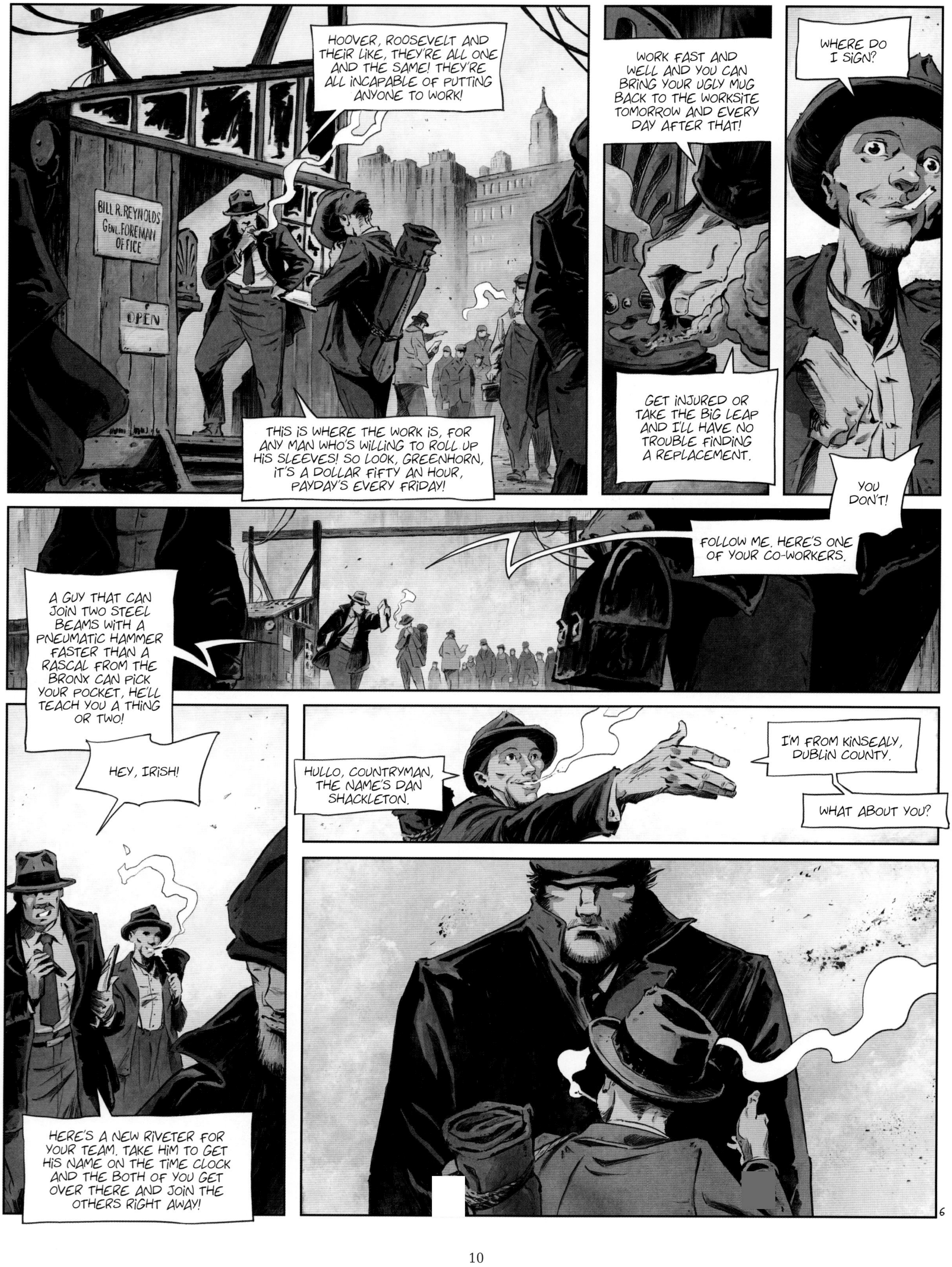
HOOVER, ROOSEVELT AND THEIR LIKE, THEY'RE ALL ONE AND THE SAME! THEY'RE ALL INCAPABLE OF PUTTING ANYONE TO WORK!
BILL R. REYNOLDS GENL. FOREMAN OFFICE
OPEN
THIS IS WHERE THE WORK IS, FOR ANY MAN WHO'S WILLING TO ROLL UP HIS SLEEVES! SO LOOK, GREENHORN, IT'S A DOLLAR FIFTY AN HOUR, PAYDAY'S EVERY FRIDAY!
WORK FAST AND WELL AND YOU CAN BRING YOUR UGLY MUG BACK TO THE WORKSITE TOMORROW AND EVERY DAY AFTER THAT!
GET INJURED OR TAKE THE BIG LEAP AND I'LL HAVE NO TROUBLE FINDING A REPLACEMENT.
WHERE DO I SIGN?
YOU DON'T!
FOLLOW ME. HERE'S ONE OF YOUR CO-WORKERS.
A GUY THAT CAN JOIN TWO STEEL BEAMS WITH A PNEUMATIC HAMMER FASTER THAN A RASCAL FROM THE BRONX CAN PICK YOUR POCKET, HE'LL TEACH YOU A THING OR TWO!
HEY, IRISH!
HERE'S A NEW RIVETER FOR YOUR TEAM. TAKE HIM TO GET HIS NAME ON THE TIME CLOCK AND THE BOTH OF YOU GET OVER THERE AND JOIN THE OTHERS RIGHT AWAY!
HULLO, COUNTRYMAN, THE NAME'S DAN SHACKLETON.
I'M FROM KINSEALY, DUBLIN COUNTY.
WHAT ABOUT YOU?
6

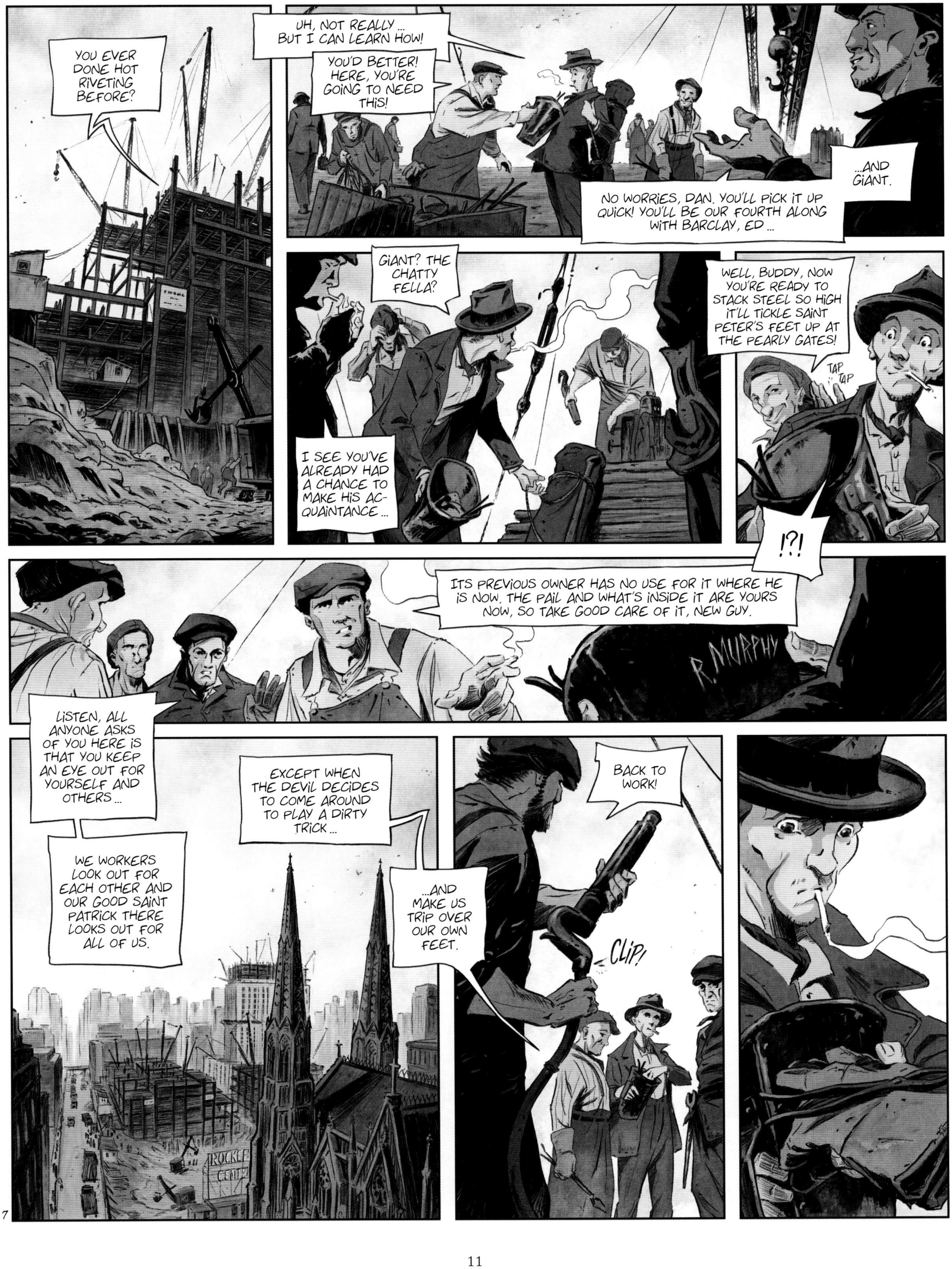

YOU EVER DONE HOT RIVETING BEFORE?
UH, NOT REALLY ... BUT I CAN LEARN HOW!
YOU'D BETTER! HERE, YOU'RE GOING TO NEED THIS!
NO WORRIES, DAN. YOU'LL PICK IT UP QUICK! YOU'LL BE OUR FOURTH ALONG WITH BARCLAY, ED ...
...AND GIANT.
GIANT? THE CHATTY FELLA?
I SEE YOU'VE ALREADY HAD A CHANCE TO MAKE HIS ACQUAINTANCE ...
WELL, BUDDY, NOW YOU'RE READY TO STACK STEEL SO HIGH IT'LL TICKLE SAINT PETER'S FEET UP AT THE PEARLY GATES!
TAP TAP
!?!
ITS PREVIOUS OWNER HAS NO USE FOR IT WHERE HE IS NOW. THE PAIL AND WHAT'S INSIDE IT ARE YOURS NOW, SO TAKE GOOD CARE OF IT, NEW GUY.
R. MURPHY
LISTEN, ALL ANYONE ASKS OF YOU HERE IS THAT YOU KEEP AN EYE OUT FOR YOURSELF AND OTHERS ...
WE WORKERS LOOK OUT FOR EACH OTHER AND OUR GOOD SAINT PATRICK THERE LOOKS OUT FOR ALL OF US.
EXCEPT WHEN THE DEVIL DECIDES TO COME AROUND TO PLAY A DIRTY TRICK ...
...AND MAKE US TRIP OVER OUR OWN FEET.
BACK TO WORK!
CLIP!

7

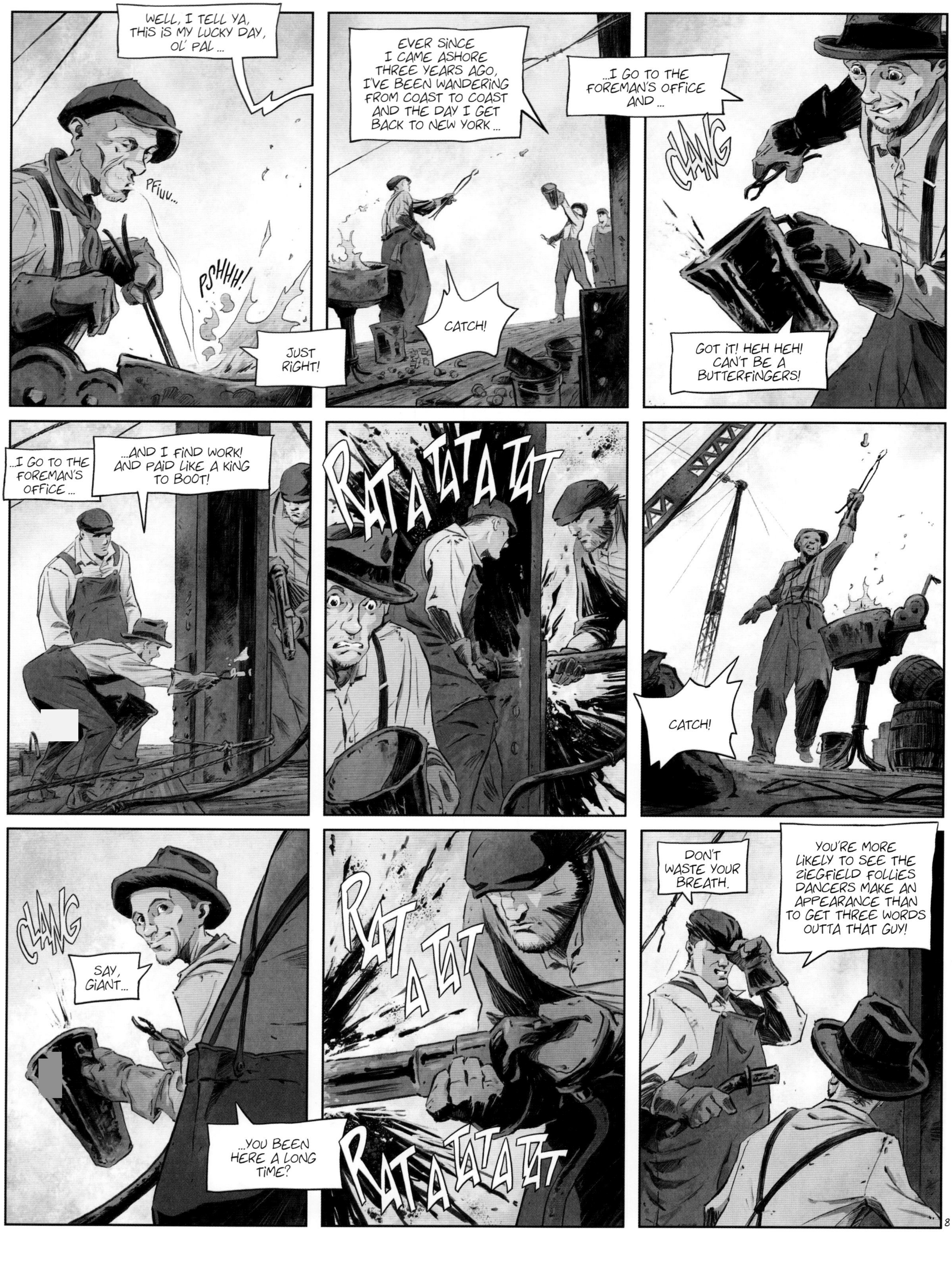

WELL, I TELL YA, THIS IS MY LUCKY DAY, OL' PAL ...
PFIUU...
PSHHH!
JUST RIGHT!
EVER SINCE I CAME ASHORE THREE YEARS AGO, I'VE BEEN WANDERING FROM COAST TO COAST AND THE DAY I GET BACK TO NEW YORK ...
CATCH!
...I GO TO THE FOREMAN'S OFFICE AND ...
CLANG
GOT IT! HEH HEH! CAN'T BE A BUTTERFINGERS!
...I GO TO THE FOREMAN'S OFFICE ...
...AND I FIND WORK! AND PAID LIKE A KING TO BOOT!
RATATATATAT
CATCH!
CLANG
SAY, GIANT...
...YOU BEEN HERE A LONG TIME?
RATATATAT
RATATATATAT
DON'T WASTE YOUR BREATH.
YOU'RE MORE LIKELY TO SEE THE ZIEGFIELD FOLLIES DANCERS MAKE AN APPEARANCE THAN TO GET THREE WORDS OUTTA THAT GUY!
8

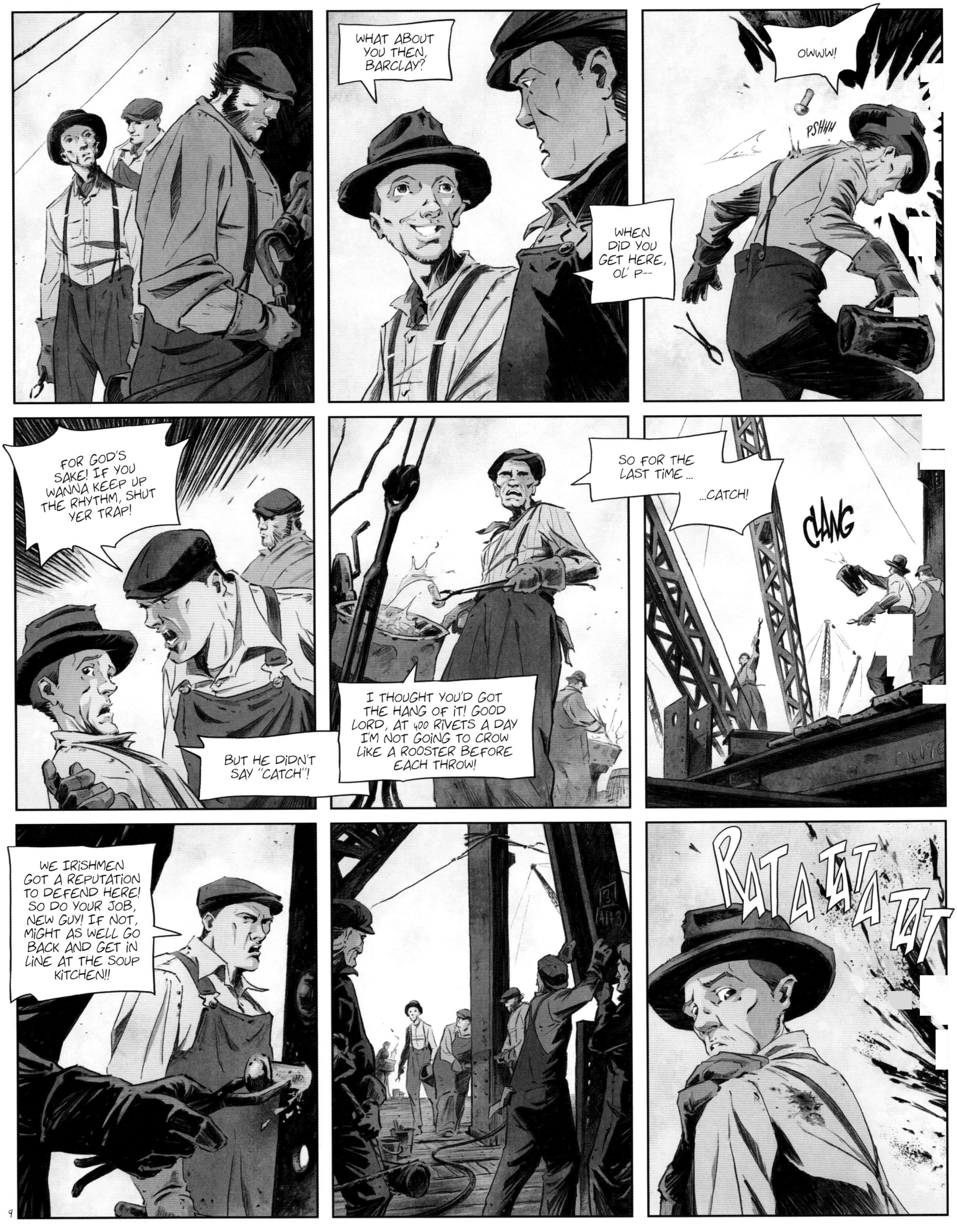
WHAT ABOUT YOU THEN, BARCLAY?
WHEN DID YOU GET HERE, OL' P--
OWWW!
PSHHH
FOR GOD'S SAKE! IF YOU WANNA KEEP UP THE RHYTHM, SHUT YER TRAP!
BUT HE DIDN'T SAY "CATCH"!
I THOUGHT YOU'D GOT THE HANG OF IT! GOOD LORD, AT 400 RIVETS A DAY I'M NOT GOING TO CROW LIKE A ROOSTER BEFORE EACH THROW!
SO FOR THE LAST TIME ...
...CATCH!
CLANG
WE IRISHMEN GOT A REPUTATION TO DEFEND HERE! SO DO YOUR JOB, NEW GUY! IF NOT, MIGHT AS WELL GO BACK AND GET IN LINE AT THE SOUP KITCHEN!!
RATATATATAT

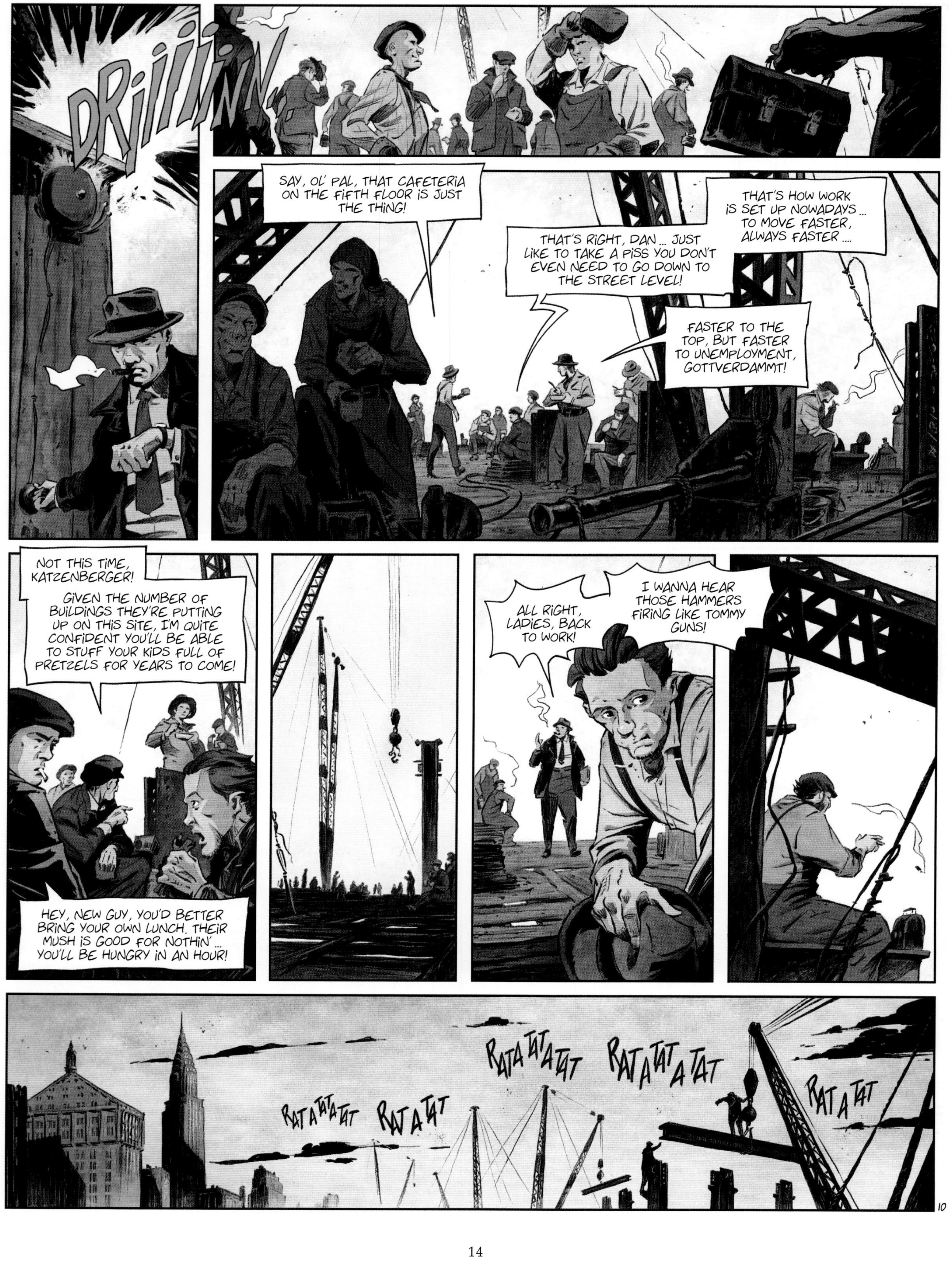
DRiiiiiiNN...
SAY, OL' PAL, THAT CAFETERIA ON THE FIFTH FLOOR IS JUST THE THING!
THAT'S RIGHT, DAN ... JUST LIKE TO TAKE A PISS YOU DON'T EVEN NEED TO GO DOWN TO THE STREET LEVEL!
THAT'S HOW WORK IS SET UP NOWADAYS ... TO MOVE FASTER, ALWAYS FASTER ....
FASTER TO THE TOP, BUT FASTER TO UNEMPLOYMENT, GOTTVERDAMMT!
NOT THIS TIME, KATZENBERGER!
GIVEN THE NUMBER OF BUILDINGS THEY'RE PUTTING UP ON THIS SITE, I'M QUITE CONFIDENT YOU'LL BE ABLE TO STUFF YOUR KIDS FULL OF PRETZELS FOR YEARS TO COME!
HEY, NEW GUY, YOU'D BETTER BRING YOUR OWN LUNCH. THEIR MUSH IS GOOD FOR NOTHIN' ... YOU'LL BE HUNGRY IN AN HOUR!
ALL RIGHT, LADIES, BACK TO WORK!
I WANNA HEAR THOSE HAMMERS FIRING LIKE TOMMY GUNS!
RATATATATAT
RATATAT
RATATATATAT
RATATATATAT
RATATAT
10

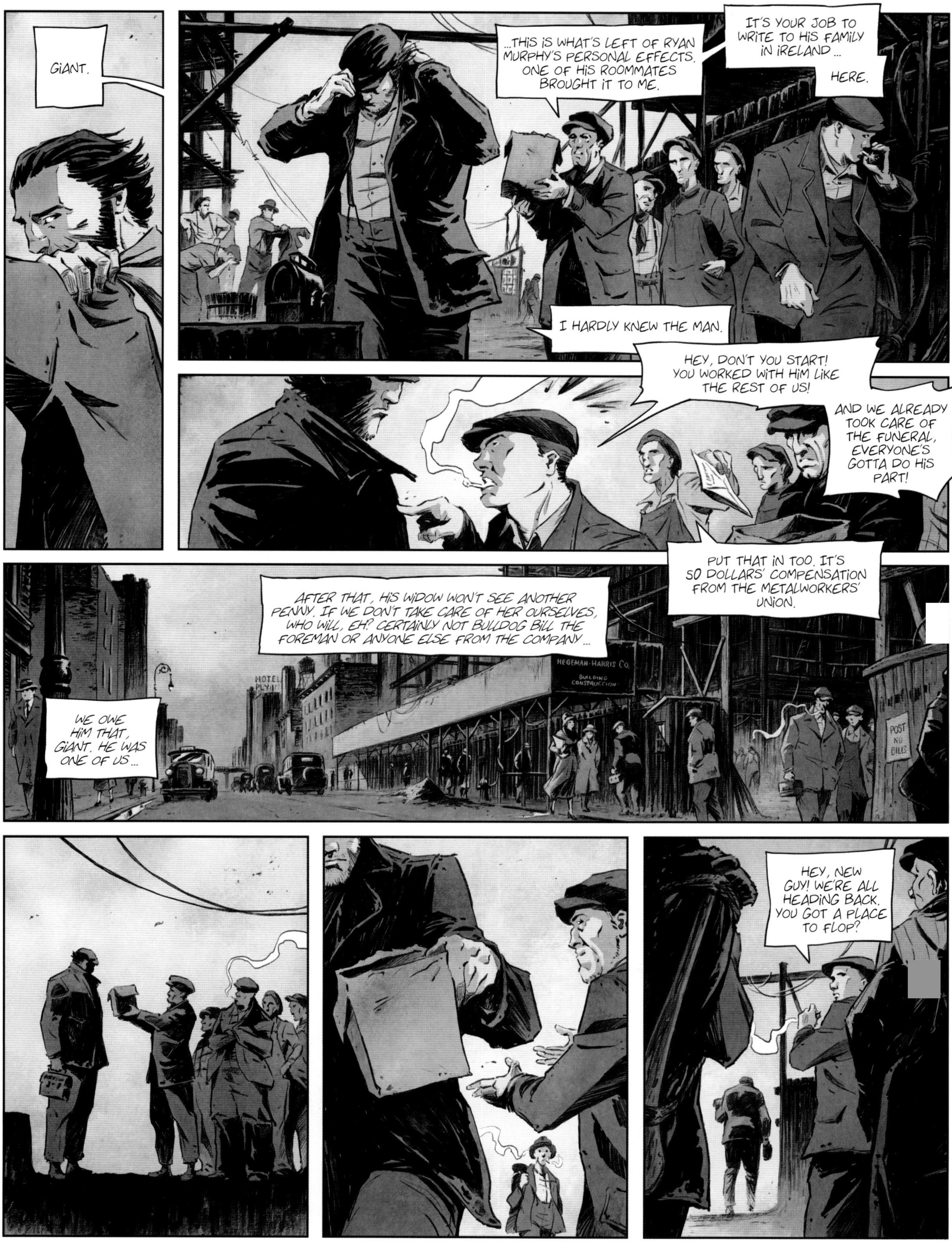
GIANT.
...THIS IS WHAT'S LEFT OF RYAN MURPHY'S PERSONAL EFFECTS. ONE OF HIS ROOMMATES BROUGHT IT TO ME.
IT'S YOUR JOB TO WRITE TO HIS FAMILY IN IRELAND ...
HERE.
I HARDLY KNEW THE MAN.
HEY, DON'T YOU START! YOU WORKED WITH HIM LIKE THE REST OF US!
AND WE ALREADY TOOK CARE OF THE FUNERAL, EVERYONE'S GOTTA DO HIS PART!
PUT THAT IN TOO. IT'S 50 DOLLARS' COMPENSATION FROM THE METALWORKERS' UNION.
AFTER THAT, HIS WIDOW WON'T SEE ANOTHER PENNY. IF WE DON'T TAKE CARE OF HER OURSELVES, WHO WILL, EH? CERTAINLY NOT BULLDOG BILL THE FOREMAN OR ANYONE ELSE FROM THE COMPANY...
HEGEMAN-HARRIS CO.
BUILDING CONSTRUCTION
HOTEL
POST NO BILLS
WE OWE HIM THAT, GIANT. HE WAS ONE OF US...
HEY, NEW GUY! WE'RE ALL HEADING BACK. YOU GOT A PLACE TO FLOP?

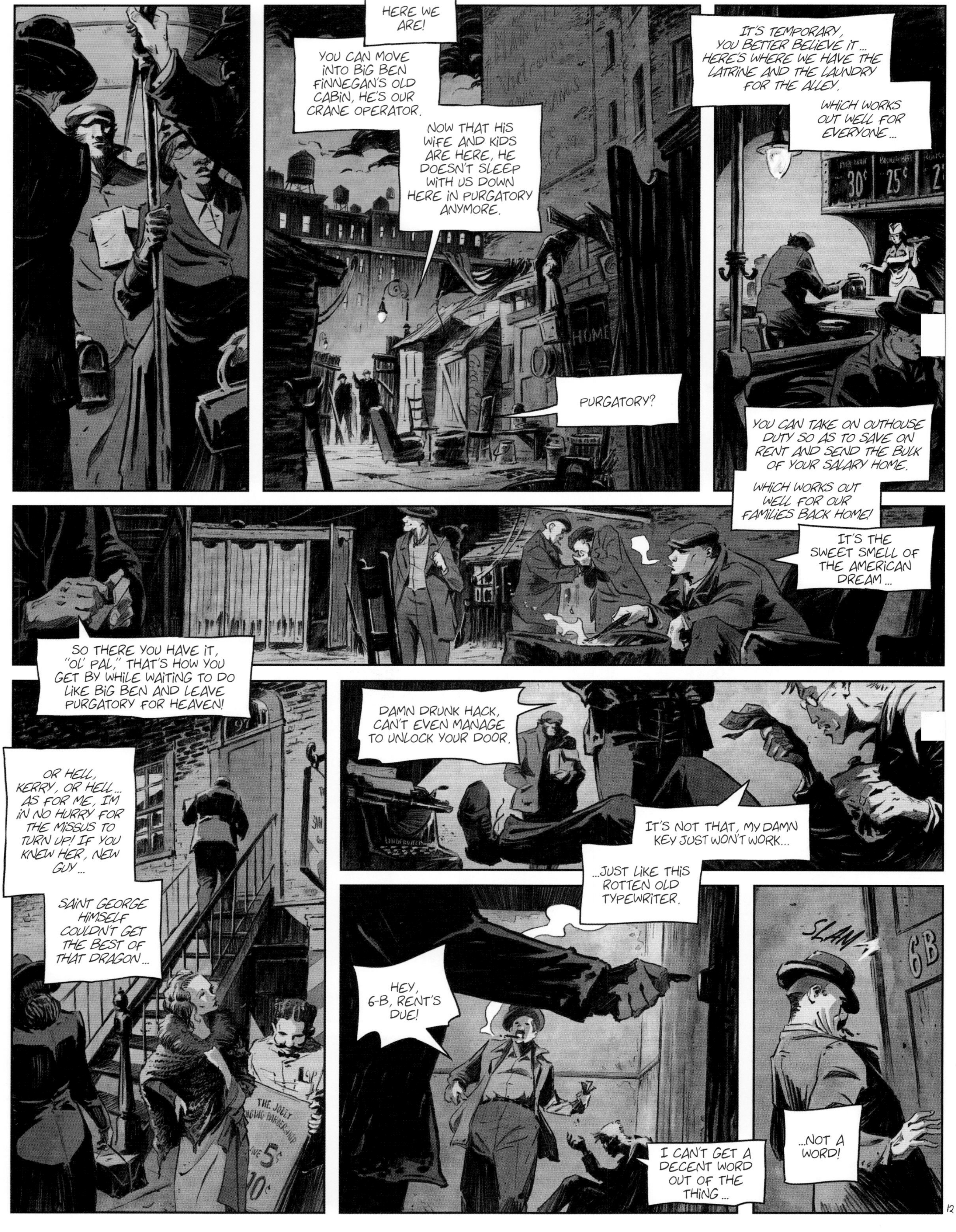
HERE WE ARE!
YOU CAN MOVE INTO BIG BEN FINNEGAN'S OLD CABIN, HE'S OUR CRANE OPERATOR.
NOW THAT HIS WIFE AND KIDS ARE HERE, HE DOESN'T SLEEP WITH US DOWN HERE IN PURGATORY ANYMORE.
PURGATORY?
IT'S TEMPORARY, YOU BETTER BELIEVE IT ... HERE'S WHERE WE HAVE THE LATRINE AND THE LAUNDRY FOR THE ALLEY.
WHICH WORKS OUT WELL FOR EVERYONE ...
30¢
25¢
YOU CAN TAKE ON OUTHOUSE DUTY SO AS TO SAVE ON RENT AND SEND THE BULK OF YOUR SALARY HOME.
WHICH WORKS OUT WELL FOR OUR FAMILIES BACK HOME!
IT'S THE SWEET SMELL OF THE AMERICAN DREAM ...
SO THERE YOU HAVE IT, "OL' PAL," THAT'S HOW YOU GET BY WHILE WAITING TO DO LIKE BIG BEN AND LEAVE PURGATORY FOR HEAVEN!
OR HELL, KERRY, OR HELL ... AS FOR ME, I'M IN NO HURRY FOR THE MISSUS TO TURN UP! IF YOU KNEW HER, NEW GUY ...
SAINT GEORGE HIMSELF COULDN'T GET THE BEST OF THAT DRAGON ...
THE JOLLY SINGING BARBERSHOP
5¢
10¢
DAMN DRUNK HACK, CAN'T EVEN MANAGE TO UNLOCK YOUR DOOR.
IT'S NOT THAT, MY DAMN KEY JUST WON'T WORK...
...JUST LIKE THIS ROTTEN OLD TYPEWRITER.
HEY, 6-B, RENT'S DUE!
I CAN'T GET A DECENT WORD OUT OF THE THING ...
SLAM
6B
...NOT A WORD!
12

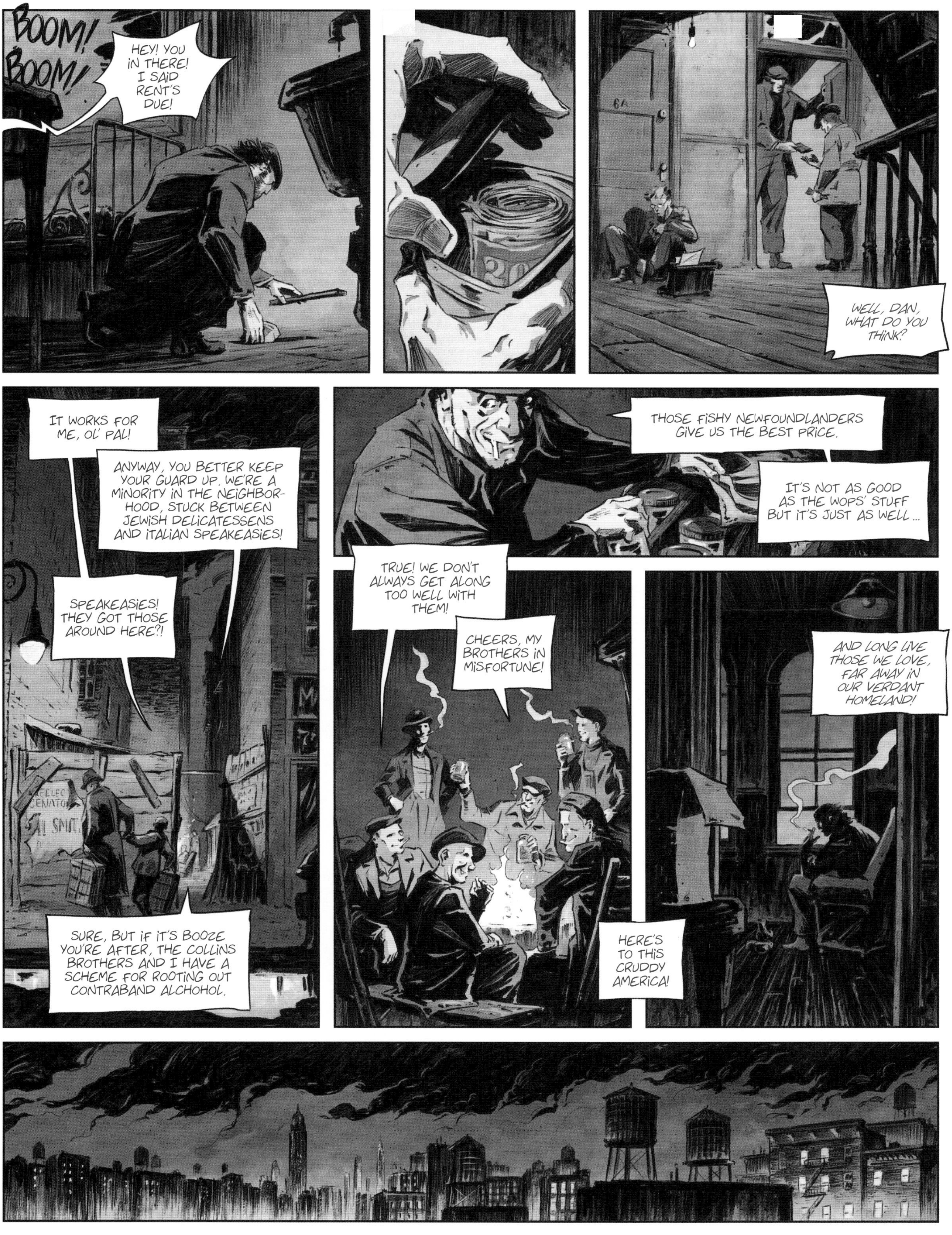
BOOM! BOOM!
HEY! YOU IN THERE! I SAID RENT'S DUE!
WELL, DAN, WHAT DO YOU THINK?
IT WORKS FOR ME, OL' PAL!
ANYWAY, YOU BETTER KEEP YOUR GUARD UP. WE'RE A MINORITY IN THE NEIGHBOR-HOOD, STUCK BETWEEN JEWISH DELICATESSENS AND ITALIAN SPEAKEASIES!
SPEAKEASIES! THEY GOT THOSE AROUND HERE?!
SURE, BUT IF IT'S BOOZE YOU'RE AFTER, THE COLLINS BROTHERS AND I HAVE A SCHEME FOR ROOTING OUT CONTRABAND ALCHOHOL.
THOSE FISHY NEWFOUNDLANDERS GIVE US THE BEST PRICE.
IT'S NOT AS GOOD AS THE WOPS' STUFF BUT IT'S JUST AS WELL ...
TRUE! WE DON'T ALWAYS GET ALONG TOO WELL WITH THEM!
CHEERS, MY BROTHERS IN MISFORTUNE!
HERE'S TO THIS CRUDDY AMERICA!
AND LONG LIVE THOSE WE LOVE, FAR AWAY IN OUR VERDANT HOMELAND!

13

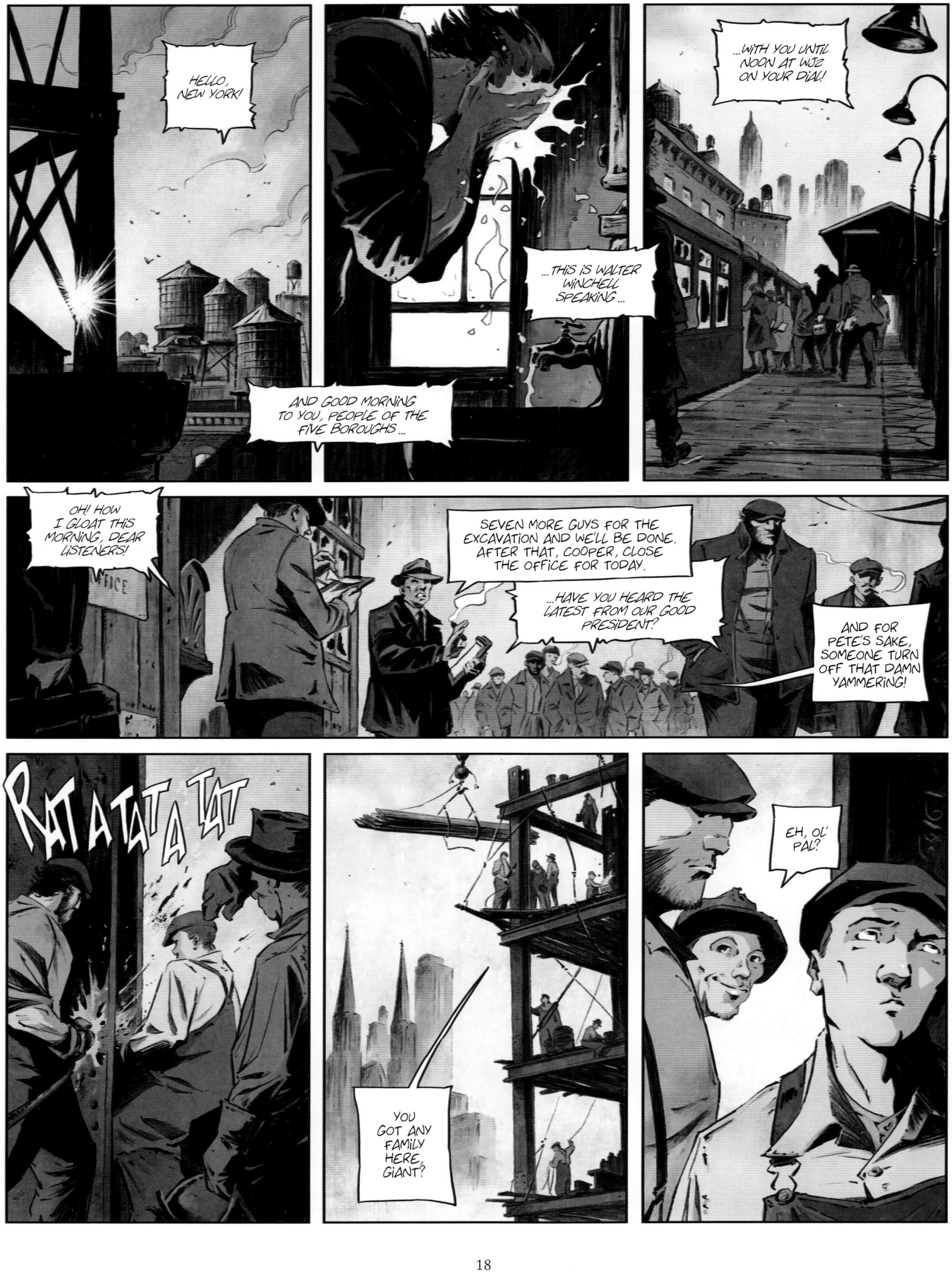
HELLO, NEW YORK!
AND GOOD MORNING TO YOU, PEOPLE OF THE FIVE BOROUGHS...
...THIS IS WALTER WINCHELL SPEAKING...
...WITH YOU UNTIL NOON AT WJZ ON YOUR DIAL!
OH! HOW I GLOAT THIS MORNING, DEAR LISTENERS!
OFFICE
SEVEN MORE GUYS FOR THE EXCAVATION AND WE'LL BE DONE. AFTER THAT, COOPER, CLOSE THE OFFICE FOR TODAY.
...HAVE YOU HEARD THE LATEST FROM OUR GOOD PRESIDENT?
AND FOR PETE'S SAKE, SOMEONE TURN OFF THAT DAMN YAMMERING!
RAT A TAT A TAT
YOU GOT ANY FAMILY HERE, GIANT?
EH, OL' PAL?
14

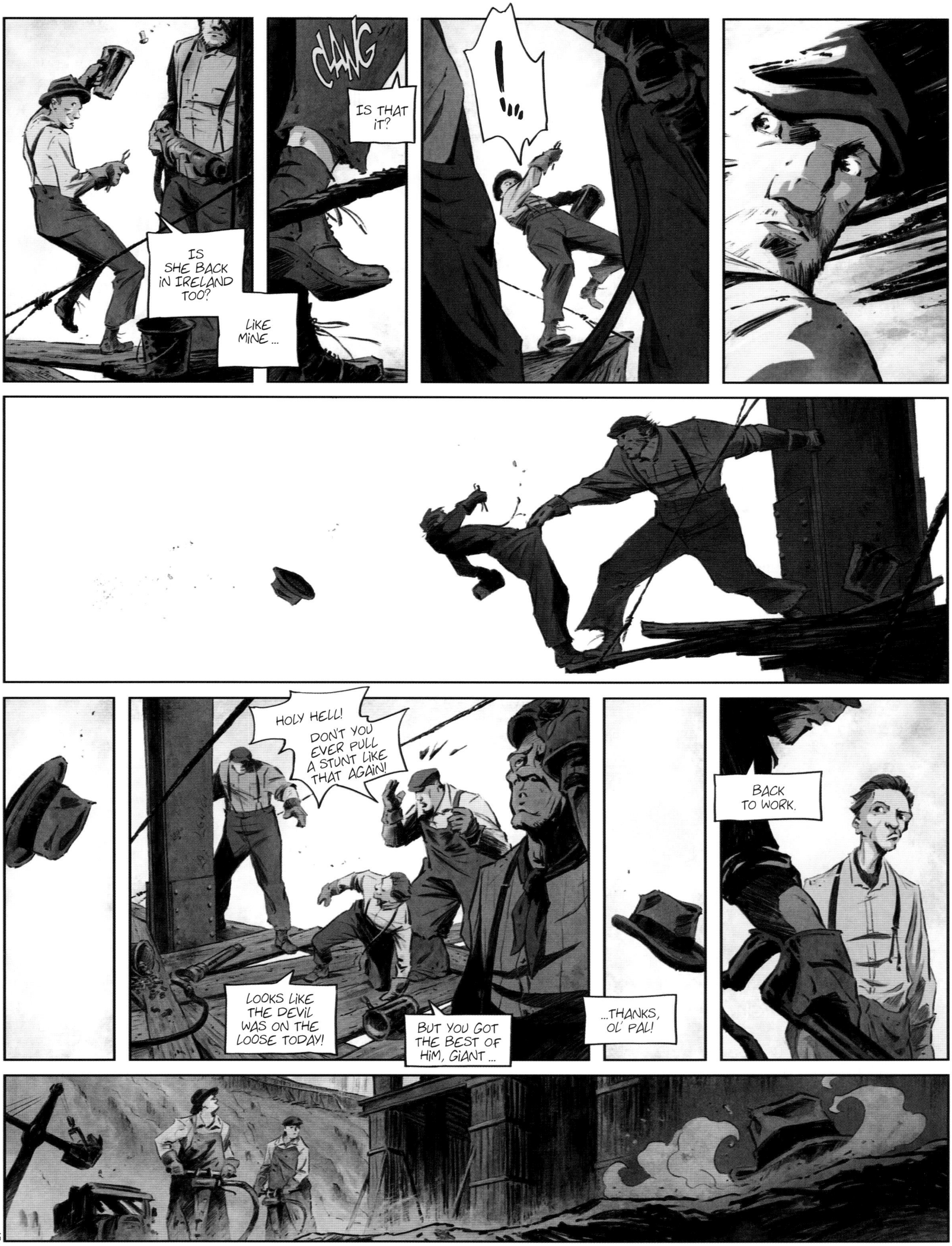
IS SHE BACK IN IRELAND TOO?
LIKE MINE ...
CLANG
IS THAT IT?
!
HOLY HELL!
DON'T YOU EVER PULL A STUNT LIKE THAT AGAIN!
LOOKS LIKE THE DEVIL WAS ON THE LOOSE TODAY!
BUT YOU GOT THE BEST OF HIM, GIANT ...
...THANKS, OL' PAL!
BACK TO WORK.
15

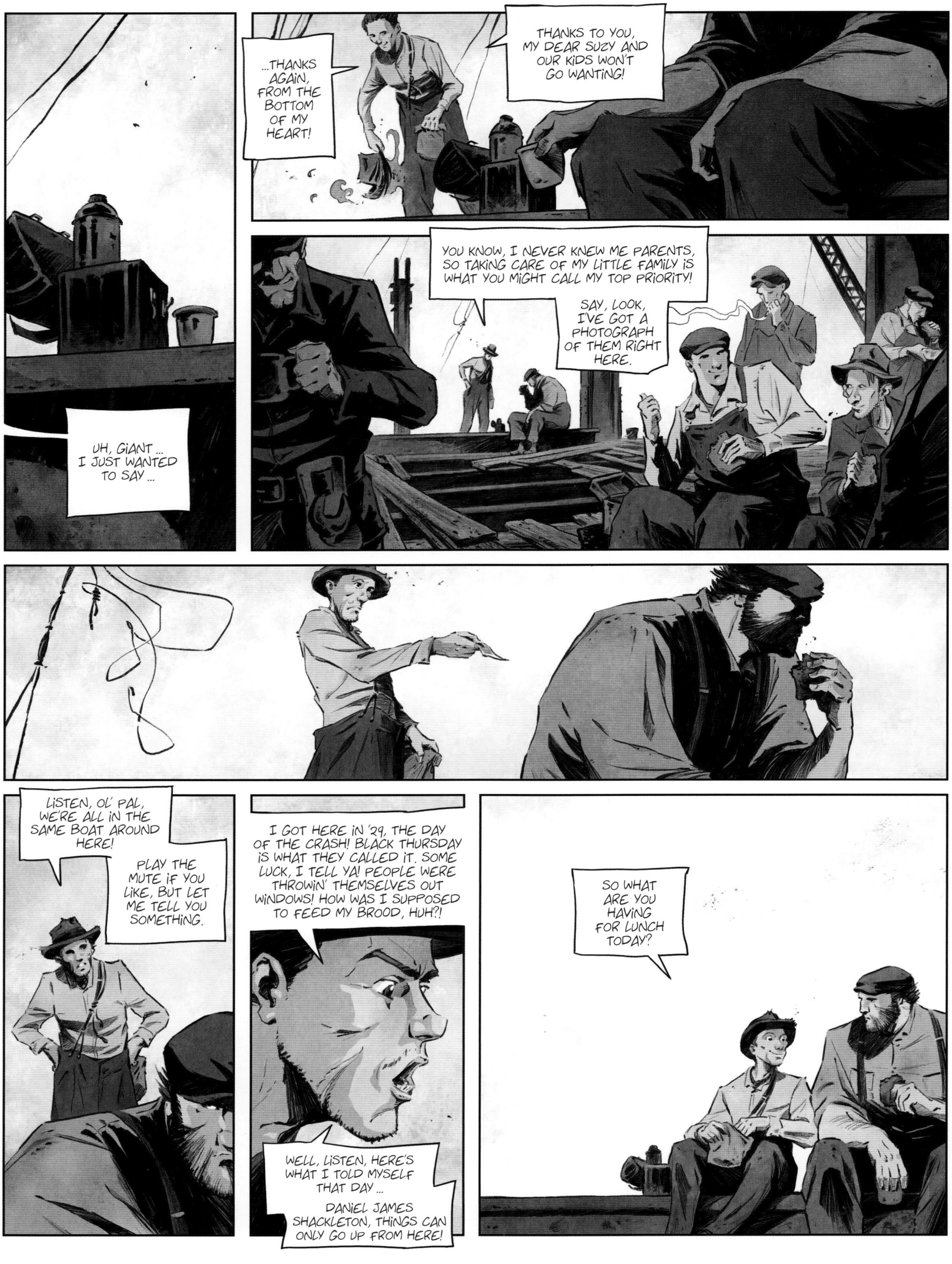
UH, GIANT ... I JUST WANTED TO SAY ...
...THANKS AGAIN, FROM THE BOTTOM OF MY HEART!
THANKS TO YOU, MY DEAR SUZY AND OUR KIDS WON'T GO WANTING!
YOU KNOW, I NEVER KNEW ME PARENTS, SO TAKING CARE OF MY LITTLE FAMILY IS WHAT YOU MIGHT CALL MY TOP PRIORITY!
SAY, LOOK, I'VE GOT A PHOTOGRAPH OF THEM RIGHT HERE.
LISTEN, OL' PAL, WE'RE ALL IN THE SAME BOAT AROUND HERE!
PLAY THE MUTE IF YOU LIKE, BUT LET ME TELL YOU SOMETHING.
I GOT HERE IN '29, THE DAY OF THE CRASH! BLACK THURSDAY IS WHAT THEY CALLED IT. SOME LUCK, I TELL YA! PEOPLE WERE THROWIN' THEMSELVES OUT WINDOWS! HOW WAS I SUPPOSED TO FEED MY BROOD, HUH?!
WELL, LISTEN, HERE'S WHAT I TOLD MYSELF THAT DAY ...
DANIEL JAMES SHACKLETON, THINGS CAN ONLY GO UP FROM HERE!
SO WHAT ARE YOU HAVING FOR LUNCH TODAY?
16

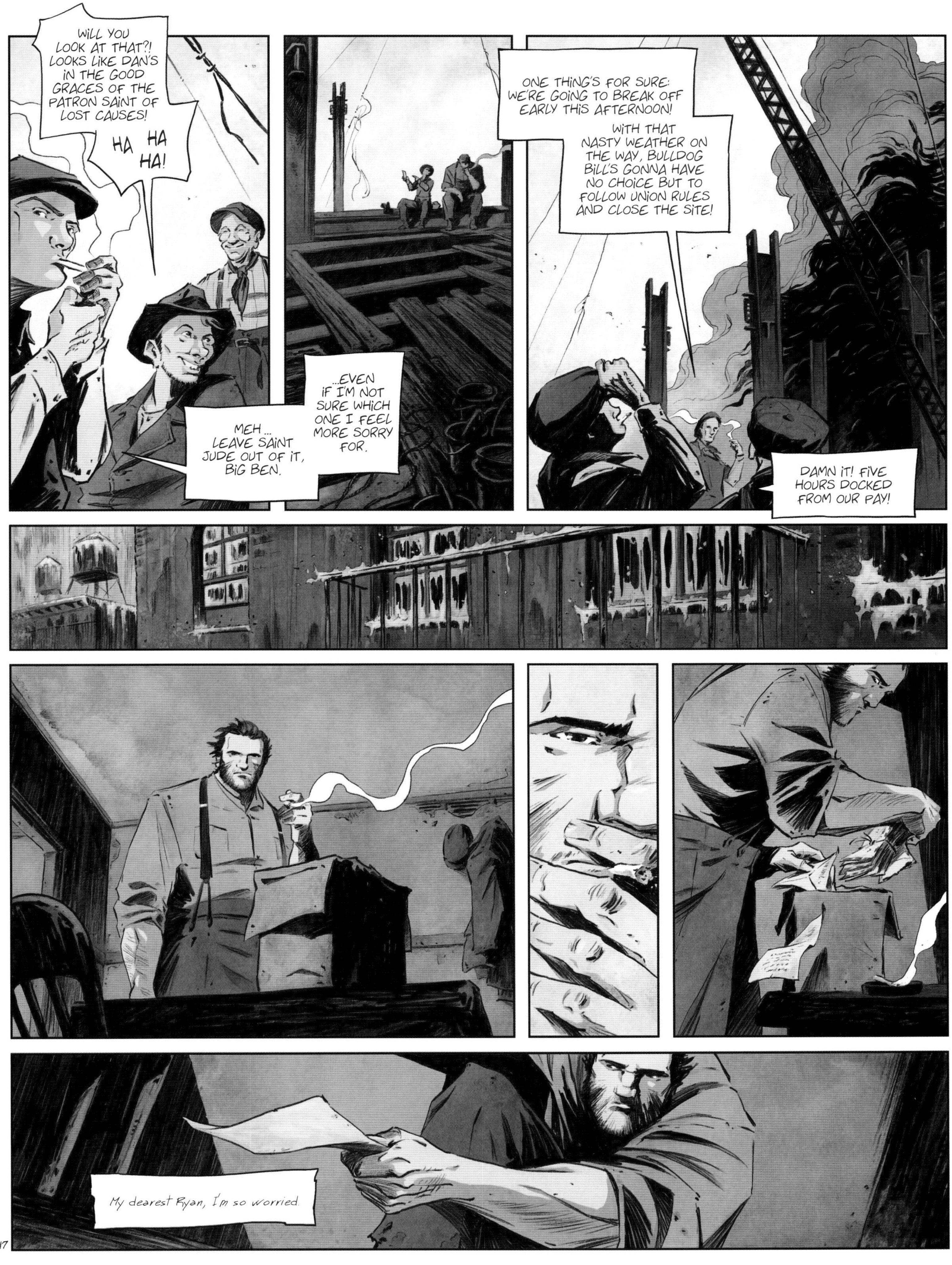
WILL YOU LOOK AT THAT?! LOOKS LIKE DAN'S IN THE GOOD GRACES OF THE PATRON SAINT OF LOST CAUSES!
HA HA HA!
MEH ... LEAVE SAINT JUDE OUT OF IT, BIG BEN.
...EVEN IF I'M NOT SURE WHICH ONE I FEEL MORE SORRY FOR.
ONE THING'S FOR SURE: WE'RE GOING TO BREAK OFF EARLY THIS AFTERNOON!
WITH THAT NASTY WEATHER ON THE WAY, BULLDOG BILL'S GONNA HAVE NO CHOICE BUT TO FOLLOW UNION RULES AND CLOSE THE SITE!
DAMN IT! FIVE HOURS DOCKED FROM OUR PAY!
My dearest Ryan, I'm so worried.
17

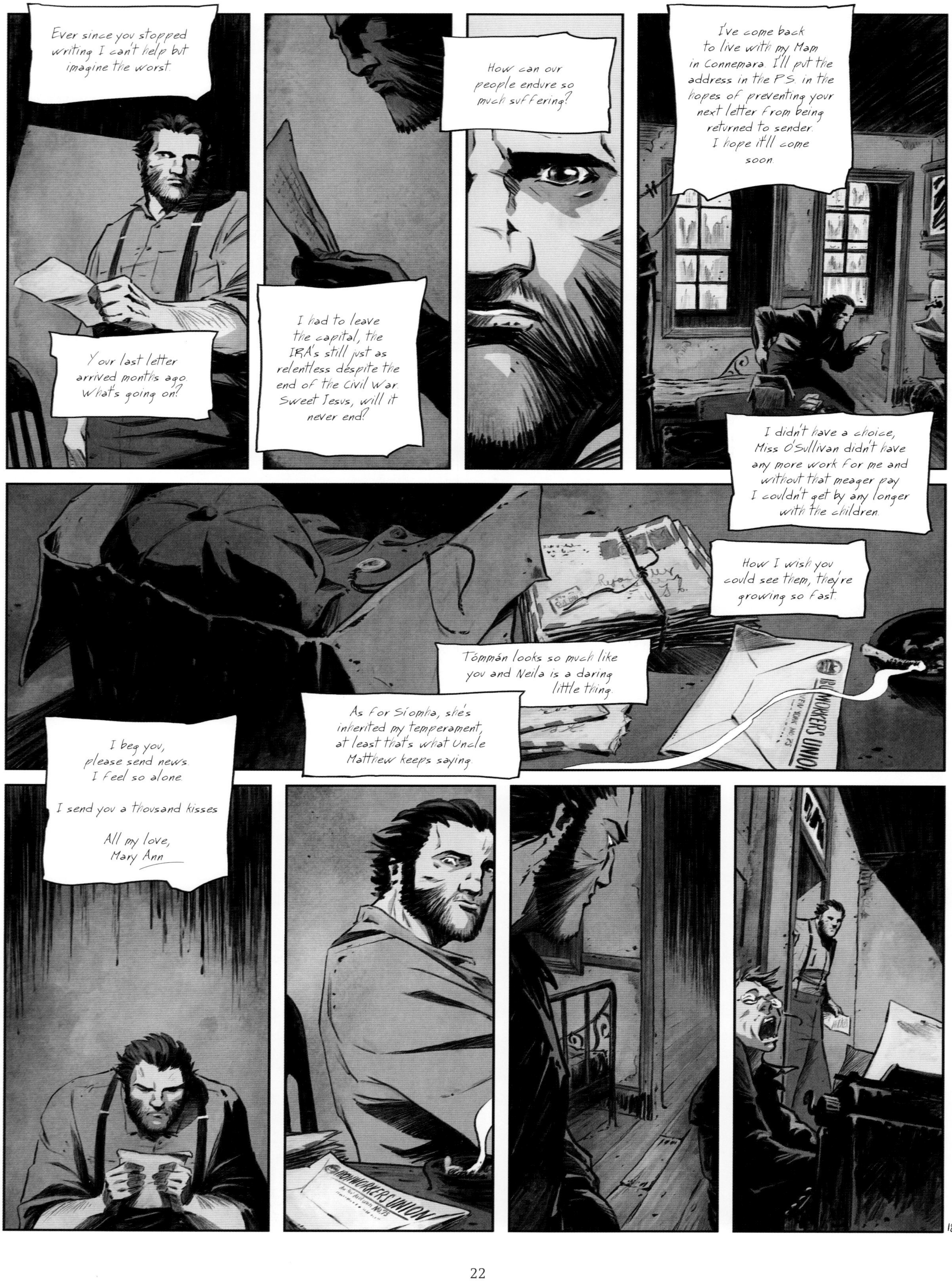

Ever since you stopped writing I can't help but imagine the worst.
Your last letter arrived months ago. What's going on?
How can our people endure so much suffering?
I had to leave the capital, the IRA's still just as relentless despite the end of the Civil War. Sweet Jesus, will it never end?
I've come back to live with my Mam in Connemara. I'll put the address in the P.S. in the hopes of preventing your next letter from being returned to sender. I hope it'll come soon.
I didn't have a choice, Miss O'Sullivan didn't have any more work for me and without that meager pay I couldn't get by any longer with the children.
How I wish you could see them, they're growing so fast.
Tómmán looks so much like you and Neila is a daring little thing.
As for Síomha, she's inherited my temperament, at least that's what Uncle Matthew keeps saying.
I beg you, please send news. I feel so alone.
I send you a thousand kisses
All my love, Mary Ann
IRONWORKERS UNION
18

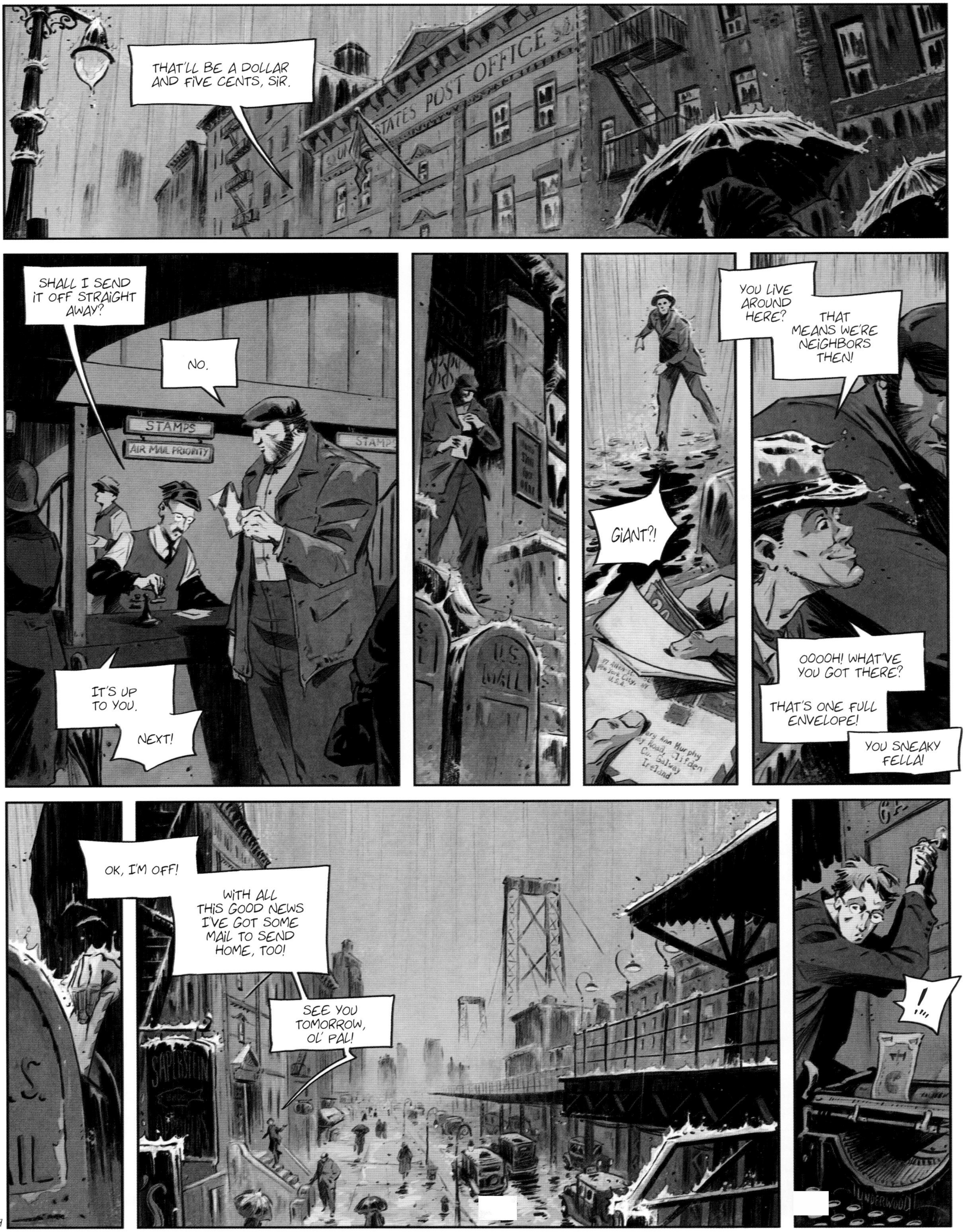
STATES POST OFFICE
THAT'LL BE A DOLLAR AND FIVE CENTS, SIR.
STAMPS
AIR MAIL PRIORITY
SHALL I SEND IT OFF STRAIGHT AWAY?
NO.
IT'S UP TO YOU.
NEXT!
U.S. MAIL
GIANT?!
YOU LIVE AROUND HERE?
THAT MEANS WE'RE NEIGHBORS THEN!
OOOOH! WHAT'VE YOU GOT THERE?
THAT'S ONE FULL ENVELOPE!
YOU SNEAKY FELLA!
OK, I'M OFF!
WITH ALL THIS GOOD NEWS I'VE GOT SOME MAIL TO SEND HOME, TOO!
SEE YOU TOMORROW, OL' PAL!
!

14

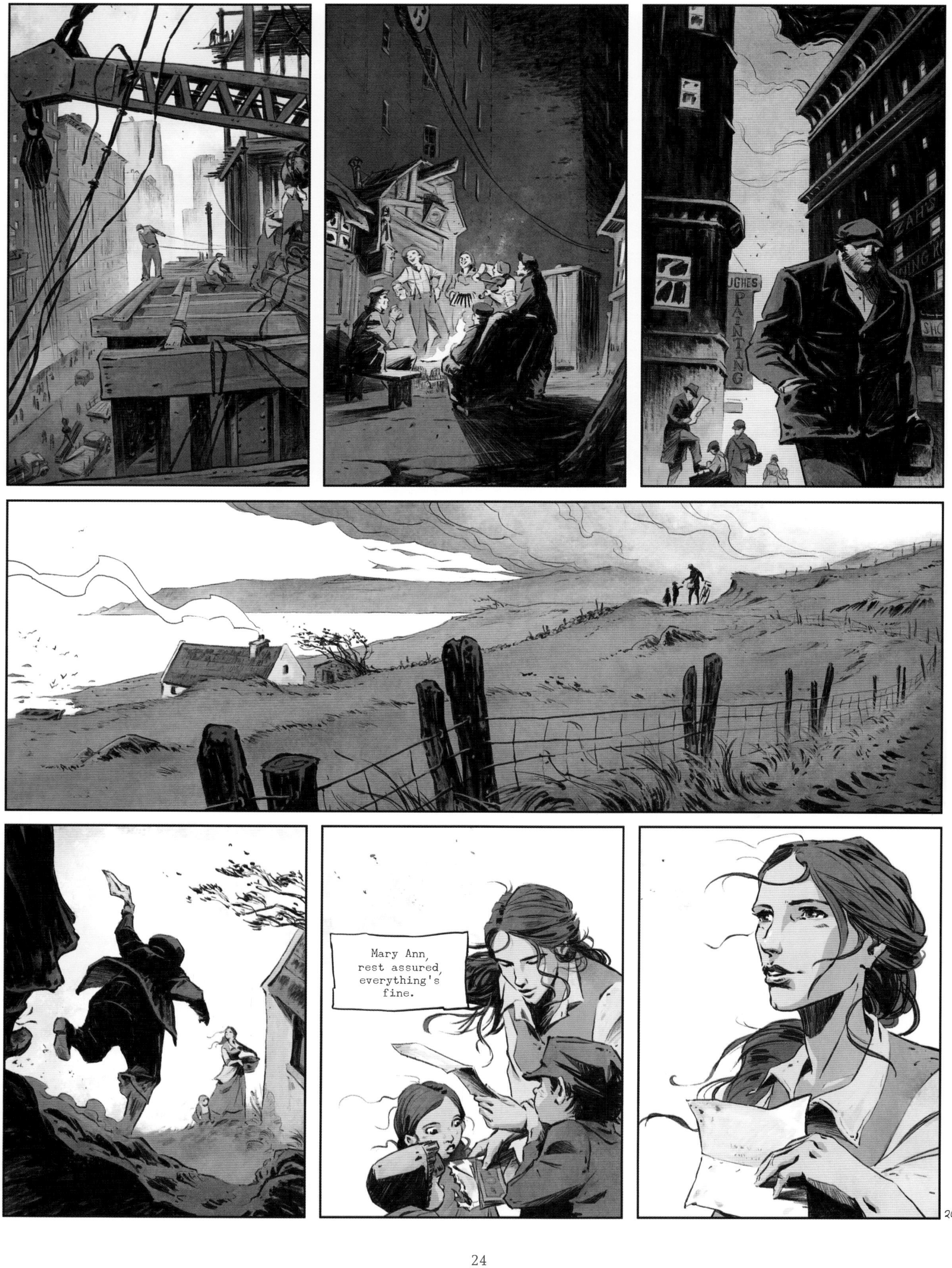
PAINTING
Mary Ann, rest assured, everything's fine.

20

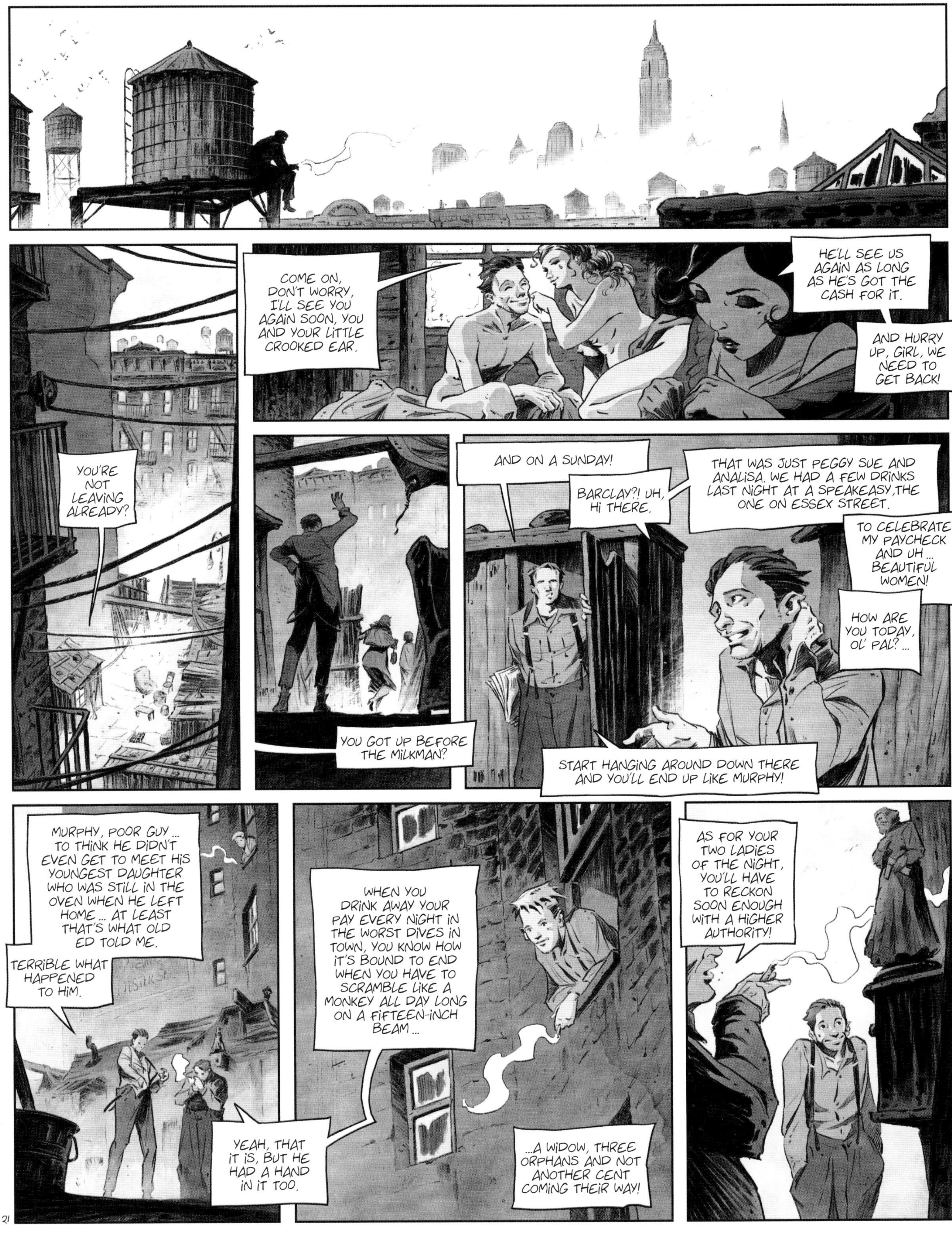
COME ON, DON'T WORRY, I'LL SEE YOU AGAIN SOON, YOU AND YOUR LITTLE CROOKED EAR.
HE'LL SEE US AGAIN AS LONG AS HE'S GOT THE CASH FOR IT.
AND HURRY UP, GIRL, WE NEED TO GET BACK!
YOU'RE NOT LEAVING ALREADY?
YOU GOT UP BEFORE THE MILKMAN?
AND ON A SUNDAY!
BARCLAY?! UH, HI THERE.
THAT WAS JUST PEGGY SUE AND ANALISA. WE HAD A FEW DRINKS LAST NIGHT AT A SPEAKEASY, THE ONE ON ESSEX STREET.
TO CELEBRATE MY PAYCHECK AND UH ... BEAUTIFUL WOMEN!
HOW ARE YOU TODAY, OL' PAL? ...
START HANGING AROUND DOWN THERE AND YOU'LL END UP LIKE MURPHY!
MURPHY, POOR GUY ... TO THINK HE DIDN'T EVEN GET TO MEET HIS YOUNGEST DAUGHTER WHO WAS STILL IN THE OVEN WHEN HE LEFT HOME ... AT LEAST THAT'S WHAT OLD ED TOLD ME.
TERRIBLE WHAT HAPPENED TO HIM.
YEAH, THAT IT IS, BUT HE HAD A HAND IN IT TOO.
WHEN YOU DRINK AWAY YOUR PAY EVERY NIGHT IN THE WORST DIVES IN TOWN, YOU KNOW HOW IT'S BOUND TO END WHEN YOU HAVE TO SCRAMBLE LIKE A MONKEY ALL DAY LONG ON A FIFTEEN-INCH BEAM ...
...A WIDOW, THREE ORPHANS AND NOT ANOTHER CENT COMING THEIR WAY!
AS FOR YOUR TWO LADIES OF THE NIGHT, YOU'LL HAVE TO RECKON SOON ENOUGH WITH A HIGHER AUTHORITY!
21

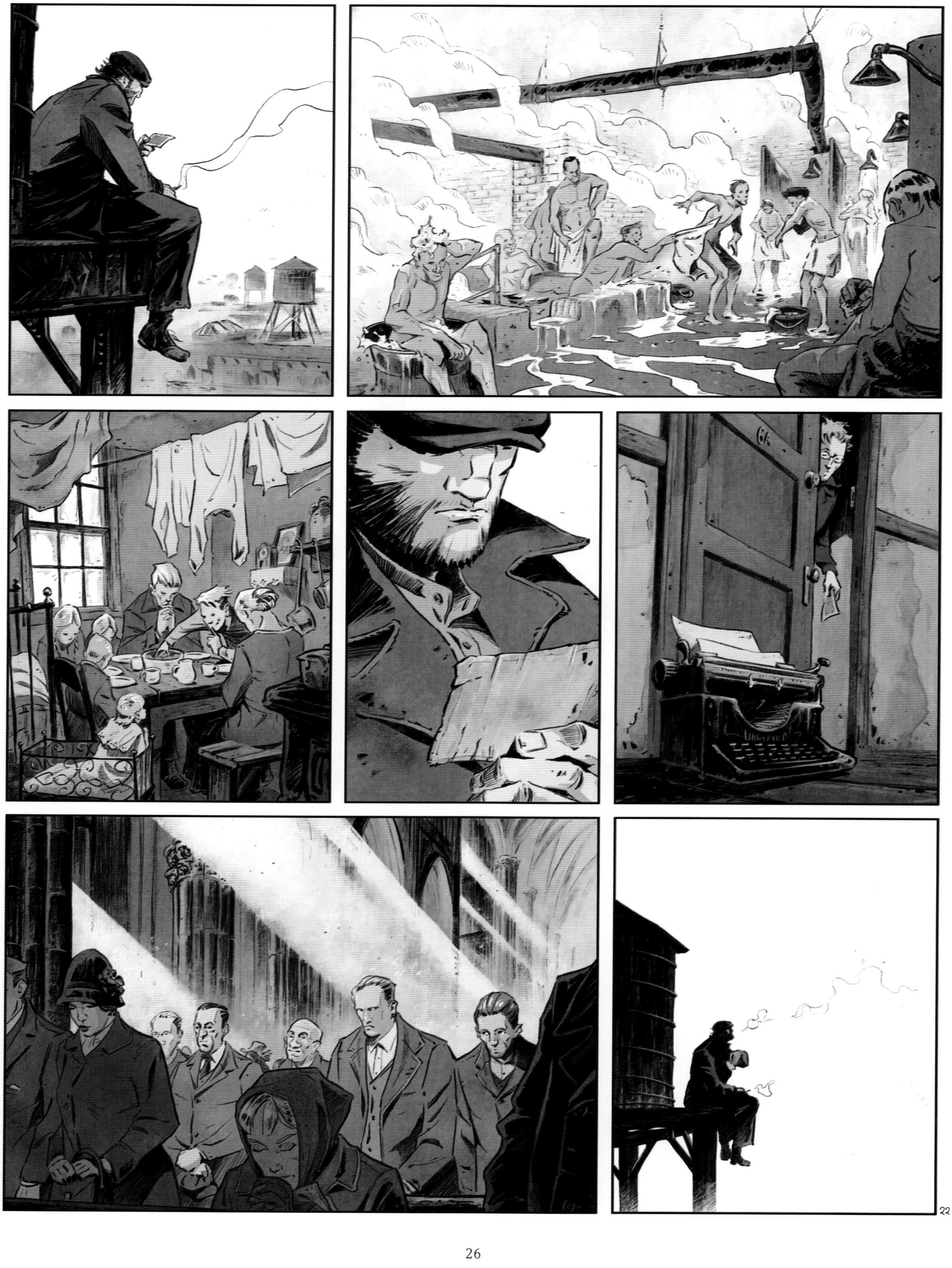

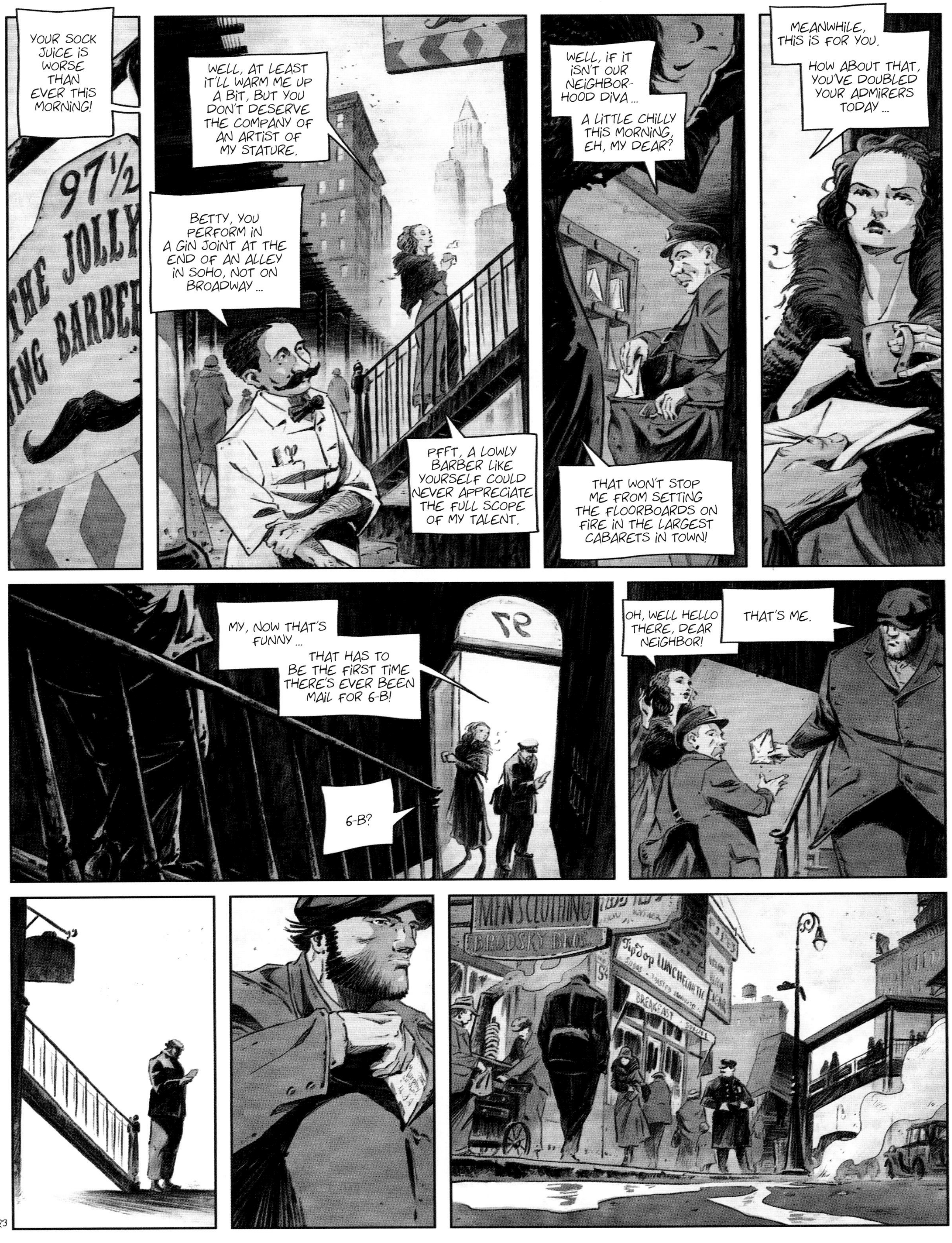
YOUR SOCK JUICE IS WORSE THAN EVER THIS MORNING!
97½
WELL, AT LEAST IT'LL WARM ME UP A BIT, BUT YOU DON'T DESERVE THE COMPANY OF AN ARTIST OF MY STATURE.
BETTY, YOU PERFORM IN A GIN JOINT AT THE END OF AN ALLEY IN SOHO, NOT ON BROADWAY ...
PFFT, A LOWLY BARBER LIKE YOURSELF COULD NEVER APPRECIATE THE FULL SCOPE OF MY TALENT.
WELL, IF IT ISN'T OUR NEIGHBOR-HOOD DIVA ...
A LITTLE CHILLY THIS MORNING, EH, MY DEAR?
THAT WON'T STOP ME FROM SETTING THE FLOORBOARDS ON FIRE IN THE LARGEST CABARETS IN TOWN!
MEANWHILE, THIS IS FOR YOU.
HOW ABOUT THAT, YOU'VE DOUBLED YOUR ADMIRERS TODAY ...
97
MY, NOW THAT'S FUNNY ...
THAT HAS TO BE THE FIRST TIME THERE'S EVER BEEN MAIL FOR 6-B!
6-B?
OH, WELL HELLO THERE, DEAR NEIGHBOR!
THAT'S ME.
MEN'S CLOTHING
BRODSKY BROS.
TipTop LUNCHEONETTE
BREAKFAST

23

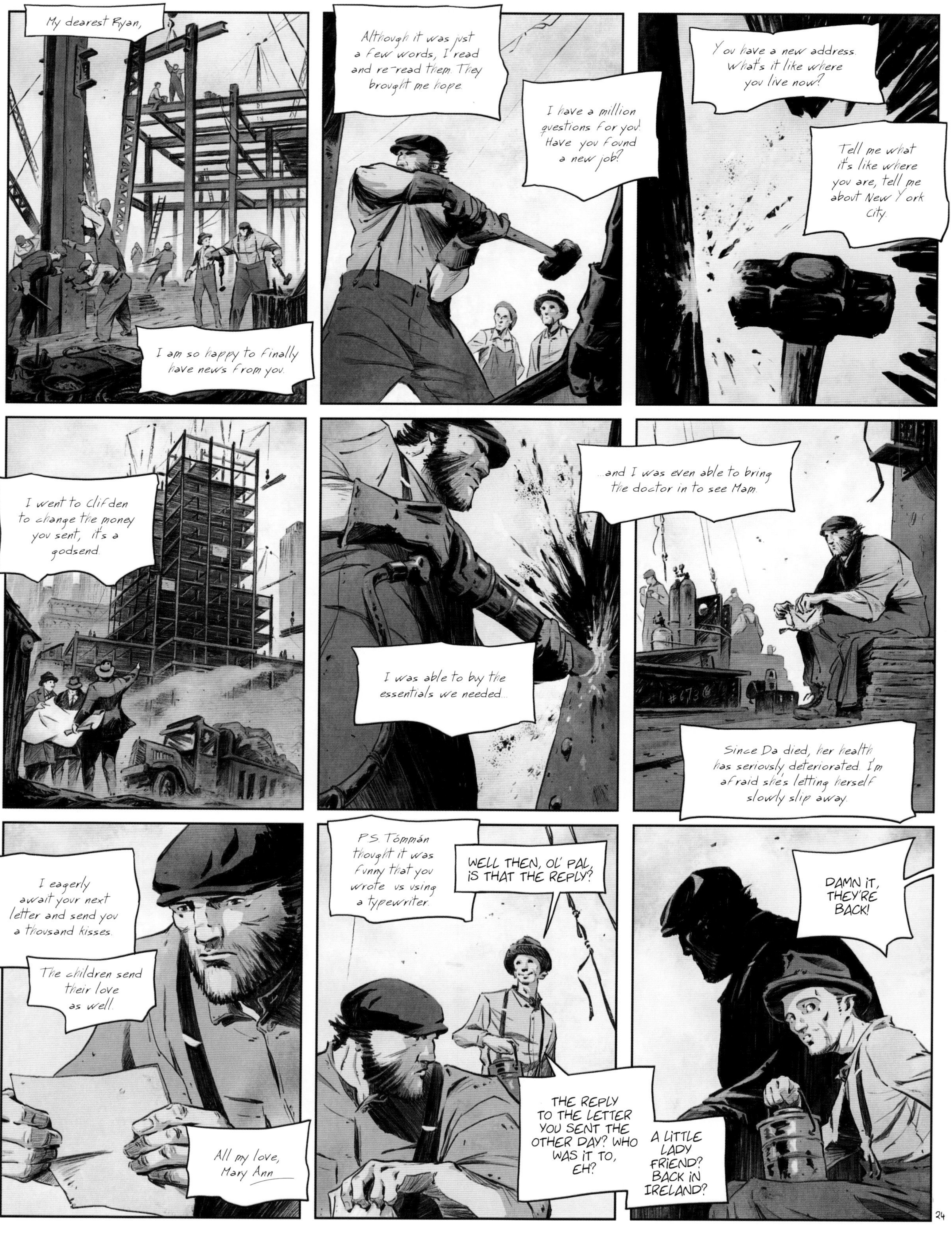
My dearest Ryan,
I am so happy to finally have news from you.
Although it was just a few words, I read and re-read them. They brought me hope.
I have a million questions for you! Have you found a new job?
You have a new address. What's it like where you live now?
Tell me what it's like where you are, tell me about New York City.
I went to Clifden to change the money you sent, it's a godsend.
I was able to buy the essentials we needed...
...and I was even able to bring the doctor in to see Mam.
Since Da died, her health has seriously deteriorated. I'm afraid she's letting herself slowly slip away.
I eagerly await your next letter and send you a thousand kisses.
The children send their love as well.
All my love, Mary Ann
P.S. Tómmán thought it was funny that you wrote us using a typewriter.
WELL THEN, OL' PAL, IS THAT THE REPLY?
THE REPLY TO THE LETTER YOU SENT THE OTHER DAY? WHO WAS IT TO, EH?
A LITTLE LADY FRIEND? BACK IN IRELAND?
DAMN IT, THEY'RE BACK!
24

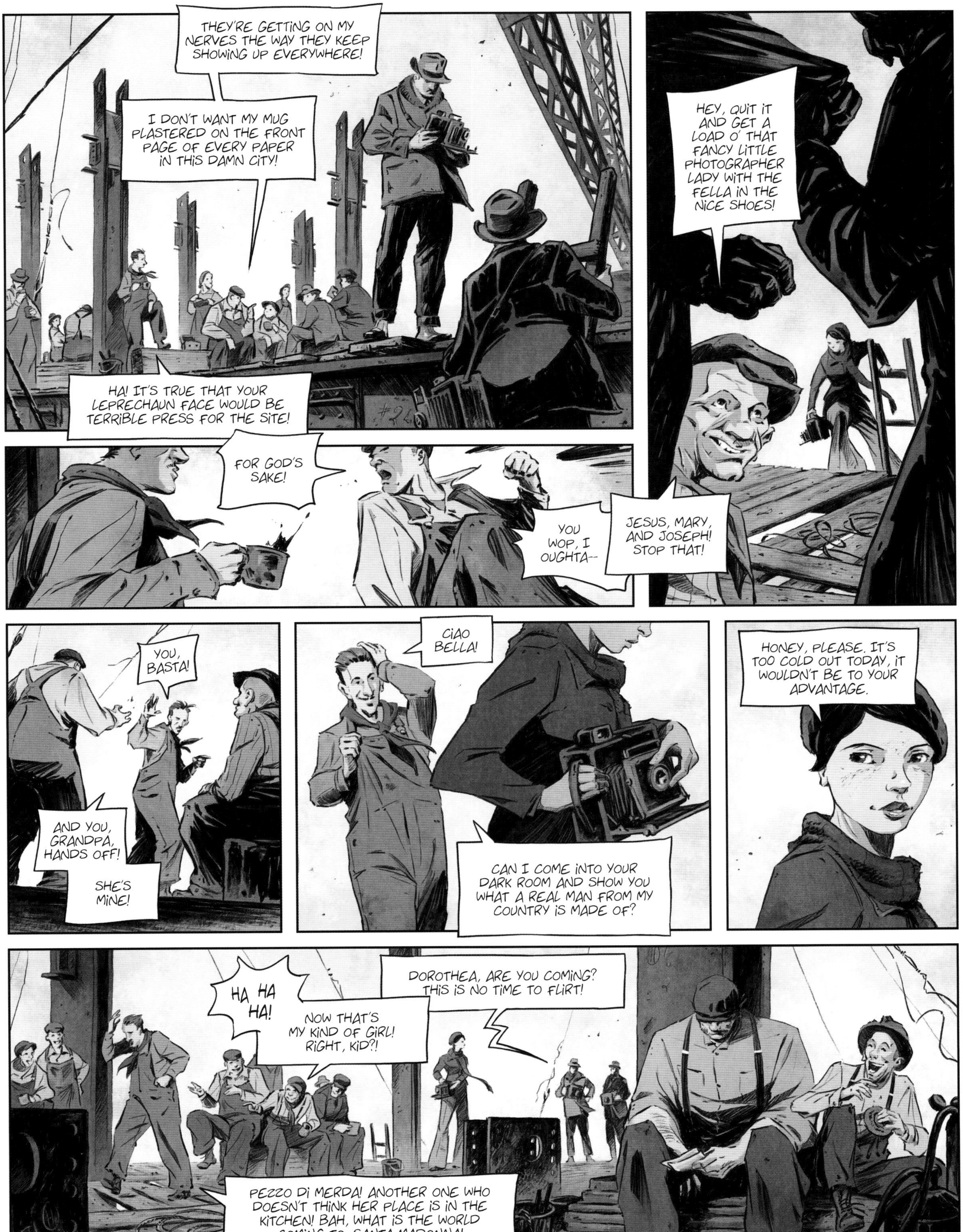
THEY'RE GETTING ON MY NERVES THE WAY THEY KEEP SHOWING UP EVERYWHERE!
I DON'T WANT MY MUG PLASTERED ON THE FRONT PAGE OF EVERY PAPER IN THIS DAMN CITY!
HA! IT'S TRUE THAT YOUR LEPRECHAUN FACE WOULD BE TERRIBLE PRESS FOR THE SITE!
HEY, QUIT IT AND GET A LOAD O' THAT FANCY LITTLE PHOTOGRAPHER LADY WITH THE FELLA IN THE NICE SHOES!
FOR GOD'S SAKE!
YOU WOP, I OUGHTA--
JESUS, MARY, AND JOSEPH! STOP THAT!
YOU, BASTA!
AND YOU, GRANDPA, HANDS OFF!
SHE'S MINE!
CIAO BELLA!
CAN I COME INTO YOUR DARK ROOM AND SHOW YOU WHAT A REAL MAN FROM MY COUNTRY IS MADE OF?
HONEY, PLEASE. IT'S TOO COLD OUT TODAY, IT WOULDN'T BE TO YOUR ADVANTAGE.
HA HA HA!
NOW THAT'S MY KIND OF GIRL! RIGHT, KID?!
DOROTHEA, ARE YOU COMING? THIS IS NO TIME TO FLIRT!
PEZZO DI MERDA! ANOTHER ONE WHO DOESN'T THINK HER PLACE IS IN THE KITCHEN! BAH, WHAT IS THE WORLD COMING TO, SANTA MADONNA!
25

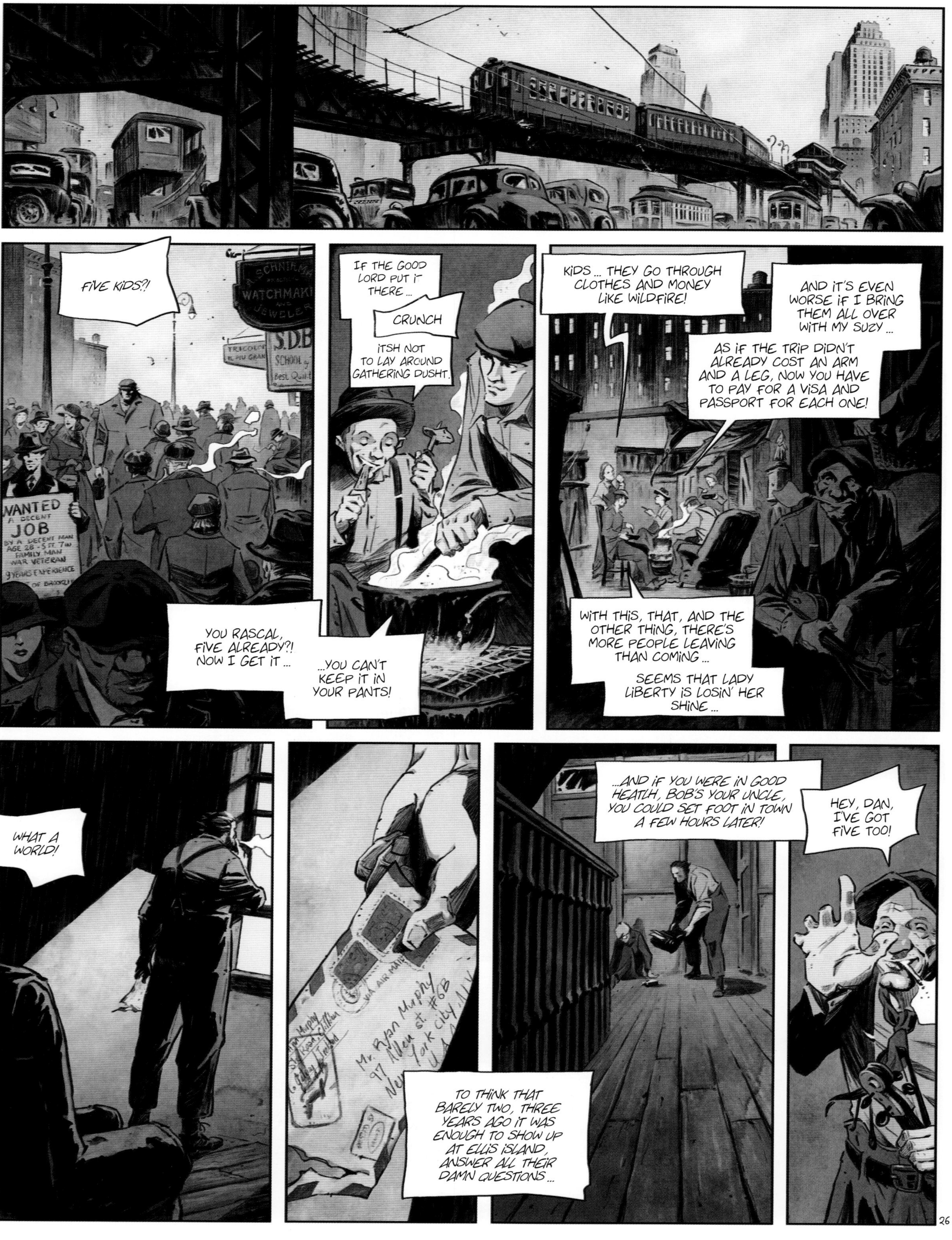
A. SCHNIRMAN WATCHMAKER AND JEWELER
S.D.B. SCHOOL
WANTED A DECENT JOB BY A DECENT MAN AGE 28 - 5 FT. 7 IN FAMILY MAN WAR VETERAN 9 YEARS EXPERIENCE
FIVE KIDS?!
YOU RASCAL, FIVE ALREADY?! NOW I GET IT ...
IF THE GOOD LORD PUT IT THERE ...
CRUNCH
ITSH NOT TO LAY AROUND GATHERING DUSHT.
...YOU CAN'T KEEP IT IN YOUR PANTS!
KIDS ... THEY GO THROUGH CLOTHES AND MONEY LIKE WILDFIRE!
AND IT'S EVEN WORSE IF I BRING THEM ALL OVER WITH MY SUZY ...
AS IF THE TRIP DIDN'T ALREADY COST AN ARM AND A LEG, NOW YOU HAVE TO PAY FOR A VISA AND PASSPORT FOR EACH ONE!
WITH THIS, THAT, AND THE OTHER THING, THERE'S MORE PEOPLE LEAVING THAN COMING ...
SEEMS THAT LADY LIBERTY IS LOSIN' HER SHINE ...
WHAT A WORLD!
VIA AIR MAIL
Mr. Ryan Murphy
97 Allen st. #6B
New York city, N.Y.
U.S.A.
TO THINK THAT BARELY TWO, THREE YEARS AGO IT WAS ENOUGH TO SHOW UP AT ELLIS ISLAND, ANSWER ALL THEIR DAMN QUESTIONS ...
...AND IF YOU WERE IN GOOD HEATH, BOB'S YOUR UNCLE, YOU COULD SET FOOT IN TOWN A FEW HOURS LATER!
HEY, DAN, I'VE GOT FIVE TOO!
26

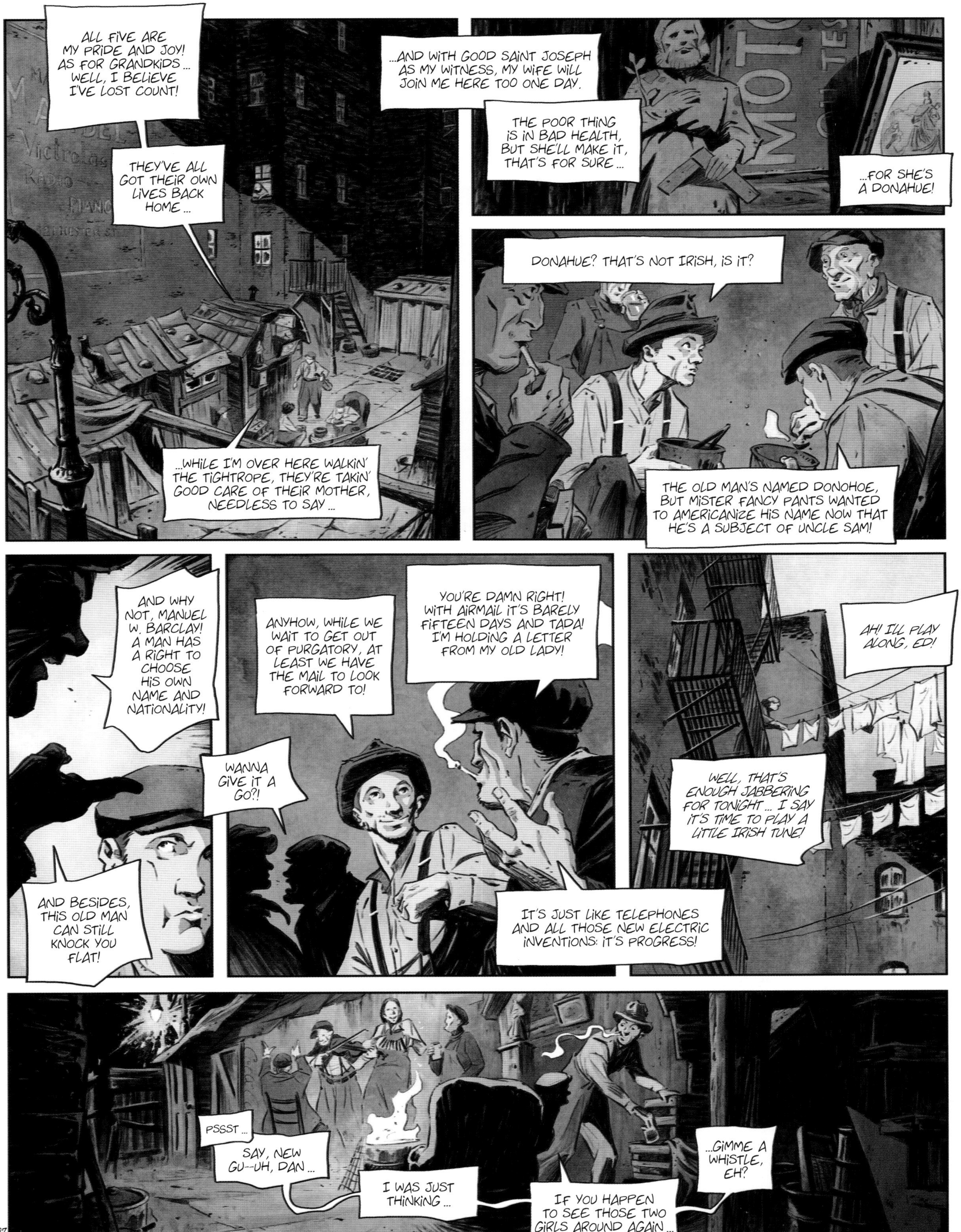
ALL FIVE ARE MY PRIDE AND JOY! AS FOR GRANDKIDS ... WELL, I BELIEVE I'VE LOST COUNT!
THEY'VE ALL GOT THEIR OWN LIVES BACK HOME ...
...WHILE I'M OVER HERE WALKIN' THE TIGHTROPE, THEY'RE TAKIN' GOOD CARE OF THEIR MOTHER, NEEDLESS TO SAY ...
...AND WITH GOOD SAINT JOSEPH AS MY WITNESS, MY WIFE WILL JOIN ME HERE TOO ONE DAY.
THE POOR THING IS IN BAD HEALTH, BUT SHE'LL MAKE IT, THAT'S FOR SURE ...
...FOR SHE'S A DONAHUE!
DONAHUE? THAT'S NOT IRISH, IS IT?
THE OLD MAN'S NAMED DONOHOE, BUT MISTER FANCY PANTS WANTED TO AMERICANIZE HIS NAME NOW THAT HE'S A SUBJECT OF UNCLE SAM!
AND WHY NOT, MANUEL W. BARCLAY! A MAN HAS A RIGHT TO CHOOSE HIS OWN NAME AND NATIONALITY!
AND BESIDES, THIS OLD MAN CAN STILL KNOCK YOU FLAT!
ANYHOW, WHILE WE WAIT TO GET OUT OF PURGATORY, AT LEAST WE HAVE THE MAIL TO LOOK FORWARD TO!
YOU'RE DAMN RIGHT! WITH AIRMAIL IT'S BARELY FIFTEEN DAYS AND TADA! I'M HOLDING A LETTER FROM MY OLD LADY!
WANNA GIVE IT A GO?!
IT'S JUST LIKE TELEPHONES AND ALL THOSE NEW ELECTRIC INVENTIONS: IT'S PROGRESS!
AH! I'LL PLAY ALONG, ED!
WELL, THAT'S ENOUGH JABBERING FOR TONIGHT ... I SAY IT'S TIME TO PLAY A LITTLE IRISH TUNE!
PSSST ...
SAY, NEW GU--UH, DAN ...
I WAS JUST THINKING ...
IF YOU HAPPEN TO SEE THOSE TWO GIRLS AROUND AGAIN ...
...GIMME A WHISTLE, EH?
27

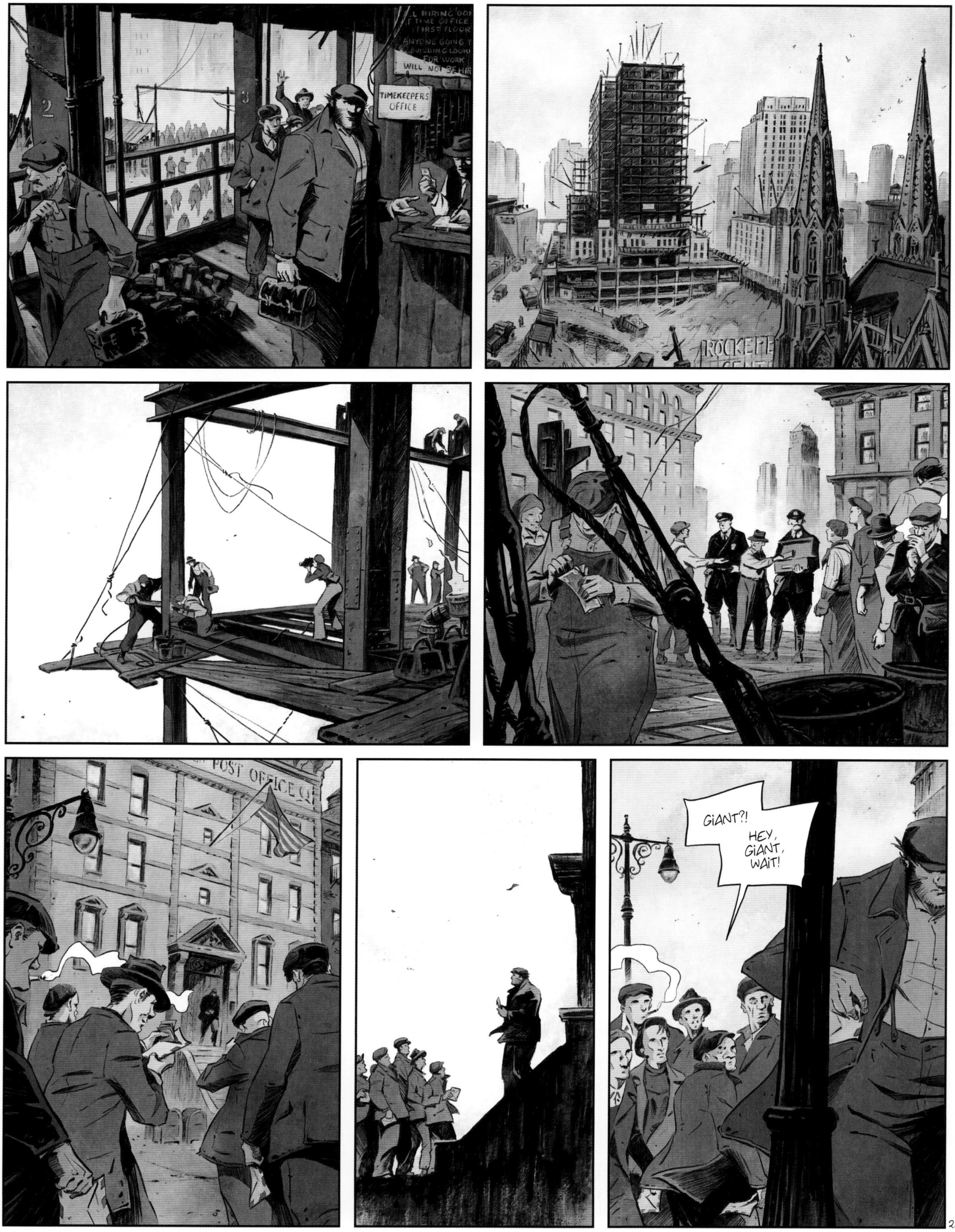
TIMEKEEPERS OFFICE
POST OFFICE
GIANT?!
HEY, GIANT, WAIT!

28

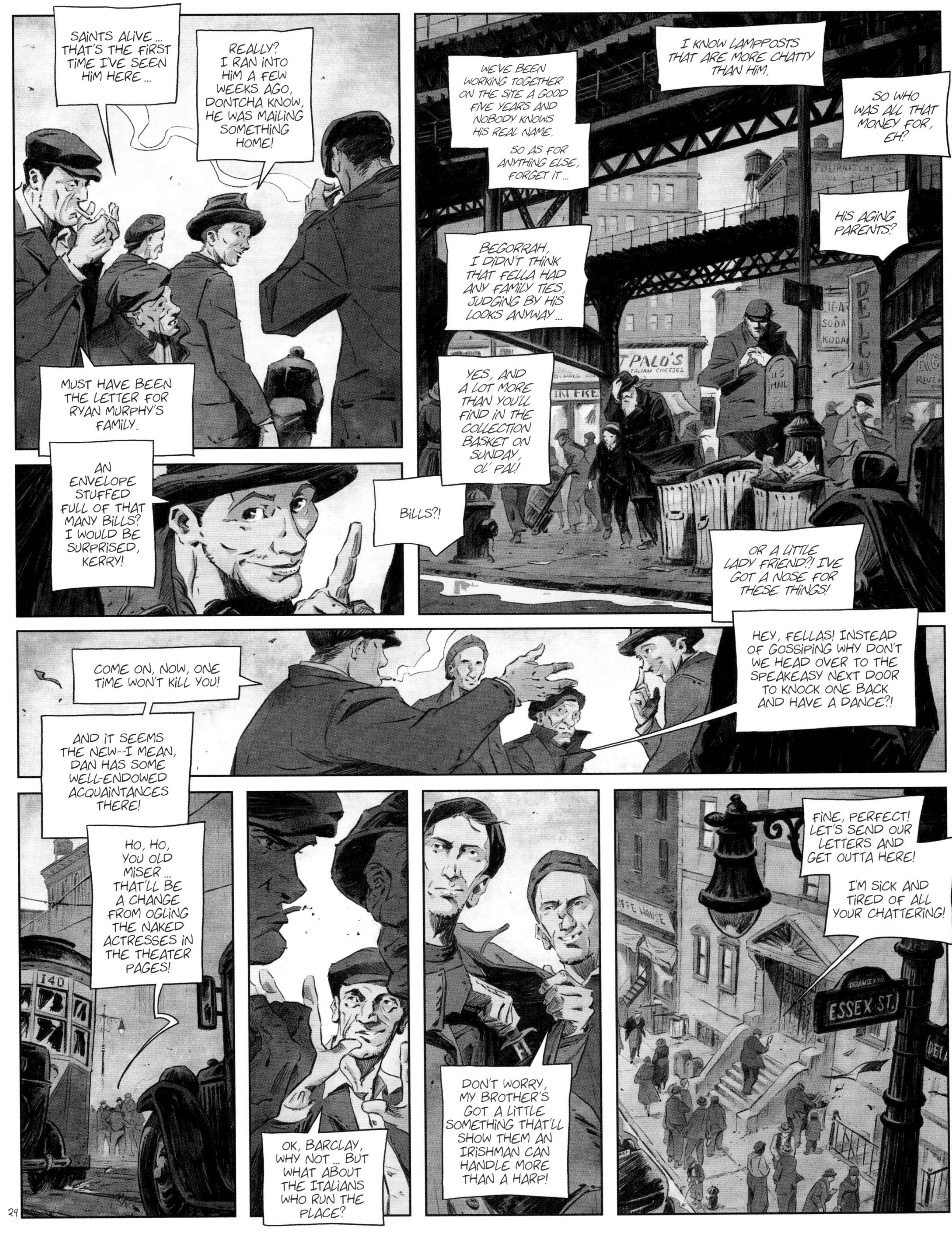
SAINTS ALIVE ... THAT'S THE FIRST TIME I'VE SEEN HIM HERE ...
REALLY? I RAN INTO HIM A FEW WEEKS AGO, DONTCHA KNOW, HE WAS MAILING SOMETHING HOME!
MUST HAVE BEEN THE LETTER FOR RYAN MURPHY'S FAMILY.
AN ENVELOPE STUFFED FULL OF THAT MANY BILLS? I WOULD BE SURPRISED, KERRY!
BILLS?!
WE'VE BEEN WORKING TOGETHER ON THE SITE A GOOD FIVE YEARS AND NOBODY KNOWS HIS REAL NAME.
SO AS FOR ANYTHING ELSE, FORGET IT ...
I KNOW LAMPPOSTS THAT ARE MORE CHATTY THAN HIM.
SO WHO WAS ALL THAT MONEY FOR, EH?
HIS AGING PARENTS?
BEGORRAH, I DIDN'T THINK THAT FELLA HAD ANY FAMILY TIES, JUDGING BY HIS LOOKS ANYWAY ...
YES, AND A LOT MORE THAN YOU'LL FIND IN THE COLLECTION BASKET ON SUNDAY, OL' PAL!
OR A LITTLE LADY FRIEND?! I'VE GOT A NOSE FOR THESE THINGS!
COME ON, NOW, ONE TIME WON'T KILL YOU!
AND IT SEEMS THE NEW--I MEAN, DAN HAS SOME WELL-ENDOWED ACQUAINTANCES THERE!
HEY, FELLAS! INSTEAD OF GOSSIPING WHY DON'T WE HEAD OVER TO THE SPEAKEASY NEXT DOOR TO KNOCK ONE BACK AND HAVE A DANCE?!
HO, HO, YOU OLD MISER ... THAT'LL BE A CHANGE FROM OGLING THE NAKED ACTRESSES IN THE THEATER PAGES!
OK, BARCLAY, WHY NOT ... BUT WHAT ABOUT THE ITALIANS WHO RUN THE PLACE?
DON'T WORRY, MY BROTHER'S GOT A LITTLE SOMETHING THAT'LL SHOW THEM AN IRISHMAN CAN HANDLE MORE THAN A HARP!
FINE, PERFECT! LET'S SEND OUR LETTERS AND GET OUTTA HERE!
I'M SICK AND TIRED OF ALL YOUR CHATTERING!
ESSEX ST.
29

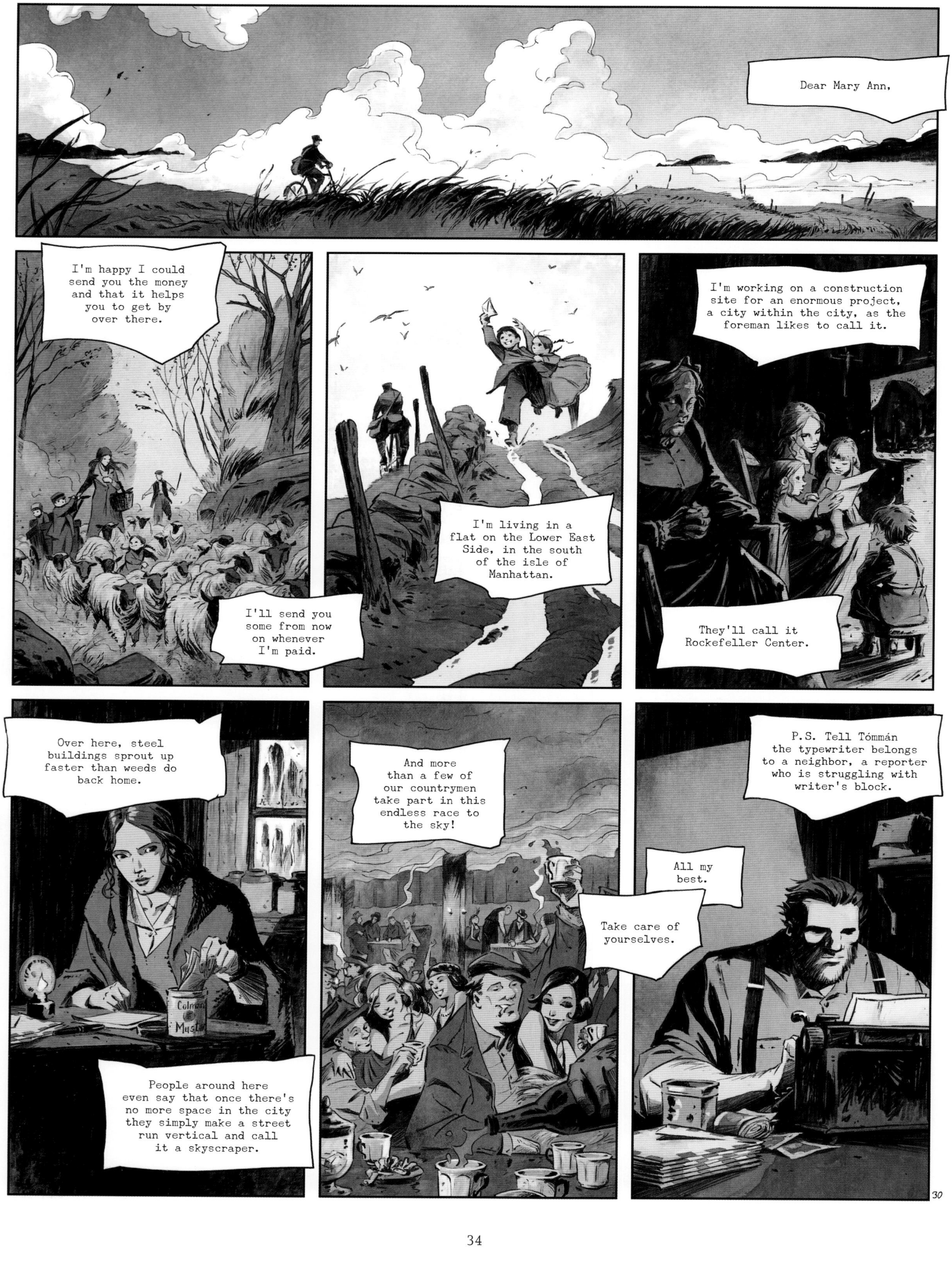
Dear Mary Ann,
I'm happy I could send you the money and that it helps you to get by over there.
I'll send you some from now on whenever I'm paid.
I'm living in a flat on the Lower East Side, in the south of the isle of Manhattan.
I'm working on a construction site for an enormous project, a city within the city, as the foreman likes to call it.
They'll call it Rockefeller Center.
Over here, steel buildings sprout up faster than weeds do back home.
People around here even say that once there's no more space in the city they simply make a street run vertical and call it a skyscraper.
And more than a few of our countrymen take part in this endless race to the sky!
P.S. Tell Tómmán the typewriter belongs to a neighbor, a reporter who is struggling with writer's block.
All my best.
Take care of yourselves.
30

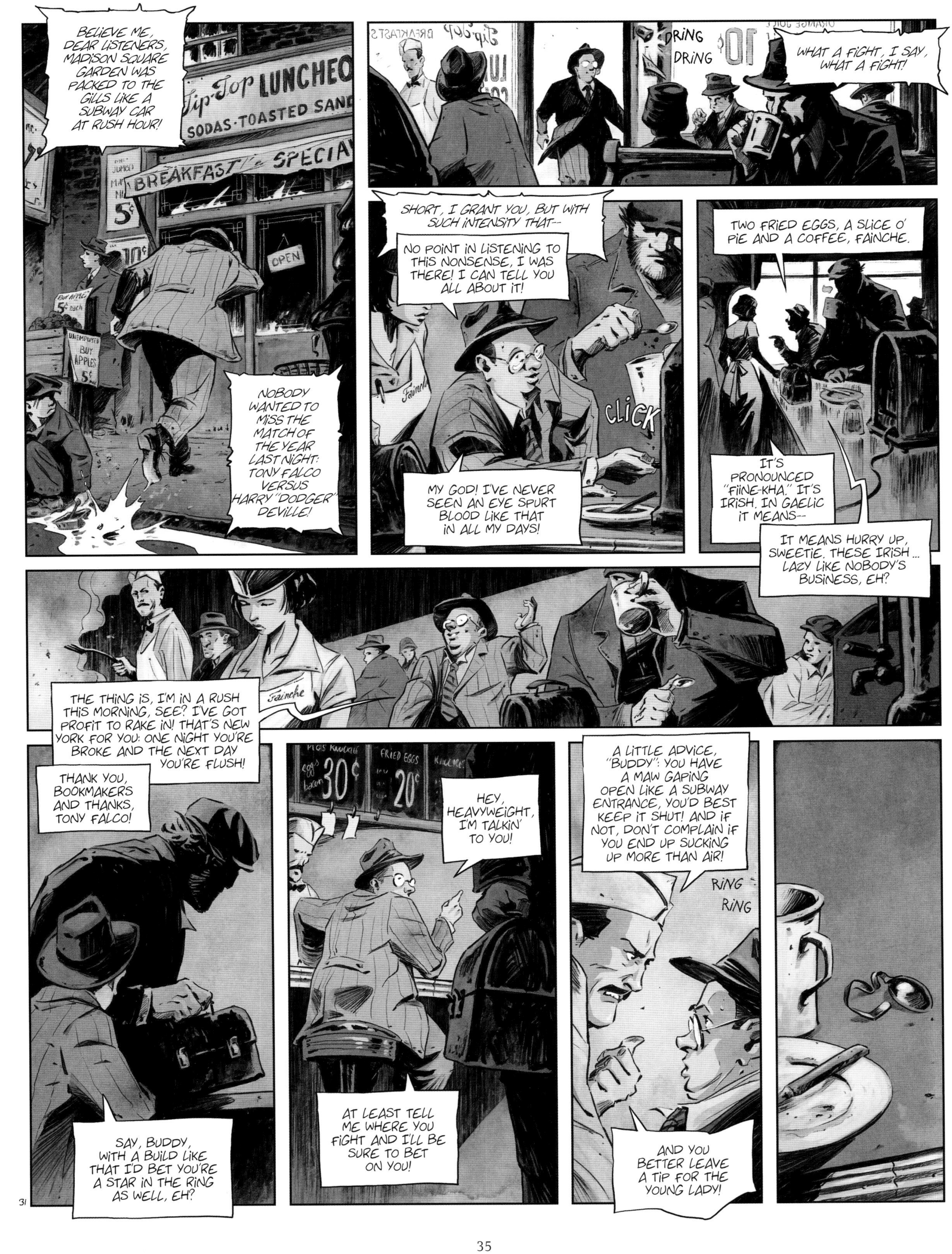
BELIEVE ME, DEAR LISTENERS, MADISON SQUARE GARDEN WAS PACKED TO THE GILLS LIKE A SUBWAY CAR AT RUSH HOUR!
Tip-Top LUNCHEO
SODAS-TOASTED SAND
BREAKFAST SPECIA
OPEN
NOBODY WANTED TO MISS THE MATCH OF THE YEAR LAST NIGHT: TONY FALCO VERSUS HARRY "DODGER" DEVILLE!
DRING DRING
WHAT A FIGHT, I SAY, WHAT A FIGHT!
SHORT, I GRANT YOU, BUT WITH SUCH INTENSITY THAT--
NO POINT IN LISTENING TO THIS NONSENSE, I WAS THERE! I CAN TELL YOU ALL ABOUT IT!
CLICK
MY GOD! I'VE NEVER SEEN AN EYE SPURT BLOOD LIKE THAT IN ALL MY DAYS!
TWO FRIED EGGS, A SLICE O' PIE AND A COFFEE, FAINCHE.
IT'S PRONOUNCED "FIINE-KHA." IT'S IRISH. IN GAELIC IT MEANS--
IT MEANS HURRY UP, SWEETIE. THESE IRISH... LAZY LIKE NOBODY'S BUSINESS, EH?
Fainche
THE THING IS, I'M IN A RUSH THIS MORNING, SEE? I'VE GOT PROFIT TO RAKE IN! THAT'S NEW YORK FOR YOU: ONE NIGHT YOU'RE BROKE AND THE NEXT DAY YOU'RE FLUSH!
THANK YOU, BOOKMAKERS AND THANKS, TONY FALCO!
SAY, BUDDY, WITH A BUILD LIKE THAT I'D BET YOU'RE A STAR IN THE RING AS WELL, EH?
FRIED EGGS
30¢
20¢
HEY, HEAVYWEIGHT, I'M TALKIN' TO YOU!
AT LEAST TELL ME WHERE YOU FIGHT AND I'LL BE SURE TO BET ON YOU!
A LITTLE ADVICE, "BUDDY": YOU HAVE A MAW GAPING OPEN LIKE A SUBWAY ENTRANCE, YOU'D BEST KEEP IT SHUT! AND IF NOT, DON'T COMPLAIN IF YOU END UP SUCKING UP MORE THAN AIR!
RING RING
AND YOU BETTER LEAVE A TIP FOR THE YOUNG LADY!
31

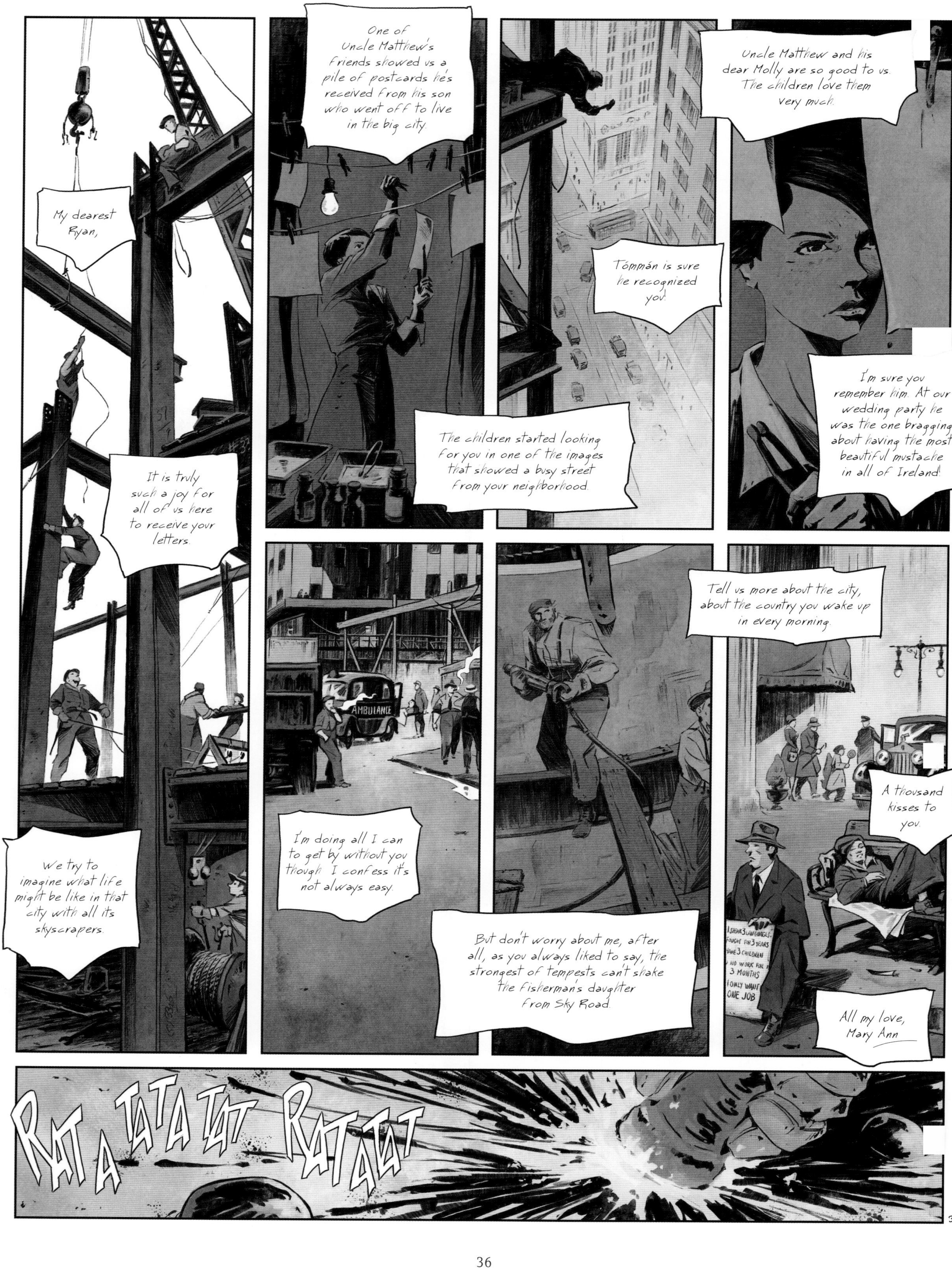

My dearest Ryan,
It is truly such a joy for all of us here to receive your letters.
We try to imagine what life might be like in that city with all its skyscrapers.
One of Uncle Matthew's friends showed us a pile of postcards he's received from his son who went off to live in the big city.
The children started looking for you in one of the images that showed a busy street from your neighborhood.
Tómmán is sure he recognized you!
Uncle Matthew and his dear Molly are so good to us. The children love them very much.
I'm sure you remember him. At our wedding party he was the one bragging about having the most beautiful mustache in all of Ireland!
AMBULANCE
I'm doing all I can to get by without you though. I confess it's not always easy.
But don't worry about me, after all, as you always liked to say, the strongest of tempests can't shake the fisherman's daughter from Sky Road.
Tell us more about the city, about the country you wake up in every morning.
A thousand kisses to you.
All my love, Mary Ann
RATATATATAT RATATAT

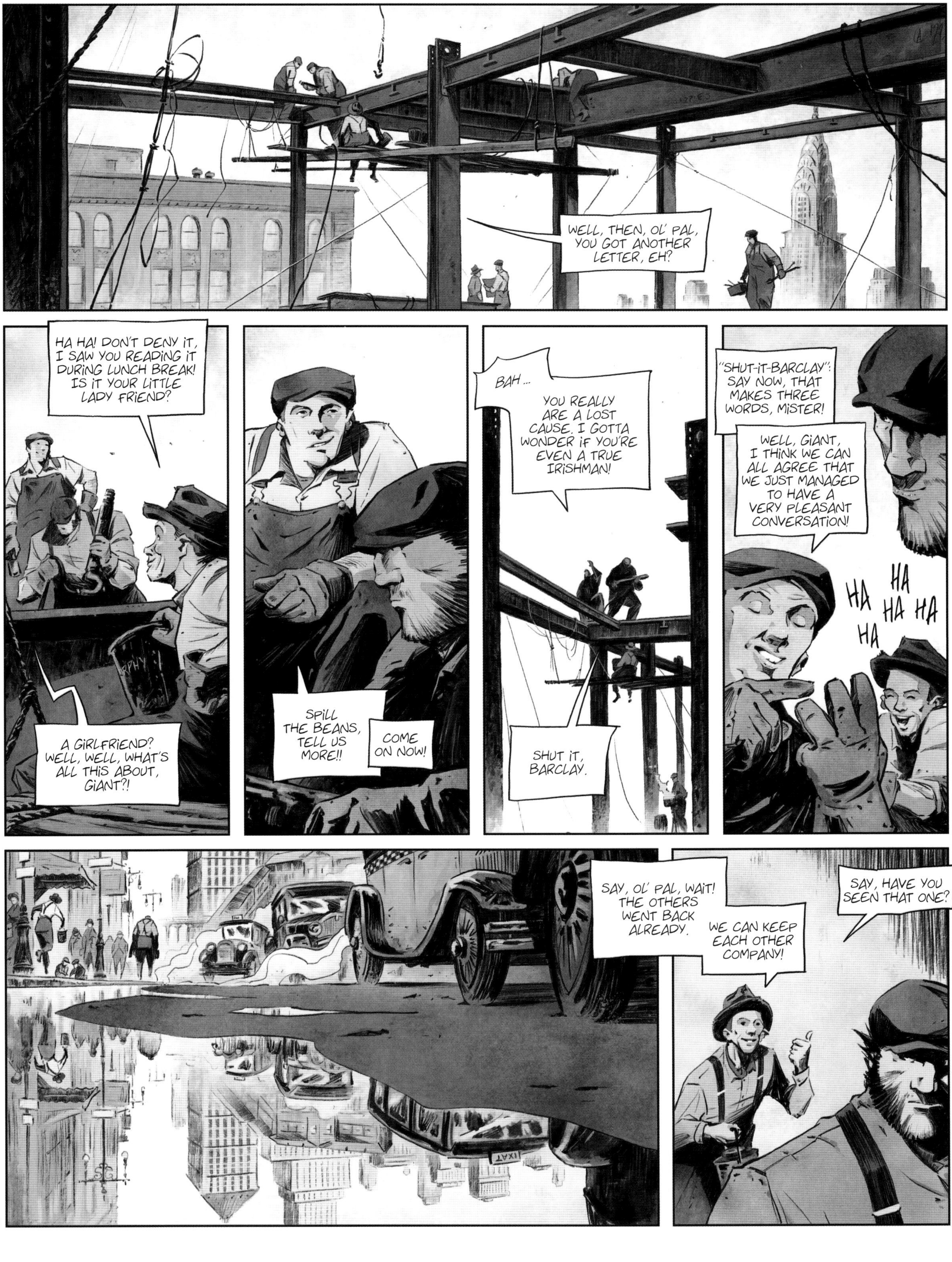
WELL, THEN, OL' PAL, YOU GOT ANOTHER LETTER, EH?
HA HA! DON'T DENY IT, I SAW YOU READING IT DURING LUNCH BREAK! IS IT YOUR LITTLE LADY FRIEND?
A GIRLFRIEND? WELL, WELL, WHAT'S ALL THIS ABOUT, GIANT?!
SPILL THE BEANS, TELL US MORE!!
COME ON NOW!
BAH ...
YOU REALLY ARE A LOST CAUSE. I GOTTA WONDER IF YOU'RE EVEN A TRUE IRISHMAN!
SHUT IT, BARCLAY.
"SHUT-IT-BARCLAY": SAY NOW, THAT MAKES THREE WORDS, MISTER!
WELL, GIANT, I THINK WE CAN ALL AGREE THAT WE JUST MANAGED TO HAVE A VERY PLEASANT CONVERSATION!
HA HA HA HA HA HA
SAY, OL' PAL, WAIT! THE OTHERS WENT BACK ALREADY.
WE CAN KEEP EACH OTHER COMPANY!
SAY, HAVE YOU SEEN THAT ONE?
33

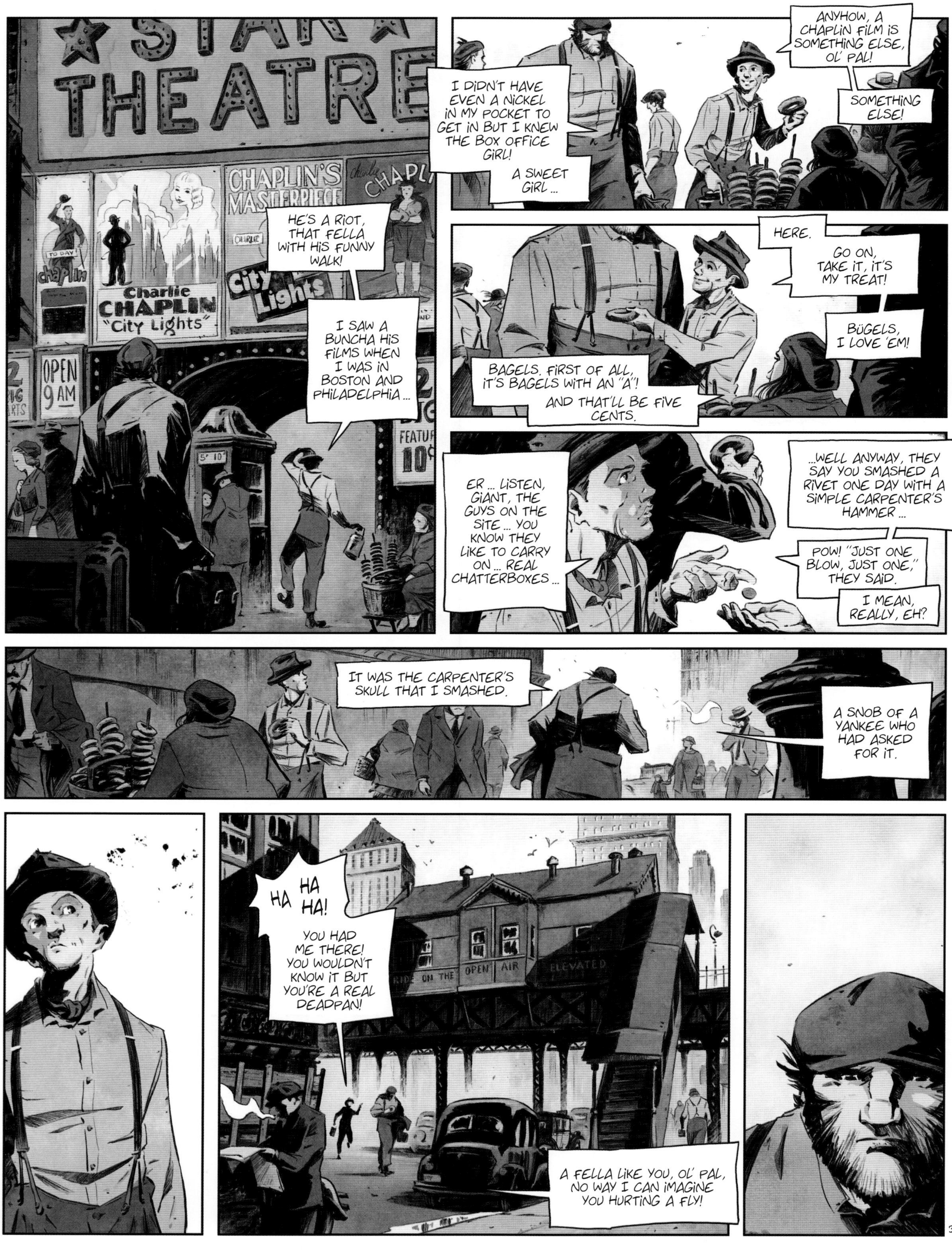
STAR THEATRE
CHAPLIN'S MASTERPIECE
Charlie CHAPLIN "City Lights"
City Lights
OPEN 9 AM
HE'S A RIOT, THAT FELLA WITH HIS FUNNY WALK!
I SAW A BUNCHA HIS FILMS WHEN I WAS IN BOSTON AND PHILADELPHIA ...
I DIDN'T HAVE EVEN A NICKEL IN MY POCKET TO GET IN BUT I KNEW THE BOX OFFICE GIRL!
A SWEET GIRL ...
ANYHOW, A CHAPLIN FILM IS SOMETHING ELSE, OL' PAL!
SOMETHING ELSE!
HERE.
GO ON, TAKE IT, IT'S MY TREAT!
BÜGELS, I LOVE 'EM!
BAGELS. FIRST OF ALL, IT'S BAGELS WITH AN "A"!
AND THAT'LL BE FIVE CENTS.
ER ... LISTEN, GIANT, THE GUYS ON THE SITE ... YOU KNOW THEY LIKE TO CARRY ON ... REAL CHATTERBOXES ...
...WELL ANYWAY, THEY SAY YOU SMASHED A RIVET ONE DAY WITH A SIMPLE CARPENTER'S HAMMER ...
POW! "JUST ONE BLOW, JUST ONE," THEY SAID.
I MEAN, REALLY, EH?
IT WAS THE CARPENTER'S SKULL THAT I SMASHED.
A SNOB OF A YANKEE WHO HAD ASKED FOR IT.
HA HA HA!
YOU HAD ME THERE! YOU WOULDN'T KNOW IT BUT YOU'RE A REAL DEADPAN!
RIDE ON THE OPEN AIR ELEVATED
A FELLA LIKE YOU, OL' PAL, NO WAY I CAN IMAGINE YOU HURTING A FLY!
34

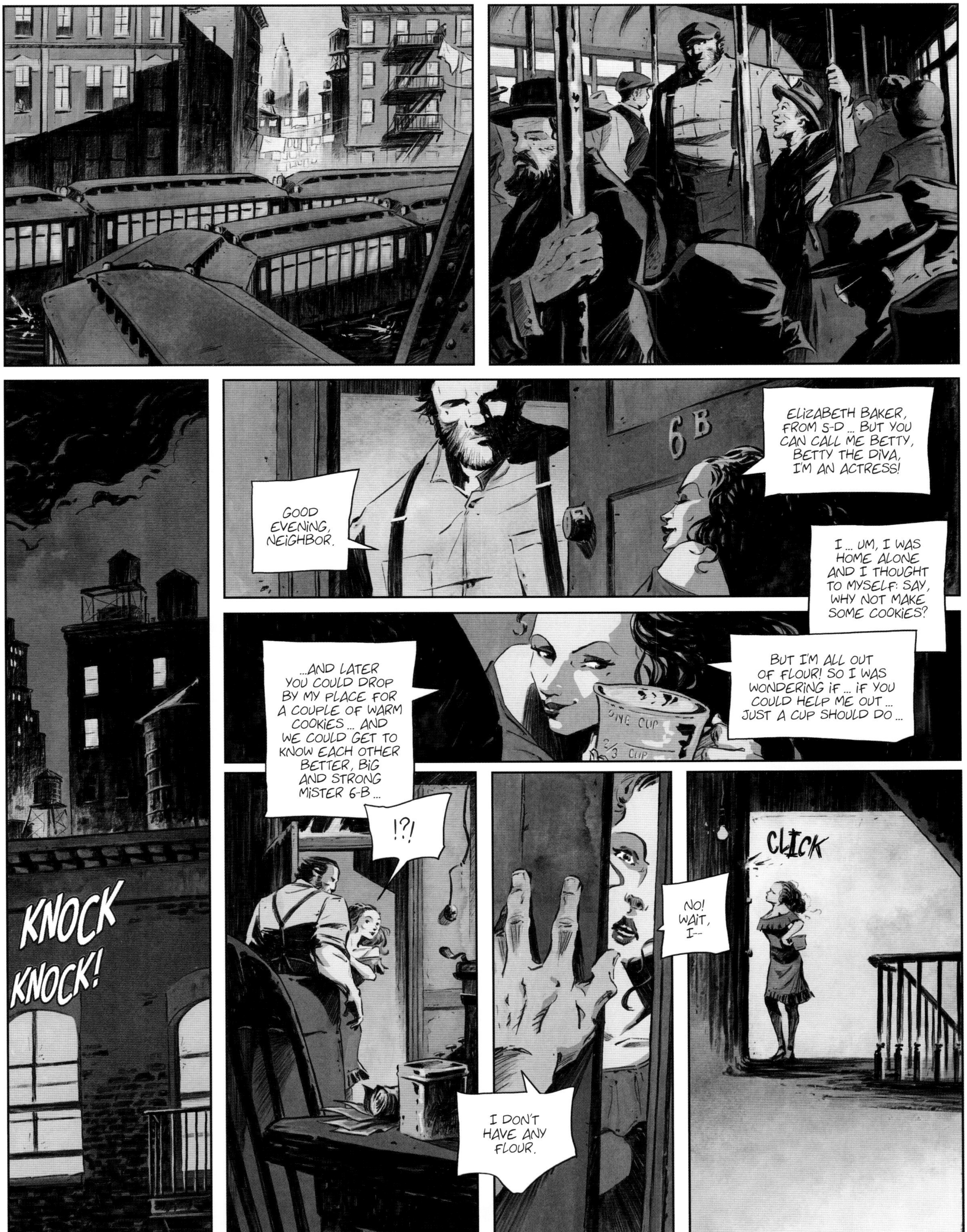

GOOD EVENING, NEIGHBOR.
ELIZABETH BAKER, FROM 5-D ... BUT YOU CAN CALL ME BETTY, BETTY THE DIVA, I'M AN ACTRESS!
I ... UM, I WAS HOME ALONE AND I THOUGHT TO MYSELF: SAY, WHY NOT MAKE SOME COOKIES?
BUT I'M ALL OUT OF FLOUR! SO I WAS WONDERING IF ... IF YOU COULD HELP ME OUT ... JUST A CUP SHOULD DO ...
...AND LATER YOU COULD DROP BY MY PLACE FOR A COUPLE OF WARM COOKIES ... AND WE COULD GET TO KNOW EACH OTHER BETTER, BIG AND STRONG MISTER 6-B ...
KNOCK
KNOCK!
!?!
I DON'T HAVE ANY FLOUR.
NO! WAIT, I--
CLICK

35

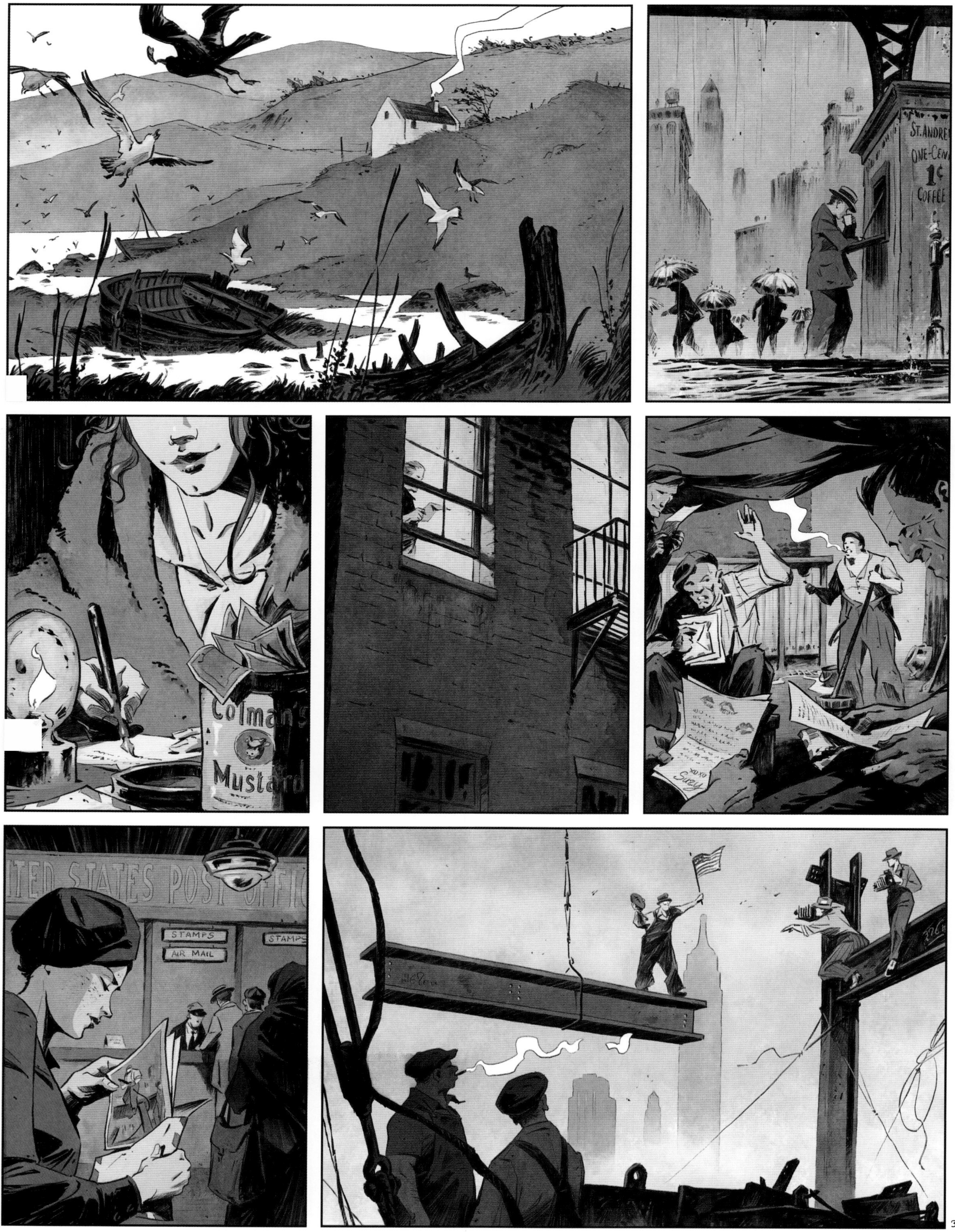
ST. ANDRE
ONE-CEN
1¢
COFFEE
Colman's
Mustard
XOXO
Suzy
ITED STATES POST OFFIC
STAMPS
AIR MAIL
STAMPS

36

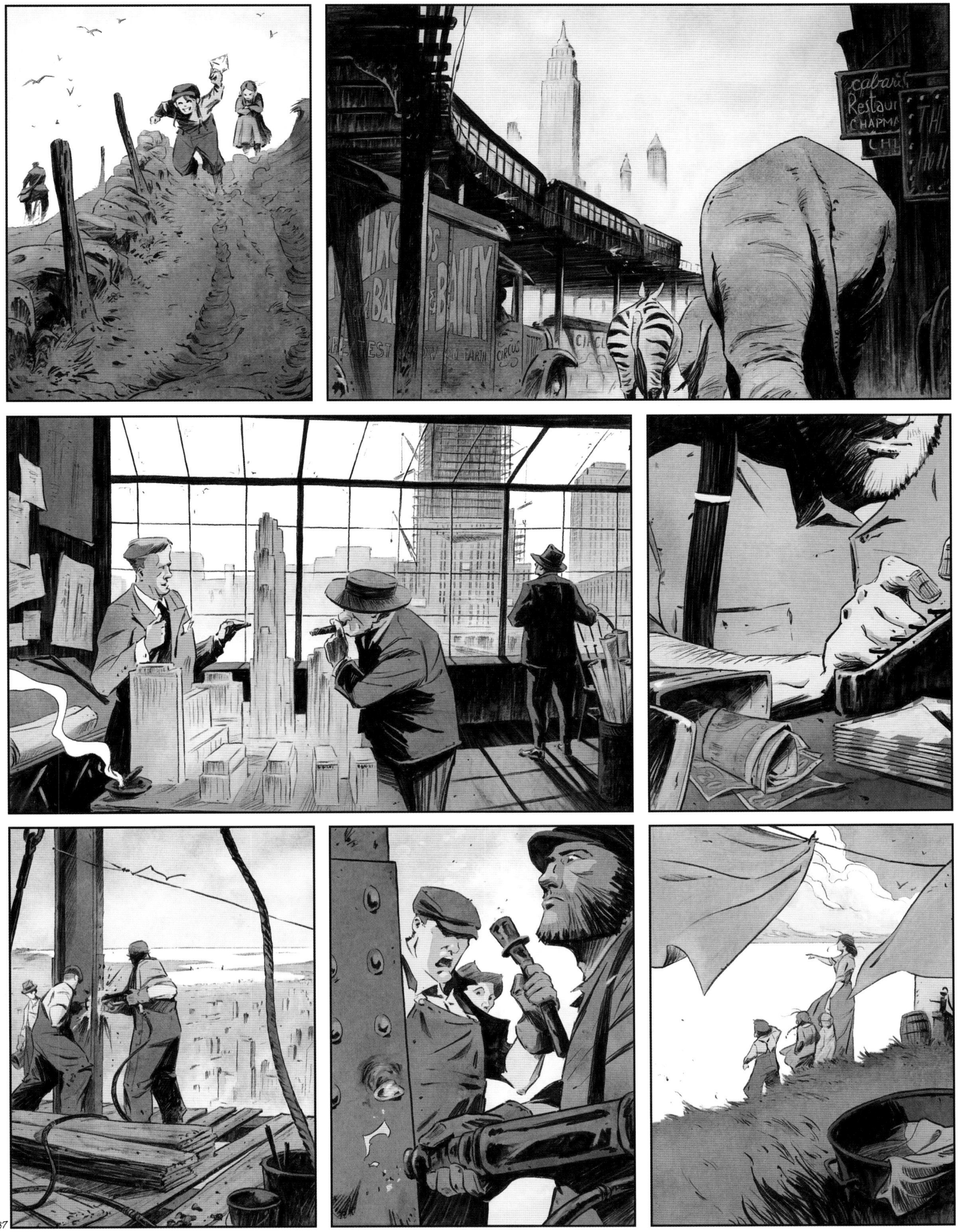
Restau
CHAPMA
BAILEY
CIRCUS

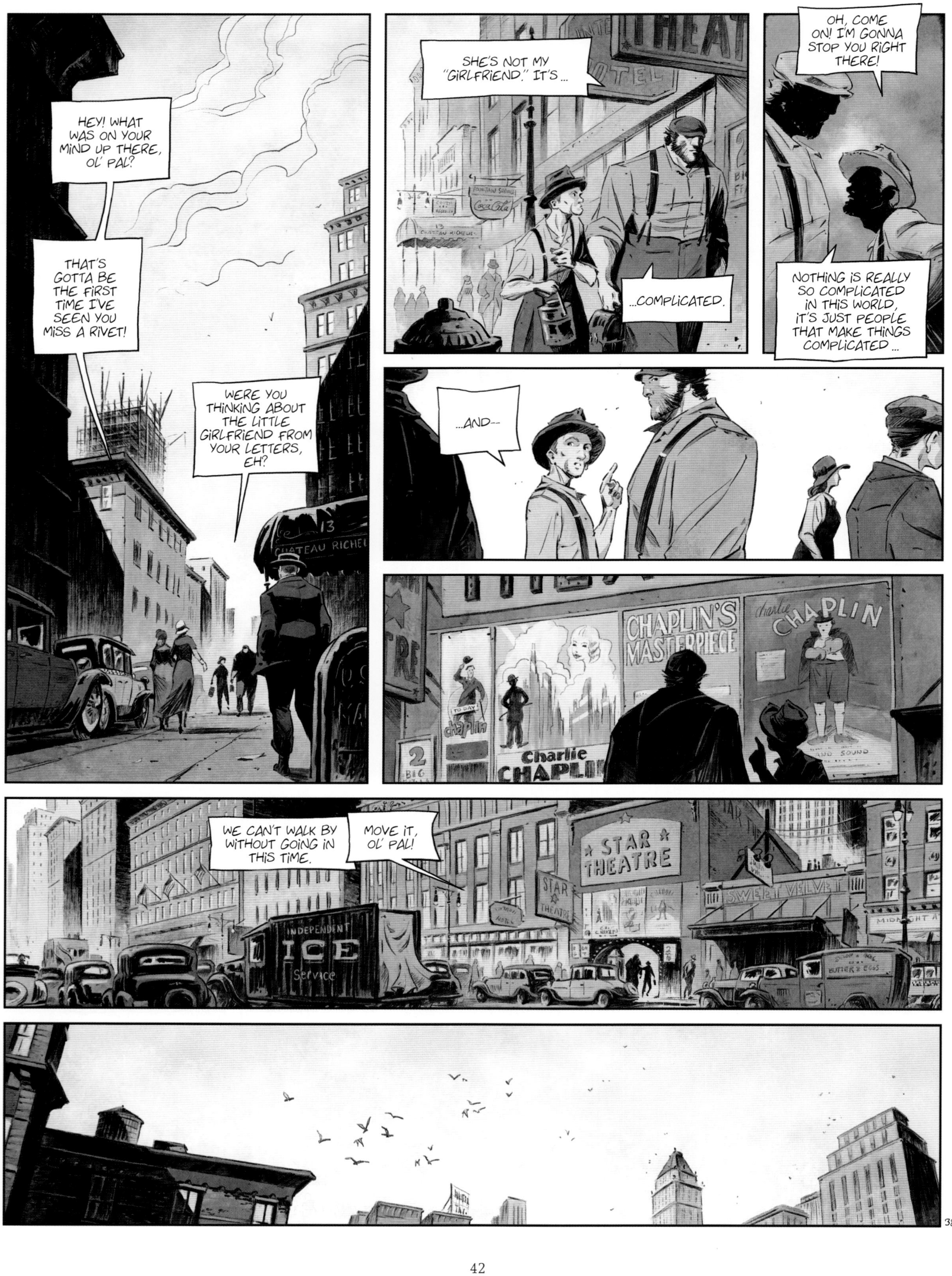
HEY! WHAT WAS ON YOUR MIND UP THERE, OL' PAL?
THAT'S GOTTA BE THE FIRST TIME I'VE SEEN YOU MISS A RIVET!
WERE YOU THINKING ABOUT THE LITTLE GIRLFRIEND FROM YOUR LETTERS, EH?
SHE'S NOT MY "GIRLFRIEND." IT'S ...
...COMPLICATED.
OH, COME ON! I'M GONNA STOP YOU RIGHT THERE!
NOTHING IS REALLY SO COMPLICATED IN THIS WORLD, IT'S JUST PEOPLE THAT MAKE THINGS COMPLICATED ...
...AND--
CHAPLIN'S MASTERPIECE
Charlie CHAPLIN
Charlie CHAPLIN
WE CAN'T WALK BY WITHOUT GOING IN THIS TIME.
MOVE IT, OL' PAL!
STAR THEATRE
INDEPENDENT ICE Service
38

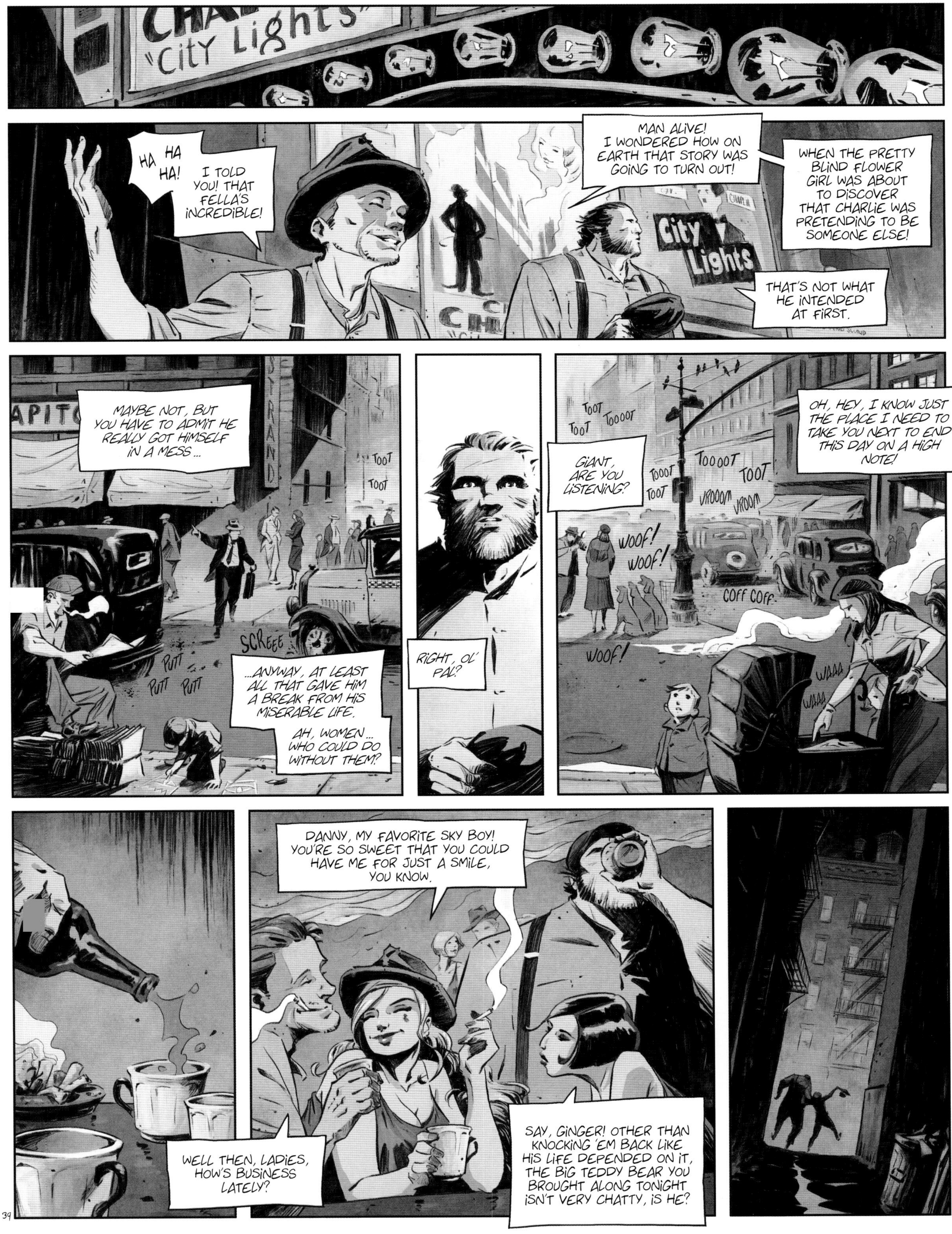
"City Lights"
HA HA HA!
I TOLD YOU! THAT FELLA'S INCREDIBLE!
MAN ALIVE! I WONDERED HOW ON EARTH THAT STORY WAS GOING TO TURN OUT!
WHEN THE PRETTY BLIND FLOWER GIRL WAS ABOUT TO DISCOVER THAT CHARLIE WAS PRETENDING TO BE SOMEONE ELSE!
City Lights
THAT'S NOT WHAT HE INTENDED AT FIRST.
MAYBE NOT, BUT YOU HAVE TO ADMIT HE REALLY GOT HIMSELF IN A MESS ...
STRAND
TOOT
TOOT
SCREEE
PUTT PUTT PUTT
...ANYWAY, AT LEAST ALL THAT GAVE HIM A BREAK FROM HIS MISERABLE LIFE.
AH, WOMEN ... WHO COULD DO WITHOUT THEM?
RIGHT, OL' PAL?
TOOT TOOT TOOOOT
GIANT, ARE YOU LISTENING?
TOOOT TOOT TOOOOT TOOT
VROOOM VROOOM
OH, HEY, I KNOW JUST THE PLACE I NEED TO TAKE YOU NEXT TO END THIS DAY ON A HIGH NOTE!
WOOF! WOOF!
COFF COFF
WOOF!
WAAA WAAA
DANNY, MY FAVORITE SKY BOY! YOU'RE SO SWEET THAT YOU COULD HAVE ME FOR JUST A SMILE, YOU KNOW.
WELL THEN, LADIES, HOW'S BUSINESS LATELY?
SAY, GINGER! OTHER THAN KNOCKING 'EM BACK LIKE HIS LIFE DEPENDED ON IT, THE BIG TEDDY BEAR YOU BROUGHT ALONG TONIGHT ISN'T VERY CHATTY, IS HE?
39

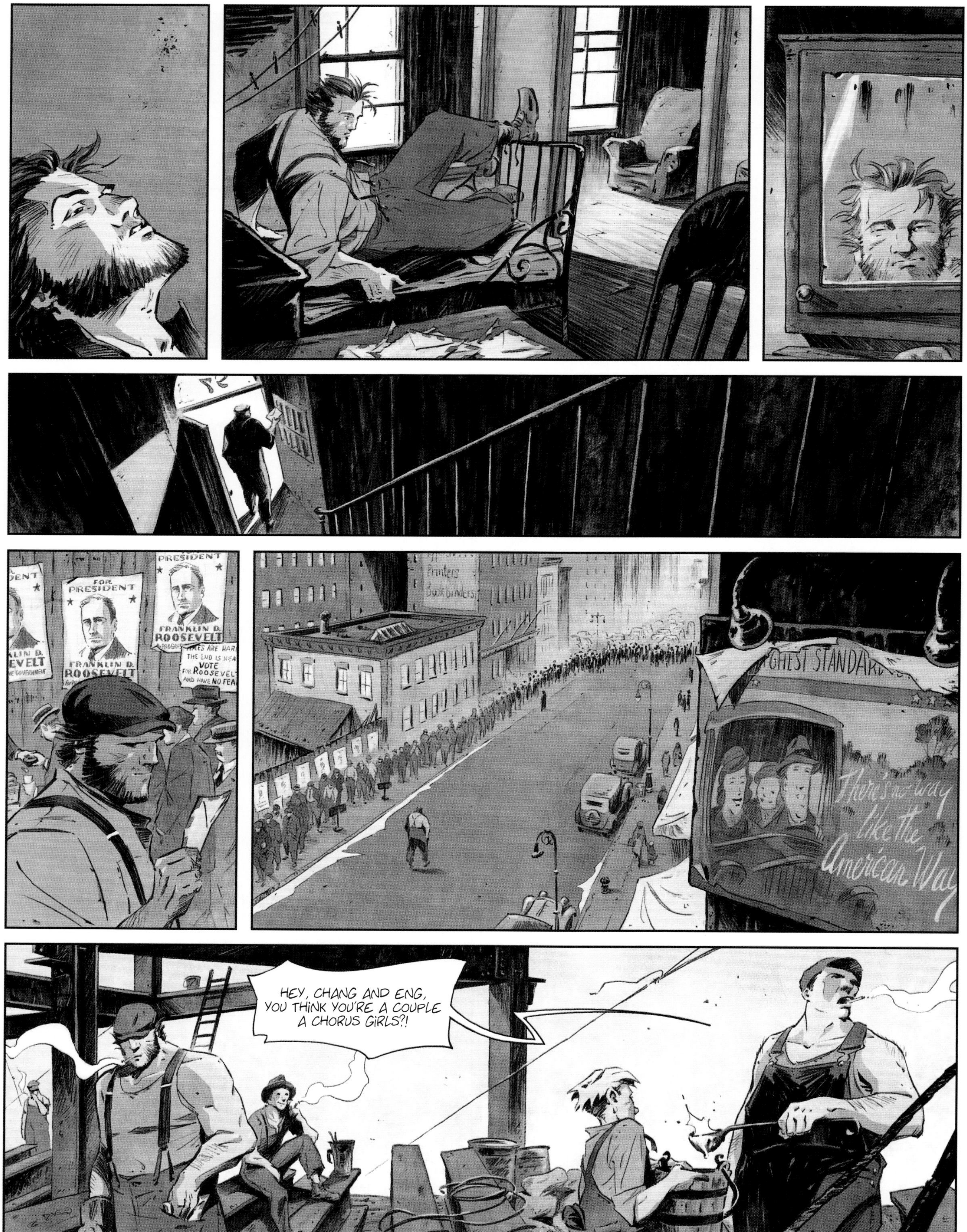
PRESIDENT
FOR PRESIDENT
FRANKLIN D. ROOSEVELT
VOTE FOR ROOSEVELT
Printers
Bookbinders
There's no way like the American Way
HEY, CHANG AND ENG, YOU THINK YOU'RE A COUPLE A CHORUS GIRLS?!

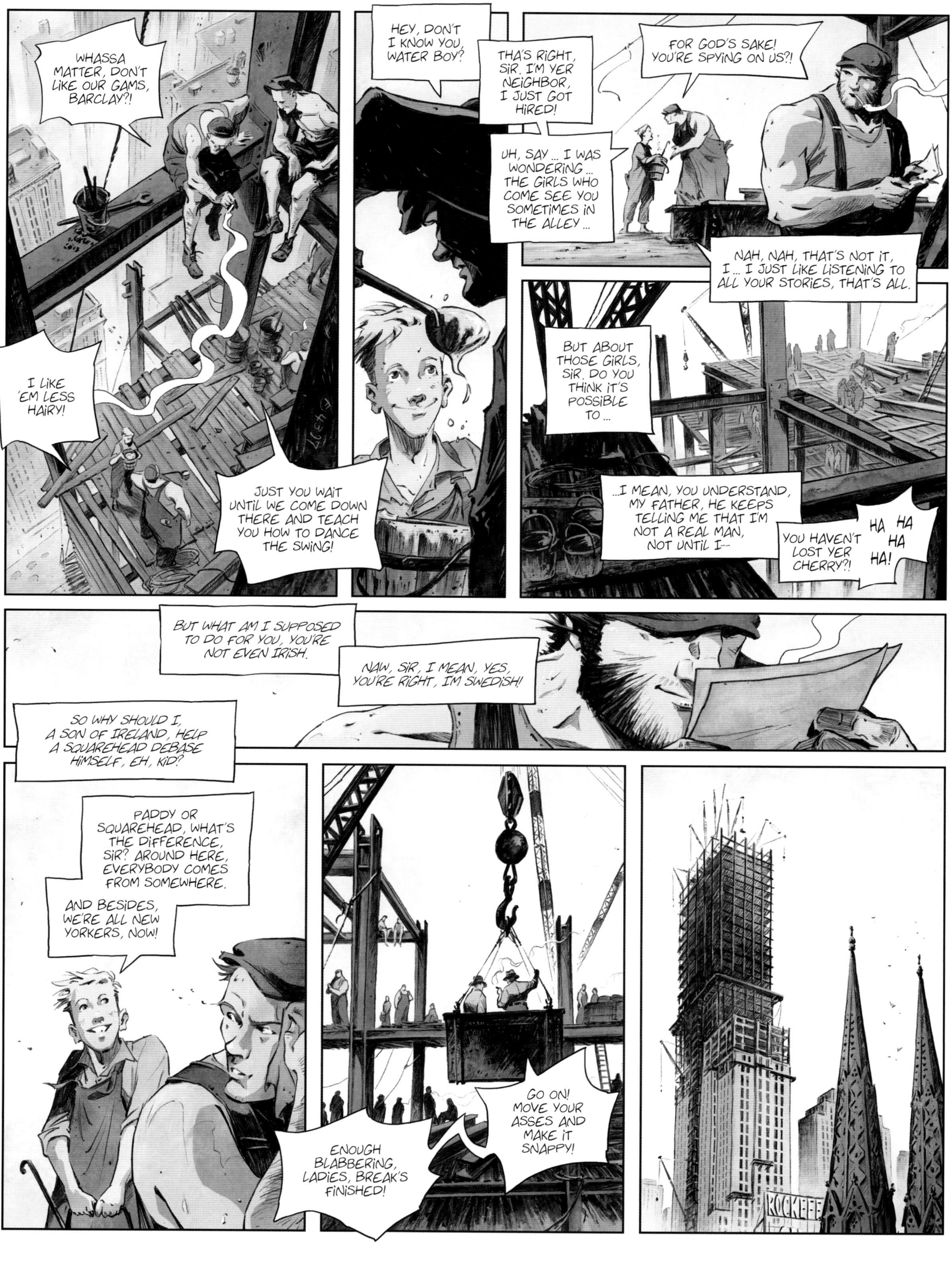
WHASSA MATTER, DON'T LIKE OUR GAMS, BARCLAY?!
I LIKE 'EM LESS HAIRY!
JUST YOU WAIT UNTIL WE COME DOWN THERE AND TEACH YOU HOW TO DANCE THE SWING!
HEY, DON'T I KNOW YOU, WATER BOY?
THA'S RIGHT, SIR. I'M YER NEIGHBOR, I JUST GOT HIRED!
UH, SAY ... I WAS WONDERING ... THE GIRLS WHO COME SEE YOU SOMETIMES IN THE ALLEY ...
FOR GOD'S SAKE! YOU'RE SPYING ON US?!
NAH, NAH, THAT'S NOT IT, I ... I JUST LIKE LISTENING TO ALL YOUR STORIES, THAT'S ALL.
BUT ABOUT THOSE GIRLS, SIR. DO YOU THINK IT'S POSSIBLE TO ...
...I MEAN, YOU UNDERSTAND, MY FATHER, HE KEEPS TELLING ME THAT I'M NOT A REAL MAN, NOT UNTIL I--
YOU HAVEN'T LOST YER CHERRY?!
HA HA HA HA!
BUT WHAT AM I SUPPOSED TO DO FOR YOU, YOU'RE NOT EVEN IRISH.
NAW, SIR, I MEAN, YES, YOU'RE RIGHT, I'M SWEDISH!
SO WHY SHOULD I, A SON OF IRELAND, HELP A SQUAREHEAD DEBASE HIMSELF, EH, KID?
PADDY OR SQUAREHEAD, WHAT'S THE DIFFERENCE, SIR? AROUND HERE, EVERYBODY COMES FROM SOMEWHERE.
AND BESIDES, WE'RE ALL NEW YORKERS, NOW!
GO ON! MOVE YOUR ASSES AND MAKE IT SNAPPY!
ENOUGH BLABBERING, LADIES, BREAK'S FINISHED!
ROCKEFE

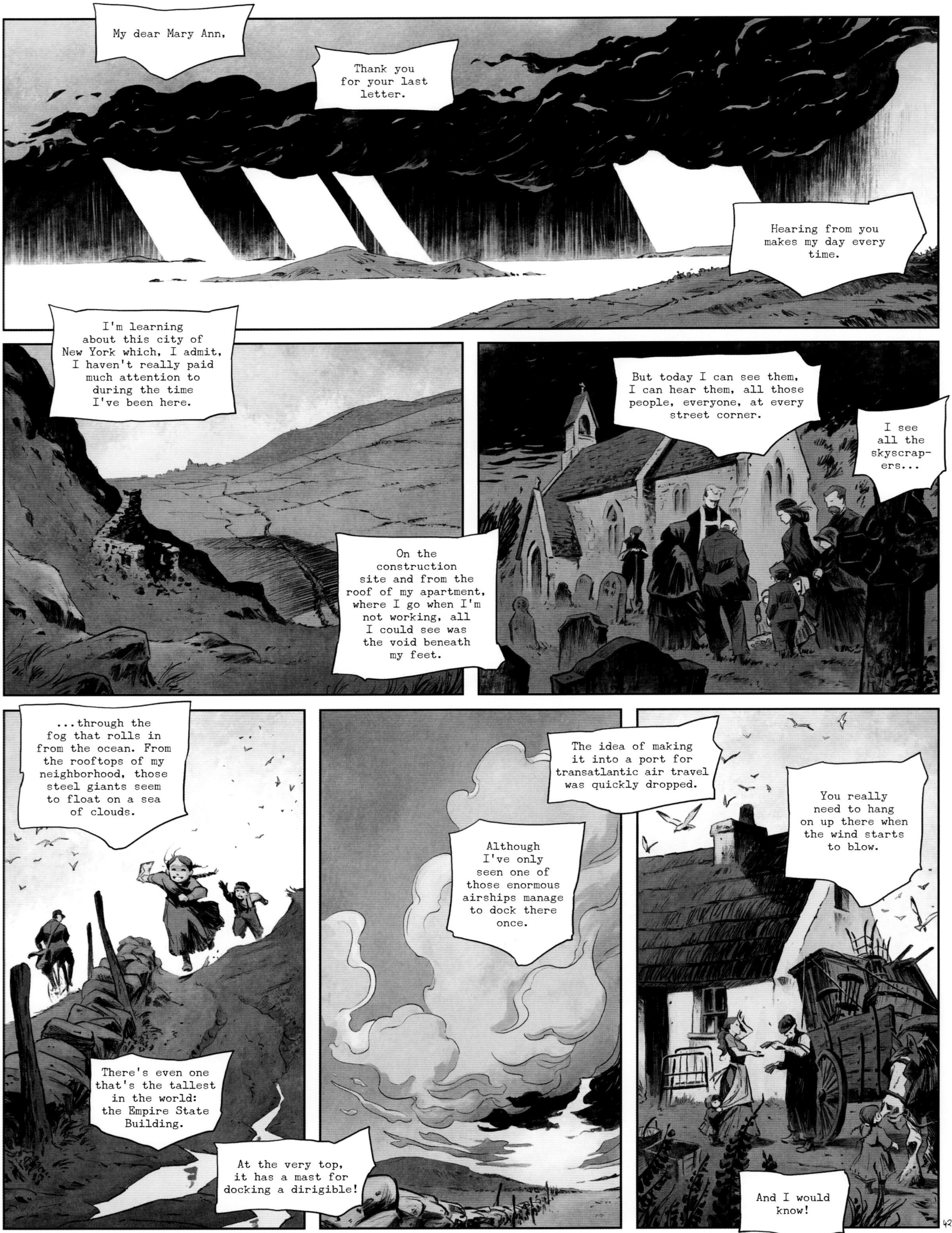
My dear Mary Ann,
Thank you for your last letter.
Hearing from you makes my day every time.
I'm learning about this city of New York which, I admit, I haven't really paid much attention to during the time I've been here.
On the construction site and from the roof of my apartment, where I go when I'm not working, all I could see was the void beneath my feet.
But today I can see them, I can hear them, all those people, everyone, at every street corner.
I see all the skyscrap-ers...
...through the fog that rolls in from the ocean. From the rooftops of my neighborhood, those steel giants seem to float on a sea of clouds.
There's even one that's the tallest in the world: the Empire State Building.
At the very top, it has a mast for docking a dirigible!
Although I've only seen one of those enormous airships manage to dock there once.
The idea of making it into a port for transatlantic air travel was quickly dropped.
You really need to hang on up there when the wind starts to blow.
And I would know!
42

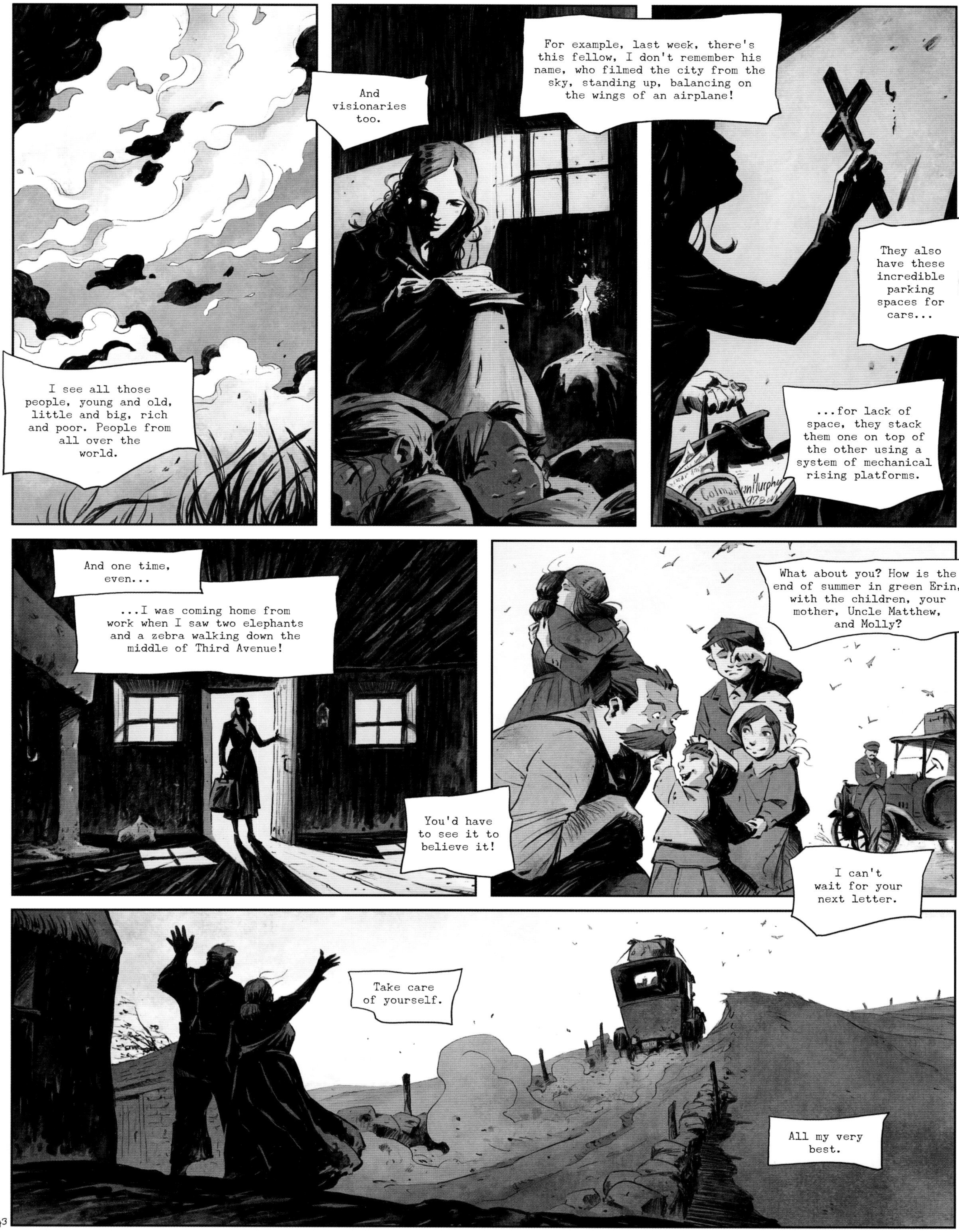
I see all those people, young and old, little and big, rich and poor. People from all over the world.
And visionaries too.
For example, last week, there's this fellow, I don't remember his name, who filmed the city from the sky, standing up, balancing on the wings of an airplane!
They also have these incredible parking spaces for cars...
...for lack of space, they stack them one on top of the other using a system of mechanical rising platforms.
And one time, even...
...I was coming home from work when I saw two elephants and a zebra walking down the middle of Third Avenue!
You'd have to see it to believe it!
What about you? How is the end of summer in green Erin, with the children, your mother, Uncle Matthew, and Molly?
I can't wait for your next letter.
Take care of yourself.
All my very best.

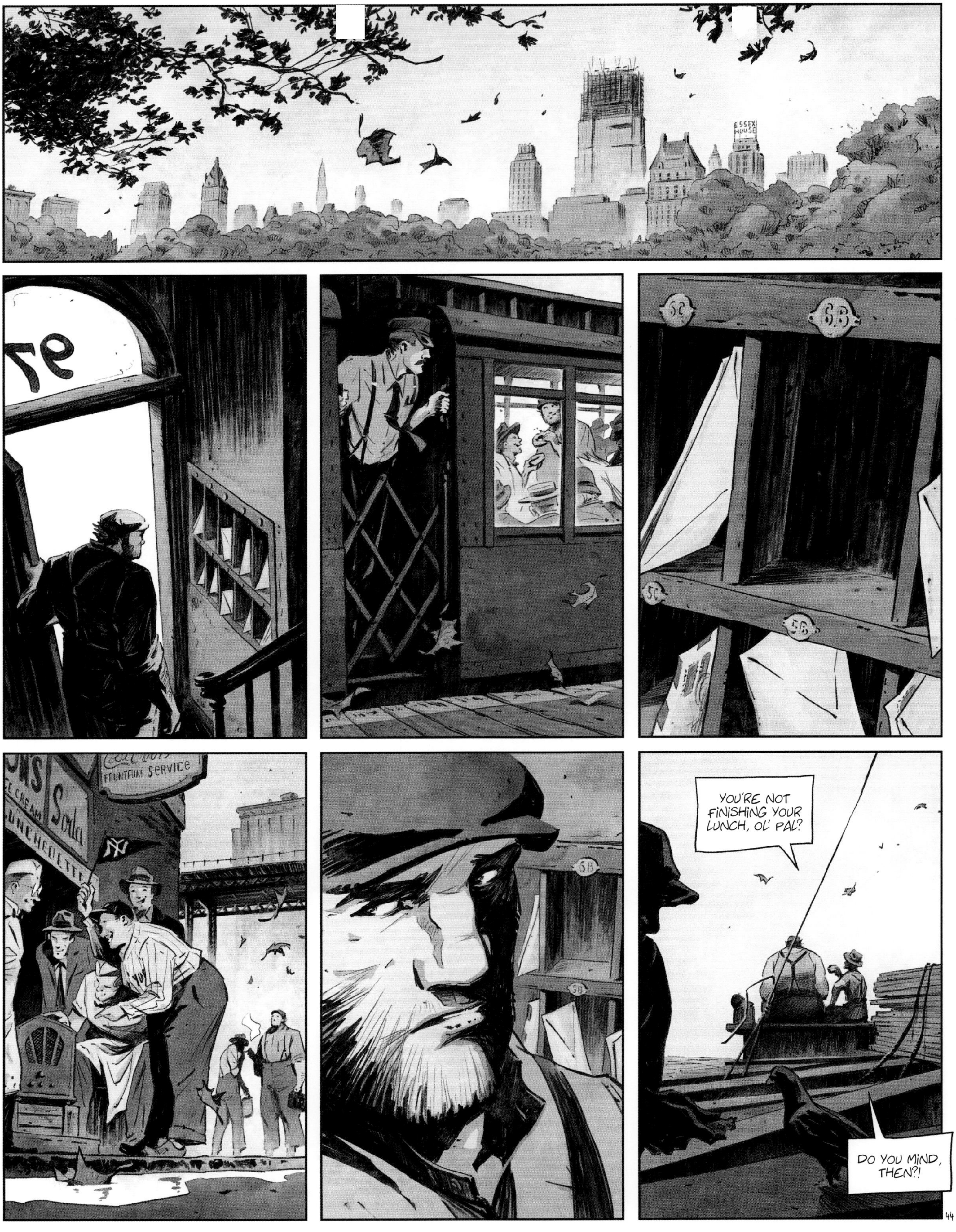
ESSEX HOUSE
97
FOUNTAIN SERVICE
Soda
ICE CREAM
LUNCHEONETTE
5B
5C
6B
YOU'RE NOT FINISHING YOUR LUNCH, OL' PAL?
DO YOU MIND, THEN?!
44

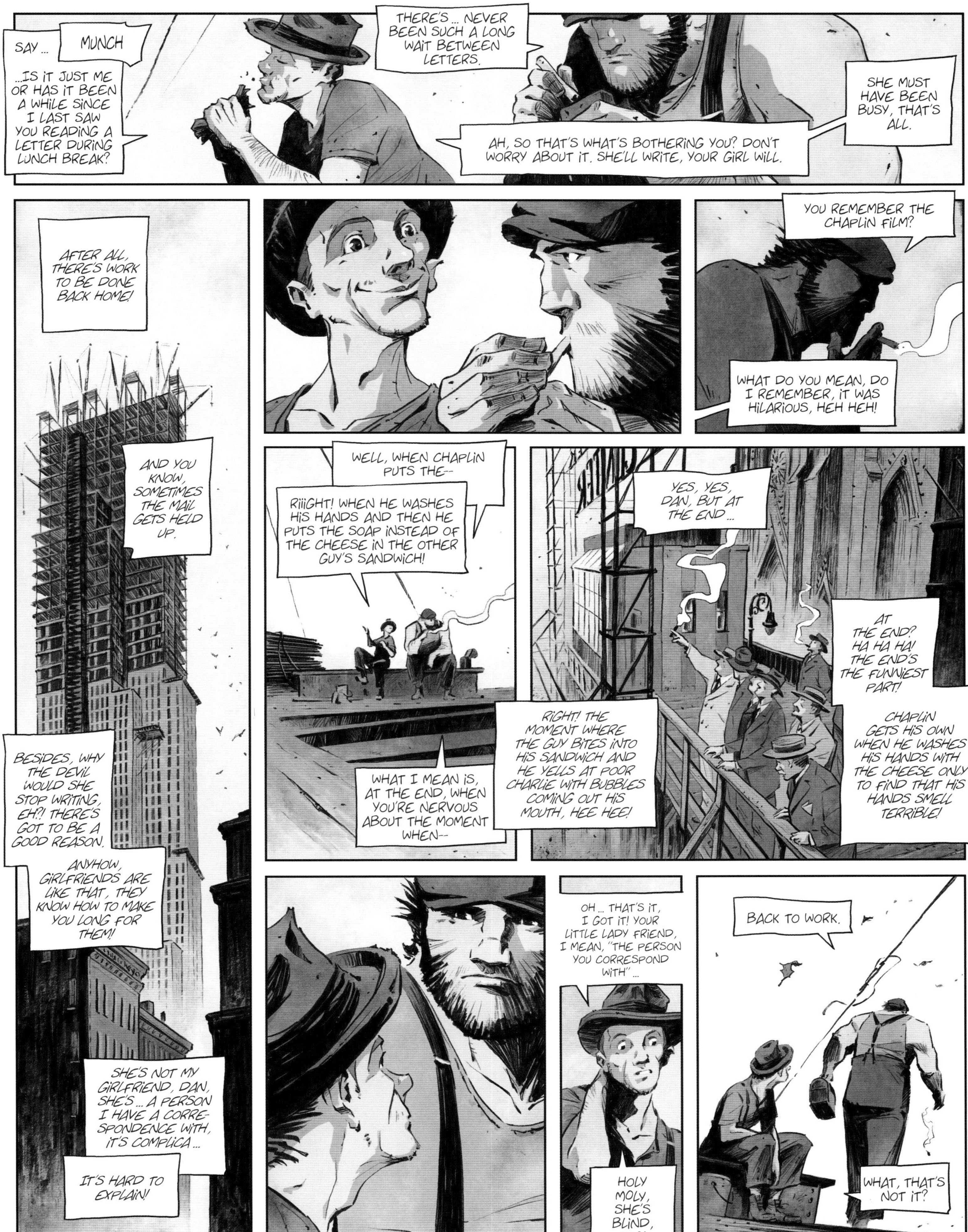

SAY ...
MUNCH
...IS IT JUST ME OR HAS IT BEEN A WHILE SINCE I LAST SAW YOU READING A LETTER DURING LUNCH BREAK?
THERE'S ... NEVER BEEN SUCH A LONG WAIT BETWEEN LETTERS.
AH, SO THAT'S WHAT'S BOTHERING YOU? DON'T WORRY ABOUT IT. SHE'LL WRITE, YOUR GIRL WILL.
SHE MUST HAVE BEEN BUSY, THAT'S ALL.
AFTER ALL, THERE'S WORK TO BE DONE BACK HOME!
AND YOU KNOW, SOMETIMES THE MAIL GETS HELD UP.
BESIDES, WHY THE DEVIL WOULD SHE STOP WRITING, EH?! THERE'S GOT TO BE A GOOD REASON.
ANYHOW, GIRLFRIENDS ARE LIKE THAT, THEY KNOW HOW TO MAKE YOU LONG FOR THEM!
SHE'S NOT MY GIRLFRIEND, DAN, SHE'S ... A PERSON I HAVE A CORRE-SPONDENCE WITH, IT'S COMPLICA ...
IT'S HARD TO EXPLAIN!
YOU REMEMBER THE CHAPLIN FILM?
WHAT DO YOU MEAN, DO I REMEMBER, IT WAS HILARIOUS, HEH HEH!
WELL, WHEN CHAPLIN PUTS THE--
RIIIGHT! WHEN HE WASHES HIS HANDS AND THEN HE PUTS THE SOAP INSTEAD OF THE CHEESE IN THE OTHER GUY'S SANDWICH!
WHAT I MEAN IS, AT THE END, WHEN YOU'RE NERVOUS ABOUT THE MOMENT WHEN--
YES, YES, DAN, BUT AT THE END ...
RIGHT! THE MOMENT WHERE THE GUY BITES INTO HIS SANDWICH AND HE YELLS AT POOR CHARLIE WITH BUBBLES COMING OUT HIS MOUTH, HEE HEE!
AT THE END? HA HA HA! THE END'S THE FUNNIEST PART!
CHAPLIN GETS HIS OWN WHEN HE WASHES HIS HANDS WITH THE CHEESE ONLY TO FIND THAT HIS HANDS SMELL TERRIBLE!
OH ... THAT'S IT, I GOT IT! YOUR LITTLE LADY FRIEND, I MEAN, "THE PERSON YOU CORRESPOND WITH" ...
HOLY MOLY, SHE'S BLIND, TOO!
BACK TO WORK.
WHAT, THAT'S NOT IT?
45

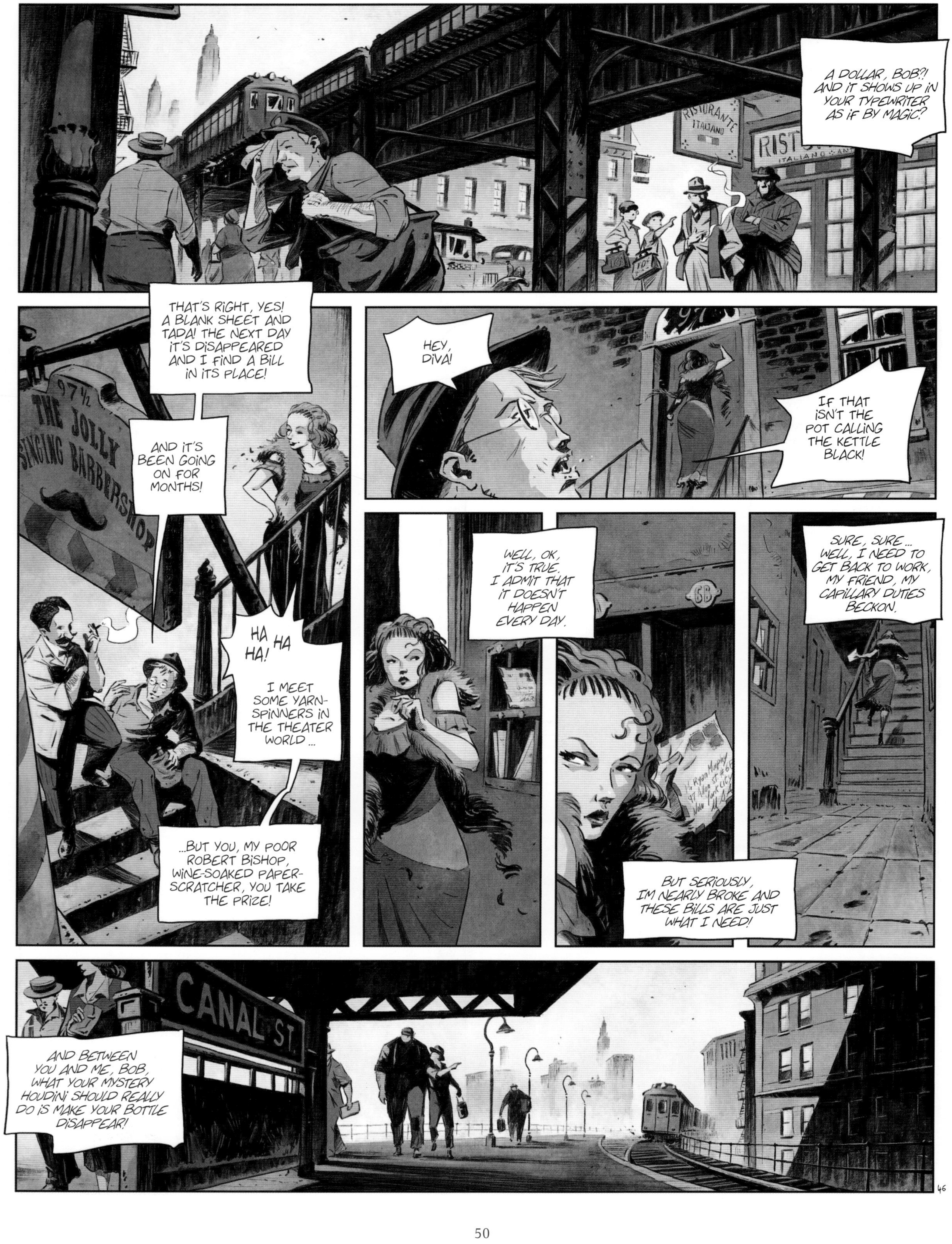

A DOLLAR, BOB?! AND IT SHOWS UP IN YOUR TYPEWRITER AS IF BY MAGIC?
RISTORANTE ITALIANO
THAT'S RIGHT, YES! A BLANK SHEET AND TADA! THE NEXT DAY IT'S DISAPPEARED AND I FIND A BILL IN ITS PLACE!
97½ THE JOLLY SINGING BARBERSHOP
AND IT'S BEEN GOING ON FOR MONTHS!
HA HA HA!
I MEET SOME YARN-SPINNERS IN THE THEATER WORLD ...
...BUT YOU, MY POOR ROBERT BISHOP, WINE-SOAKED PAPER-SCRATCHER, YOU TAKE THE PRIZE!
HEY, DIVA!
IF THAT ISN'T THE POT CALLING THE KETTLE BLACK!
WELL, OK, IT'S TRUE. I ADMIT THAT IT DOESN'T HAPPEN EVERY DAY.
SURE, SURE... WELL, I NEED TO GET BACK TO WORK, MY FRIEND, MY CAPILLARY DUTIES BECKON.
BUT SERIOUSLY, I'M NEARLY BROKE AND THESE BILLS ARE JUST WHAT I NEED!
CANAL ST.
AND BETWEEN YOU AND ME, BOB, WHAT YOUR MYSTERY HOUDINI SHOULD REALLY DO IS MAKE YOUR BOTTLE DISAPPEAR!
46

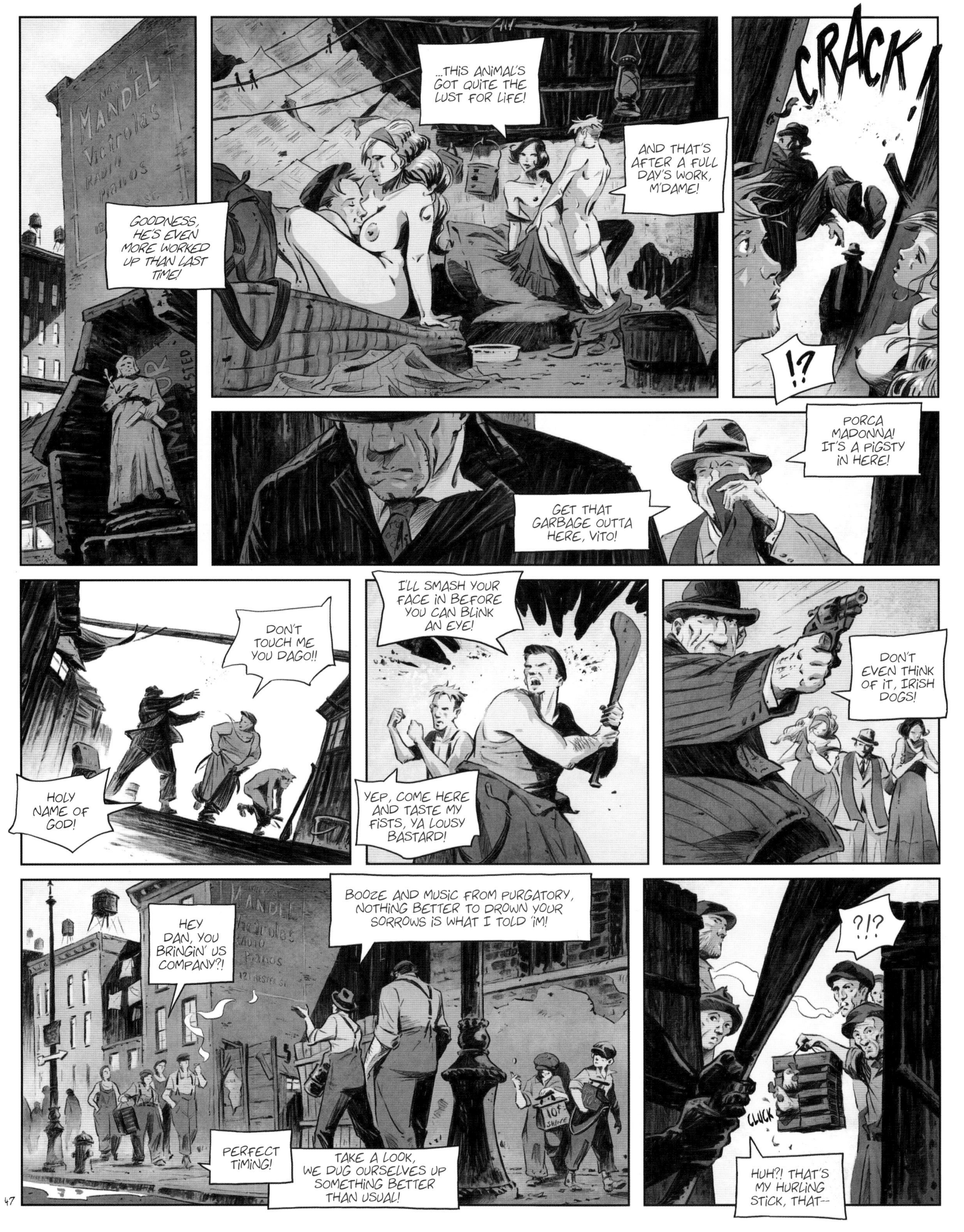
GOODNESS, HE'S EVEN MORE WORKED UP THAN LAST TIME!
...THIS ANIMAL'S GOT QUITE THE LUST FOR LIFE!
AND THAT'S AFTER A FULL DAY'S WORK, M'DAME!
CRACK!
!?
PORCA MADONNA! IT'S A PIGSTY IN HERE!
GET THAT GARBAGE OUTTA HERE, VITO!
DON'T TOUCH ME YOU DAGO!!
HOLY NAME OF GOD!
I'LL SMASH YOUR FACE IN BEFORE YOU CAN BLINK AN EYE!
YEP, COME HERE AND TASTE MY FISTS, YA LOUSY BASTARD!
DON'T EVEN THINK OF IT, IRISH DOGS!
HEY DAN, YOU BRINGIN' US COMPANY?!
BOOZE AND MUSIC FROM PURGATORY, NOTHING BETTER TO DROWN YOUR SORROWS IS WHAT I TOLD 'IM!
PERFECT TIMING!
TAKE A LOOK, WE DUG OURSELVES UP SOMETHING BETTER THAN USUAL!
?!?
CLUCK
HUH?! THAT'S MY HURLING STICK, THAT--
47

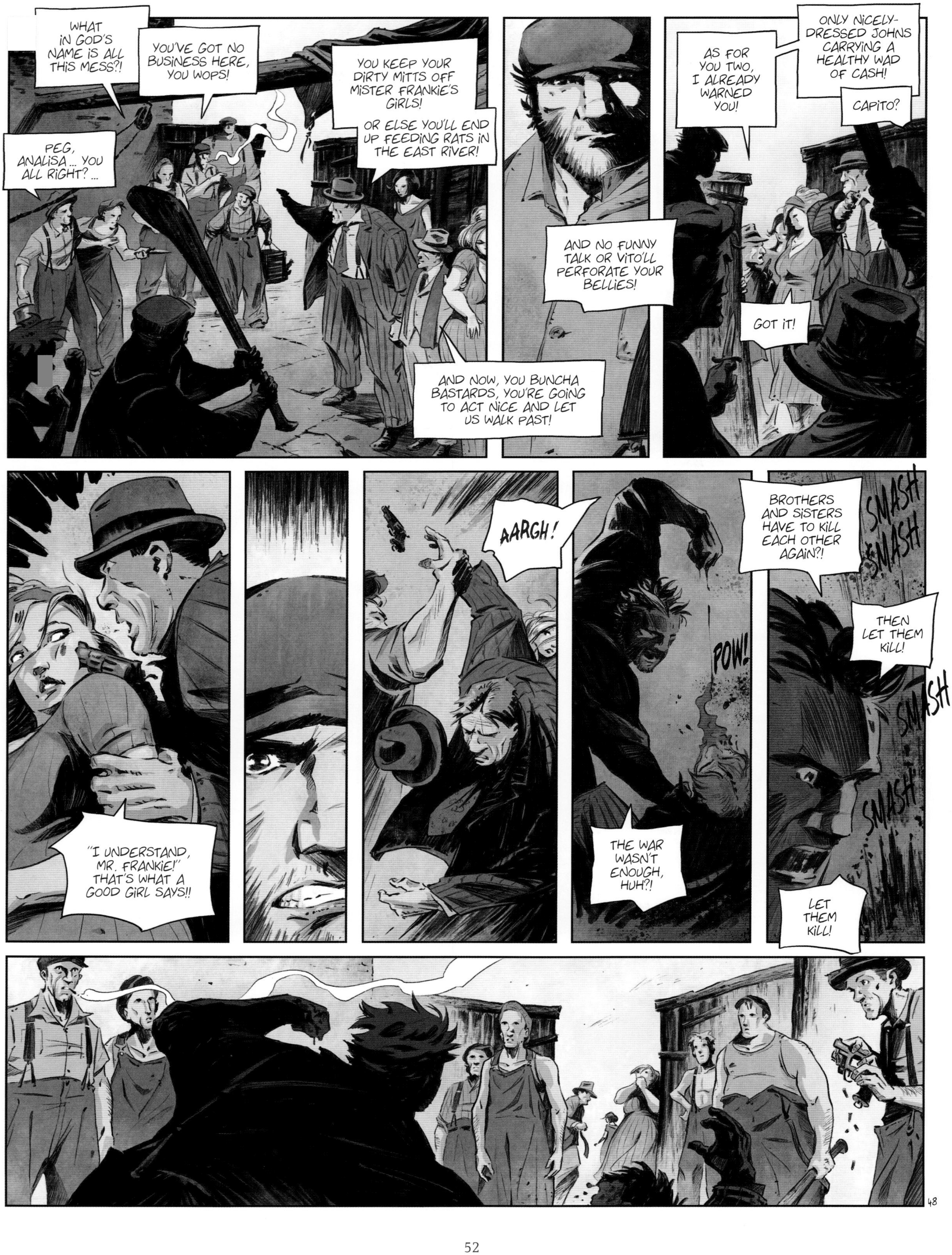

WHAT IN GOD'S NAME IS ALL THIS MESS?!
YOU'VE GOT NO BUSINESS HERE, YOU WOPS!
PEG, ANALISA... YOU ALL RIGHT? ...
YOU KEEP YOUR DIRTY MITTS OFF MISTER FRANKIE'S GIRLS!
OR ELSE YOU'LL END UP FEEDING RATS IN THE EAST RIVER!
AND NOW, YOU BUNCHA BASTARDS, YOU'RE GOING TO ACT NICE AND LET US WALK PAST!
AND NO FUNNY TALK OR VITO'LL PERFORATE YOUR BELLIES!
AS FOR YOU TWO, I ALREADY WARNED YOU!
ONLY NICELY-DRESSED JOHNS CARRYING A HEALTHY WAD OF CASH!
CAPITO?
GOT IT!
"I UNDERSTAND, MR. FRANKIE!" THAT'S WHAT A GOOD GIRL SAYS!!
AARGH!
POW!
THE WAR WASN'T ENOUGH, HUH?!
BROTHERS AND SISTERS HAVE TO KILL EACH OTHER AGAIN?!
SMASH SMASH
THEN LET THEM KILL!
SMASH
SMASH
LET THEM KILL!
48

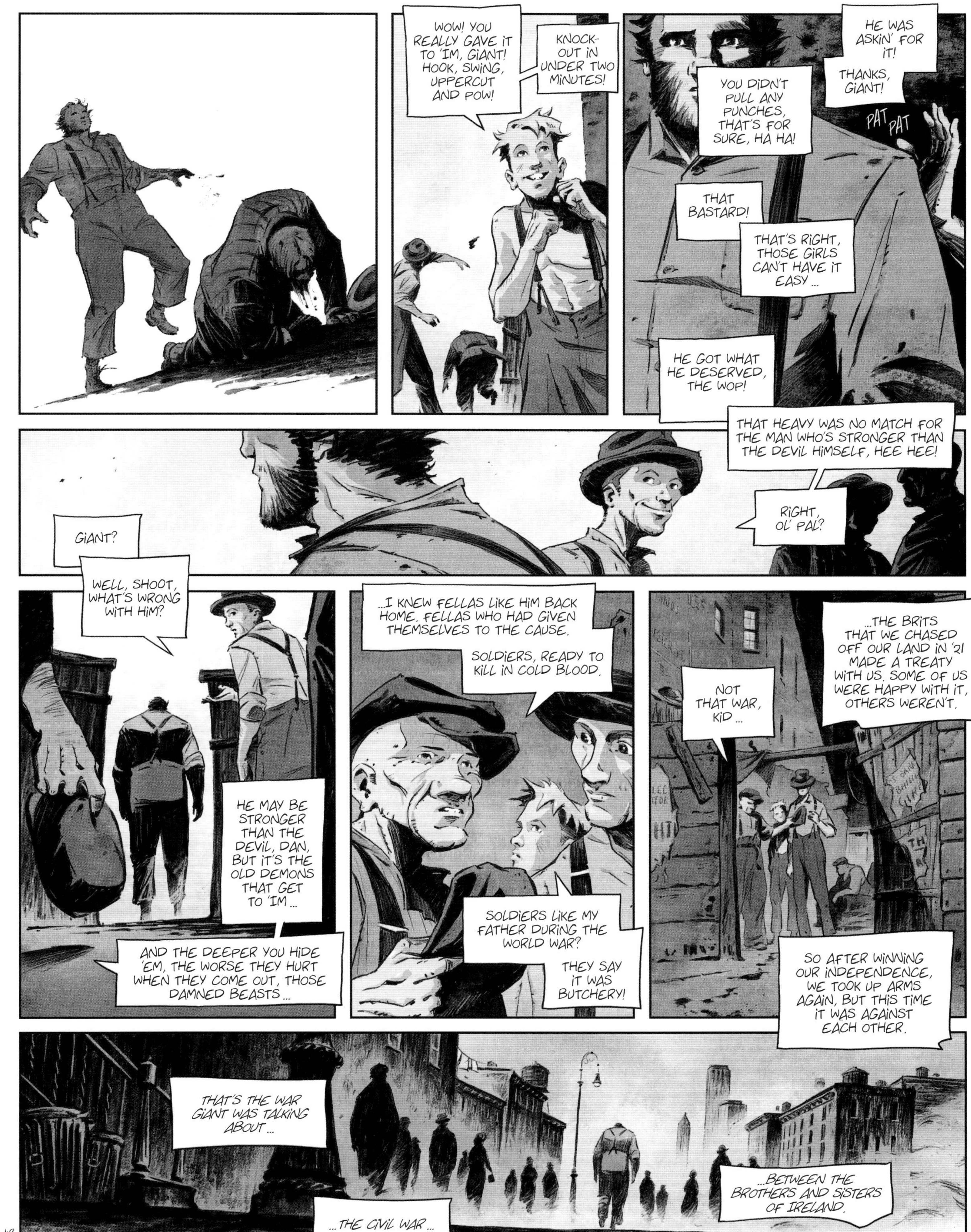
WOW! YOU REALLY GAVE IT TO 'IM, GIANT! HOOK, SWING, UPPERCUT AND POW!
KNOCK-OUT IN UNDER TWO MINUTES!
HE WAS ASKIN' FOR IT!
THANKS, GIANT!
YOU DIDN'T PULL ANY PUNCHES, THAT'S FOR SURE, HA HA!
PAT PAT
THAT BASTARD!
THAT'S RIGHT, THOSE GIRLS CAN'T HAVE IT EASY ...
HE GOT WHAT HE DESERVED, THE WOP!
THAT HEAVY WAS NO MATCH FOR THE MAN WHO'S STRONGER THAN THE DEVIL HIMSELF, HEE HEE!
GIANT?
RIGHT, OL' PAL?
WELL, SHOOT, WHAT'S WRONG WITH HIM?
HE MAY BE STRONGER THAN THE DEVIL, DAN, BUT IT'S THE OLD DEMONS THAT GET TO 'IM ...
AND THE DEEPER YOU HIDE 'EM, THE WORSE THEY HURT WHEN THEY COME OUT, THOSE DAMNED BEASTS ...
...I KNEW FELLAS LIKE HIM BACK HOME. FELLAS WHO HAD GIVEN THEMSELVES TO THE CAUSE.
SOLDIERS, READY TO KILL IN COLD BLOOD.
SOLDIERS LIKE MY FATHER DURING THE WORLD WAR?
THEY SAY IT WAS BUTCHERY!
NOT THAT WAR, KID ...
...THE BRITS THAT WE CHASED OFF OUR LAND IN '21 MADE A TREATY WITH US. SOME OF US WERE HAPPY WITH IT, OTHERS WEREN'T.
SO AFTER WINNING OUR INDEPENDENCE, WE TOOK UP ARMS AGAIN, BUT THIS TIME IT WAS AGAINST EACH OTHER.
THAT'S THE WAR GIANT WAS TALKING ABOUT ...
...THE CIVIL WAR ...
...BETWEEN THE BROTHERS AND SISTERS OF IRELAND.
49

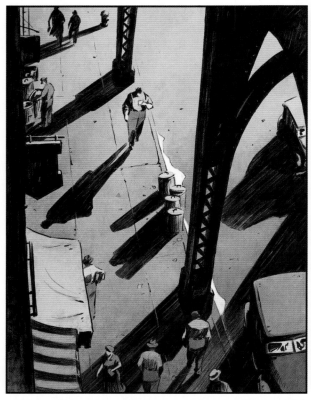

GIRDLES
H. KNOX

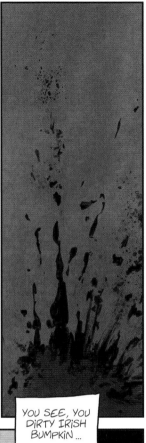

YOU SEE, YOU DIRTY IRISH BUMPKIN ...

...WHEN I HAVE A STAIN THAT BOTHERS ME ...

...I PREFER TO CLEAN IT STRAIGHT AWAY.

SCRiiiTCH...

OTHERWISE IT SETS IN ...

KLOK

...AND THEN IT BECOMES HARDER TO GET RID OF!

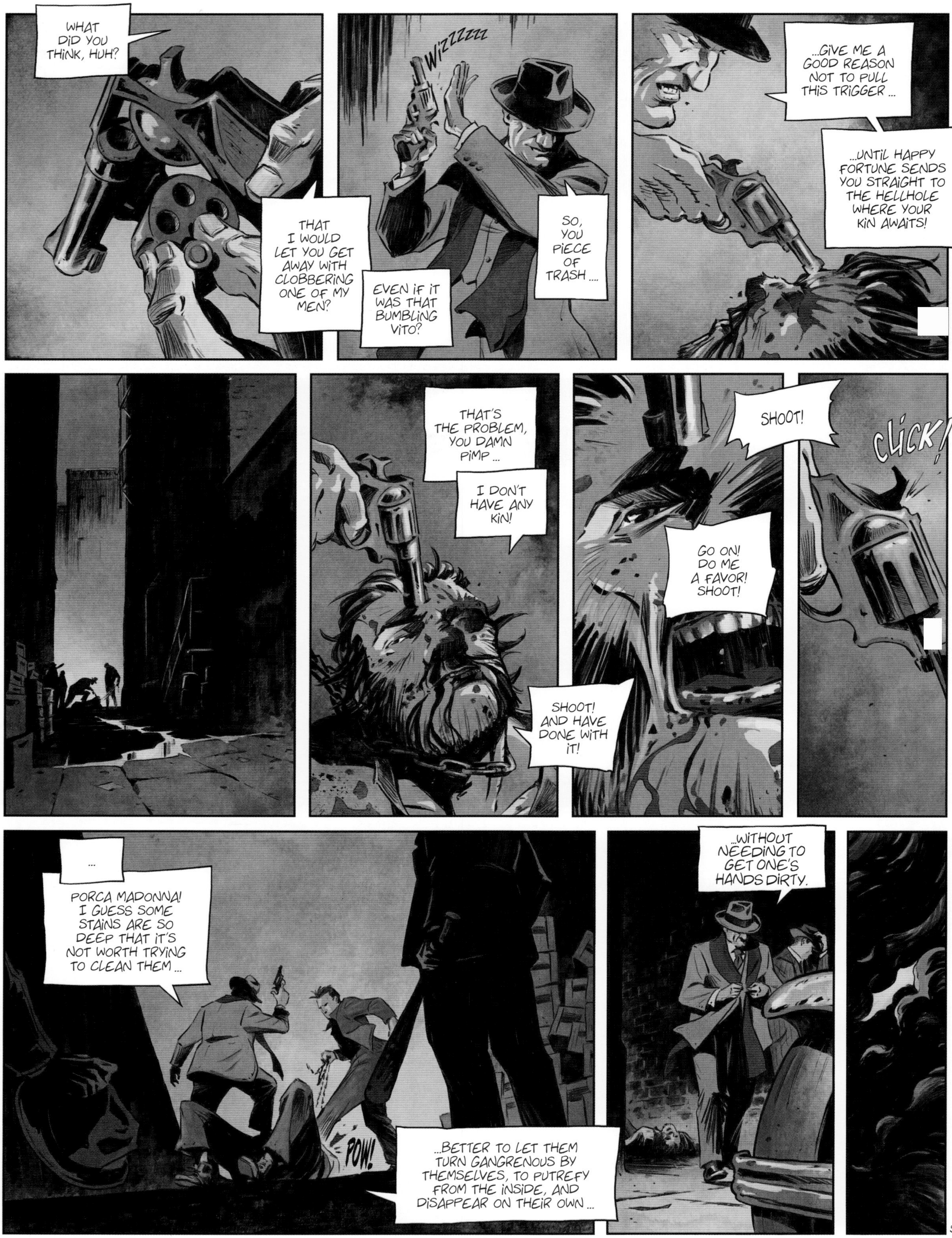
WHAT DID YOU THINK, HUH?
WIZZZZZZ
THAT I WOULD LET YOU GET AWAY WITH CLOBBERING ONE OF MY MEN?
EVEN IF IT WAS THAT BUMBLING VITO?
SO, YOU PIECE OF TRASH ....
...GIVE ME A GOOD REASON NOT TO PULL THIS TRIGGER ...
...UNTIL HAPPY FORTUNE SENDS YOU STRAIGHT TO THE HELLHOLE WHERE YOUR KIN AWAITS!
THAT'S THE PROBLEM, YOU DAMN PIMP ...
I DON'T HAVE ANY KIN!
SHOOT! AND HAVE DONE WITH IT!
SHOOT!
GO ON! DO ME A FAVOR! SHOOT!
CLICK!
...
PORCA MADONNA! I GUESS SOME STAINS ARE SO DEEP THAT IT'S NOT WORTH TRYING TO CLEAN THEM ...
POW!
...BETTER TO LET THEM TURN GANGRENOUS BY THEMSELVES, TO PUTREFY FROM THE INSIDE, AND DISAPPEAR ON THEIR OWN ...
...WITHOUT NEEDING TO GET ONE'S HANDS DIRTY.
52

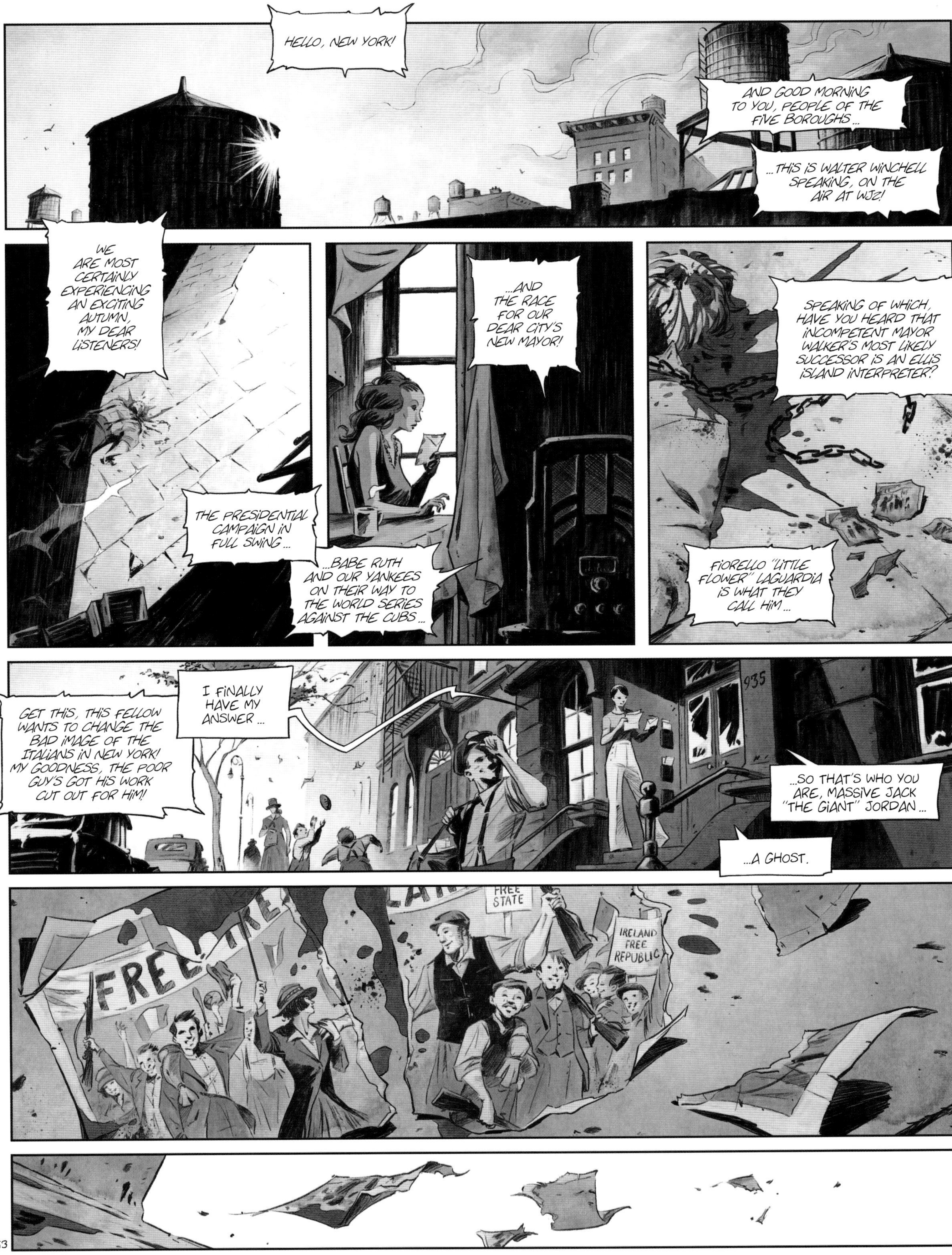

HELLO, NEW YORK!
AND GOOD MORNING TO YOU, PEOPLE OF THE FIVE BOROUGHS ...
...THIS IS WALTER WINCHELL SPEAKING, ON THE AIR AT WJZ!
WE ARE MOST CERTAINLY EXPERIENCING AN EXCITING AUTUMN, MY DEAR LISTENERS!
THE PRESIDENTIAL CAMPAIGN IN FULL SWING ...
...AND THE RACE FOR OUR DEAR CITY'S NEW MAYOR!
...BABE RUTH AND OUR YANKEES ON THEIR WAY TO THE WORLD SERIES AGAINST THE CUBS ...
SPEAKING OF WHICH, HAVE YOU HEARD THAT INCOMPETENT MAYOR WALKER'S MOST LIKELY SUCCESSOR IS AN ELLIS ISLAND INTERPRETER?
FIORELLO "LITTLE FLOWER" LAGUARDIA IS WHAT THEY CALL HIM ...
GET THIS, THIS FELLOW WANTS TO CHANGE THE BAD IMAGE OF THE ITALIANS IN NEW YORK! MY GOODNESS, THE POOR GUY'S GOT HIS WORK CUT OUT FOR HIM!
I FINALLY HAVE MY ANSWER ...
935
...SO THAT'S WHO YOU ARE, MASSIVE JACK "THE GIANT" JORDAN ...
...A GHOST.
FREE STATE
IRELAND FREE REPUBLIC
FREE
53

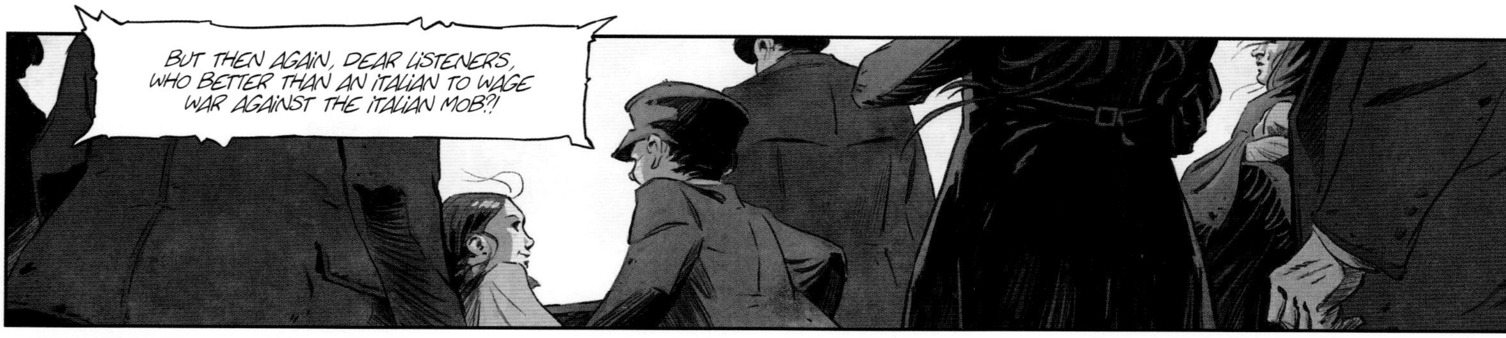
BUT THEN AGAIN, DEAR LISTENERS, WHO BETTER THAN AN ITALIAN TO WAGE WAR AGAINST THE ITALIAN MOB?!

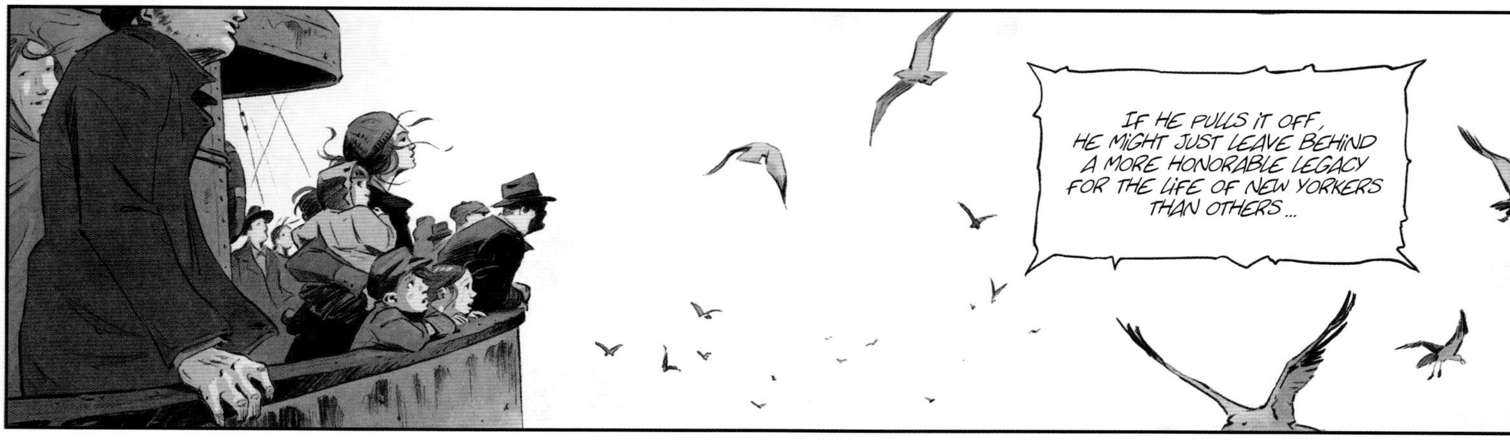
IF HE PULLS IT OFF, HE MIGHT JUST LEAVE BEHIND A MORE HONORABLE LEGACY FOR THE LIFE OF NEW YORKERS THAN OTHERS...

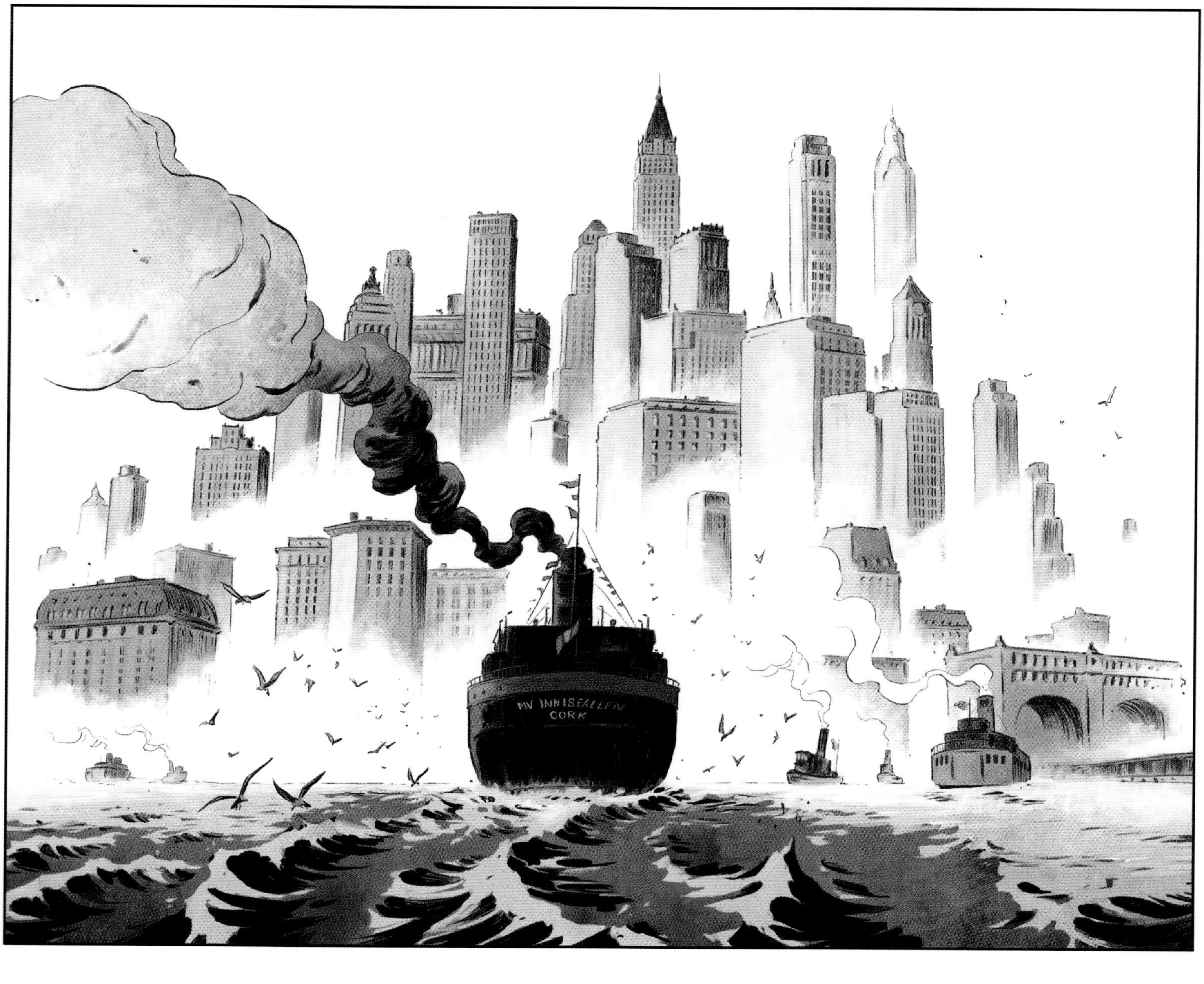
MV INNISFALLEN
CORK

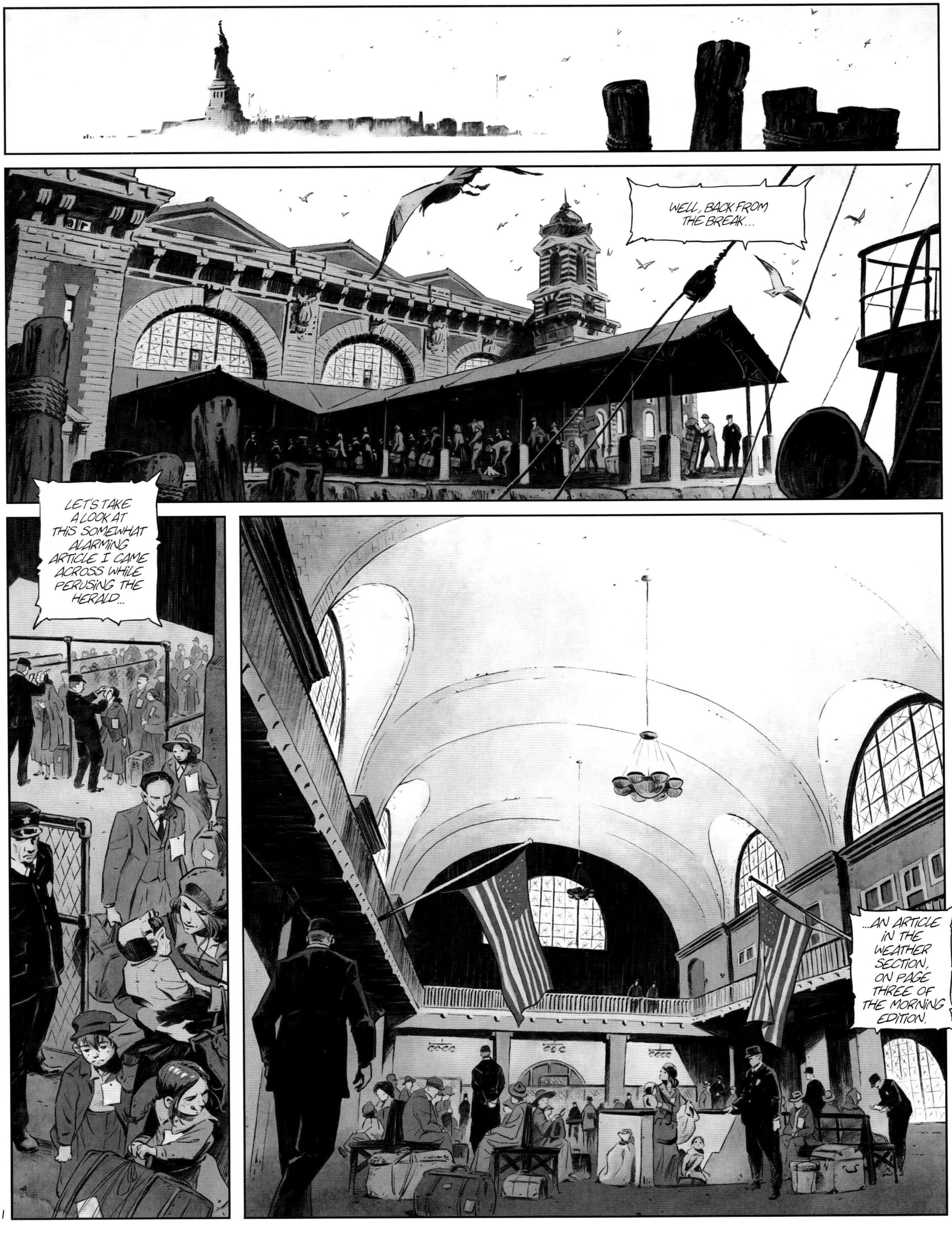
WELL, BACK FROM THE BREAK...
LET'S TAKE A LOOK AT THIS SOMEWHAT ALARMING ARTICLE I CAME ACROSS WHILE PERUSING THE HERALD...
...AN ARTICLE IN THE WEATHER SECTION, ON PAGE THREE OF THE MORNING EDITION.

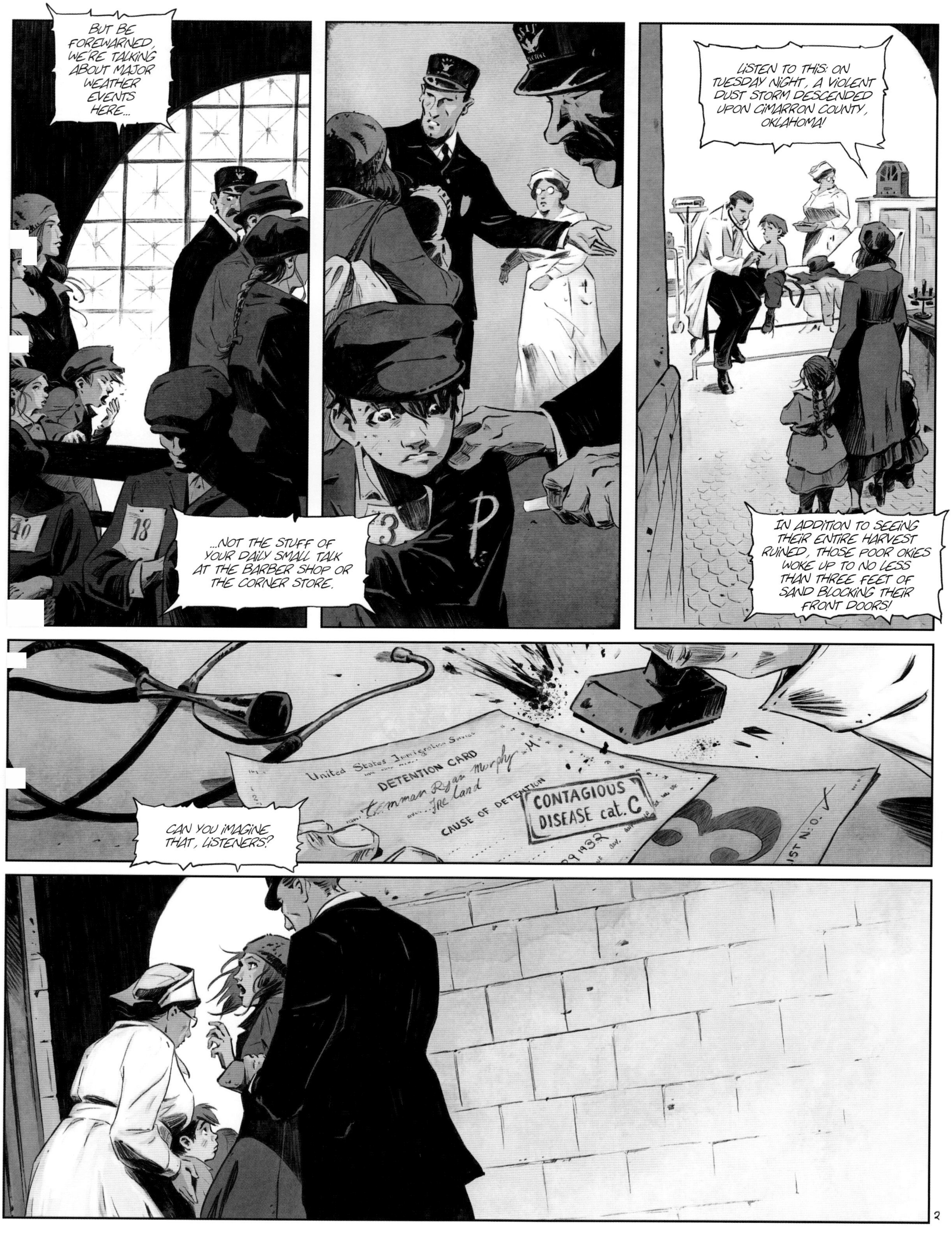
BUT BE FOREWARNED, WE'RE TALKING ABOUT MAJOR WEATHER EVENTS HERE...
...NOT THE STUFF OF YOUR DAILY SMALL TALK AT THE BARBER SHOP OR THE CORNER STORE.
LISTEN TO THIS: ON TUESDAY NIGHT, A VIOLENT DUST STORM DESCENDED UPON CIMARRON COUNTY, OKLAHOMA!
IN ADDITION TO SEEING THEIR ENTIRE HARVEST RUINED, THOSE POOR OKIES WOKE UP TO NO LESS THAN THREE FEET OF SAND BLOCKING THEIR FRONT DOORS!
United States Immigration Service
DETENTION CARD
CAUSE OF DETENTION
CONTAGIOUS DISEASE cat. C
CAN YOU IMAGINE THAT, LISTENERS?

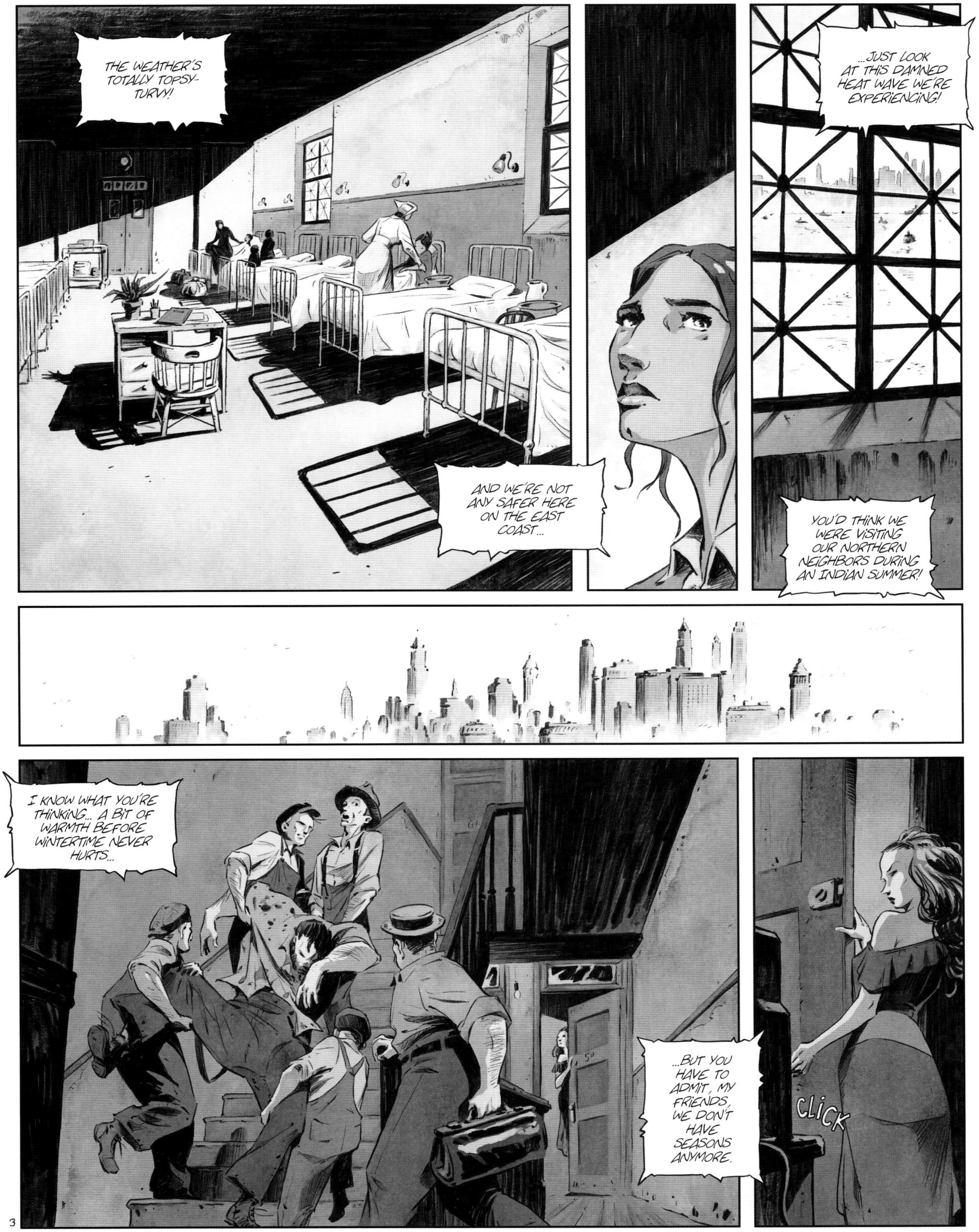
THE WEATHER'S TOTALLY TOPSY-TURVY!
AND WE'RE NOT ANY SAFER HERE ON THE EAST COAST...
...JUST LOOK AT THIS DAMNED HEAT WAVE WE'RE EXPERIENCING!
YOU'D THINK WE WERE VISITING OUR NORTHERN NEIGHBORS DURING AN INDIAN SUMMER!
I KNOW WHAT YOU'RE THINKING... A BIT OF WARMTH BEFORE WINTERTIME NEVER HURTS...
...BUT YOU HAVE TO ADMIT, MY FRIENDS, WE DON'T HAVE SEASONS ANYMORE.
CLICK

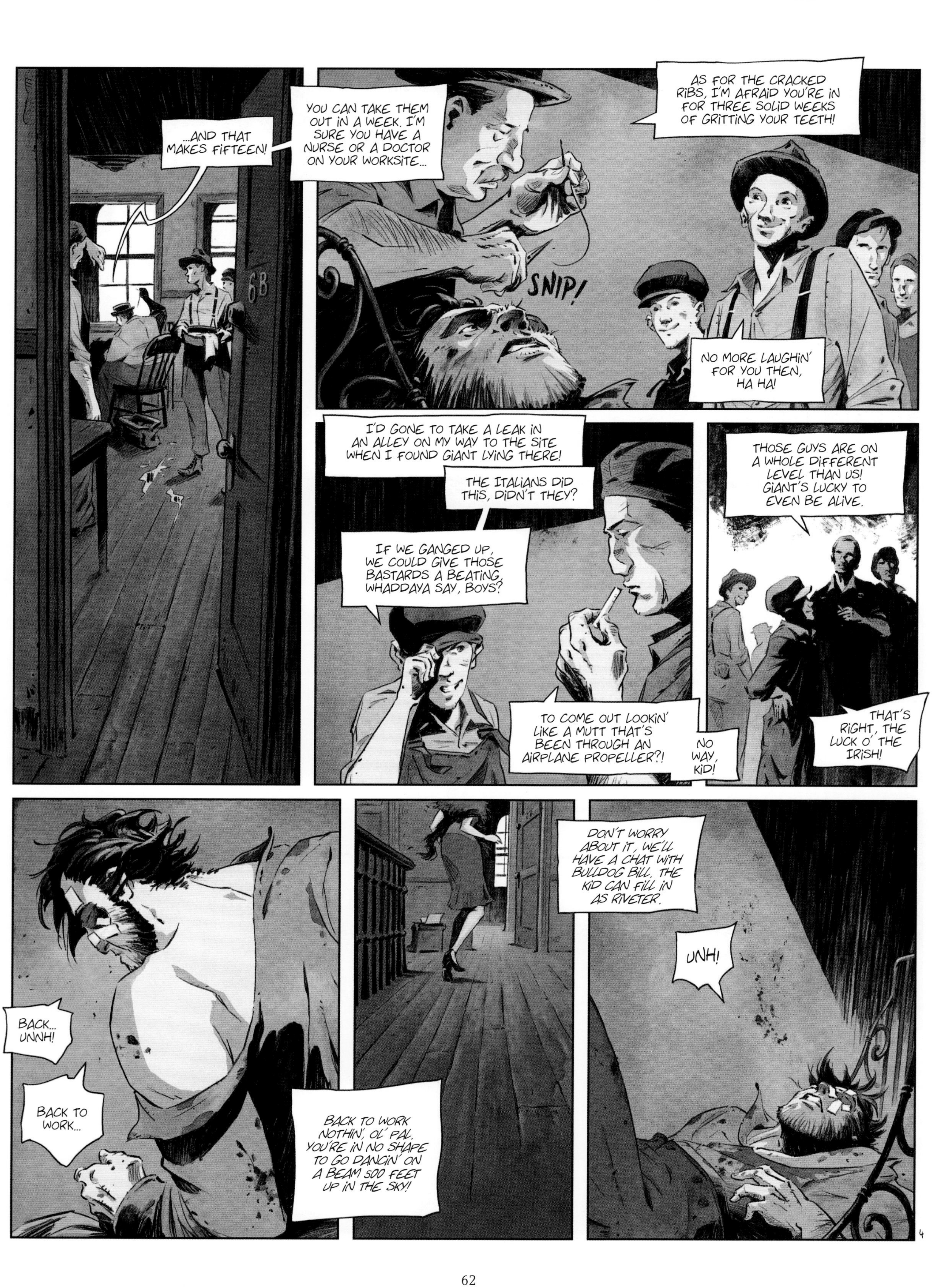
...AND THAT MAKES FIFTEEN!
YOU CAN TAKE THEM OUT IN A WEEK. I'M SURE YOU HAVE A NURSE OR A DOCTOR ON YOUR WORKSITE...
AS FOR THE CRACKED RIBS, I'M AFRAID YOU'RE IN FOR THREE SOLID WEEKS OF GRITTING YOUR TEETH!
SNIP!
NO MORE LAUGHIN' FOR YOU THEN, HA HA!
I'D GONE TO TAKE A LEAK IN AN ALLEY ON MY WAY TO THE SITE WHEN I FOUND GIANT LYING THERE!
THE ITALIANS DID THIS, DIDN'T THEY?
IF WE GANGED UP, WE COULD GIVE THOSE BASTARDS A BEATING, WHADDAYA SAY, BOYS?
TO COME OUT LOOKIN' LIKE A MUTT THAT'S BEEN THROUGH AN AIRPLANE PROPELLER?!
NO WAY, KID!
THOSE GUYS ARE ON A WHOLE DIFFERENT LEVEL THAN US! GIANT'S LUCKY TO EVEN BE ALIVE.
THAT'S RIGHT, THE LUCK O' THE IRISH!
BACK... UNNH!
BACK TO WORK...
BACK TO WORK NOTHIN', OL' PAL. YOU'RE IN NO SHAPE TO GO DANCIN' ON A BEAM 500 FEET UP IN THE SKY!
DON'T WORRY ABOUT IT, WE'LL HAVE A CHAT WITH BULLDOG BILL. THE KID CAN FILL IN AS RIVETER.
UNH!
4

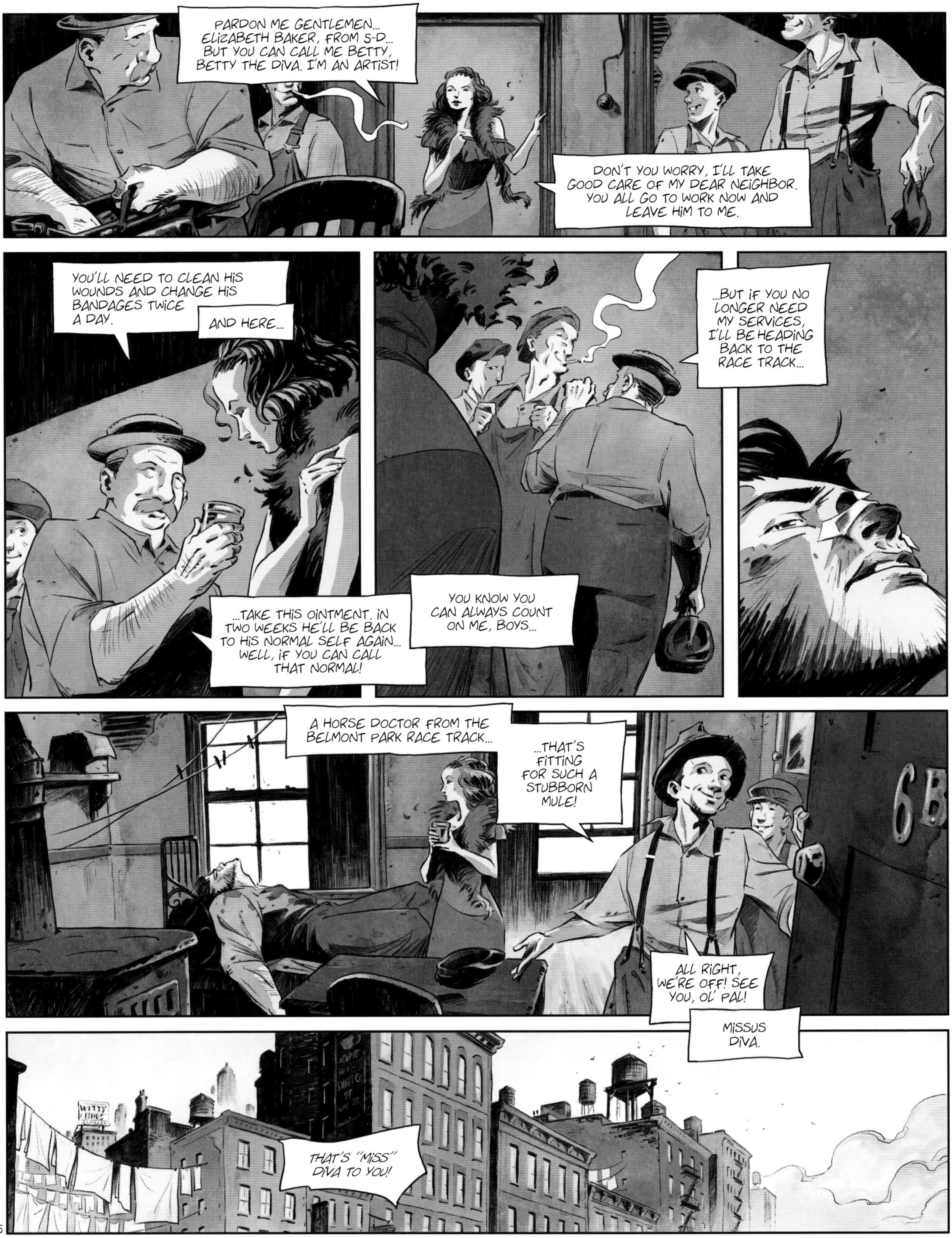
PARDON ME GENTLEMEN... ELIZABETH BAKER, FROM 5-D... BUT YOU CAN CALL ME BETTY, BETTY THE DIVA. I'M AN ARTIST!
DON'T YOU WORRY, I'LL TAKE GOOD CARE OF MY DEAR NEIGHBOR. YOU ALL GO TO WORK NOW AND LEAVE HIM TO ME.
YOU'LL NEED TO CLEAN HIS WOUNDS AND CHANGE HIS BANDAGES TWICE A DAY.
AND HERE...
...TAKE THIS OINTMENT. IN TWO WEEKS HE'LL BE BACK TO HIS NORMAL SELF AGAIN... WELL, IF YOU CAN CALL THAT NORMAL!
YOU KNOW YOU CAN ALWAYS COUNT ON ME, BOYS...
...BUT IF YOU NO LONGER NEED MY SERVICES, I'LL BE HEADING BACK TO THE RACE TRACK...
A HORSE DOCTOR FROM THE BELMONT PARK RACE TRACK...
...THAT'S FITTING FOR SUCH A STUBBORN MULE!
6 B
ALL RIGHT, WE'RE OFF! SEE YOU, OL' PAL!
MISSUS DIVA.
THAT'S "MISS" DIVA TO YOU!

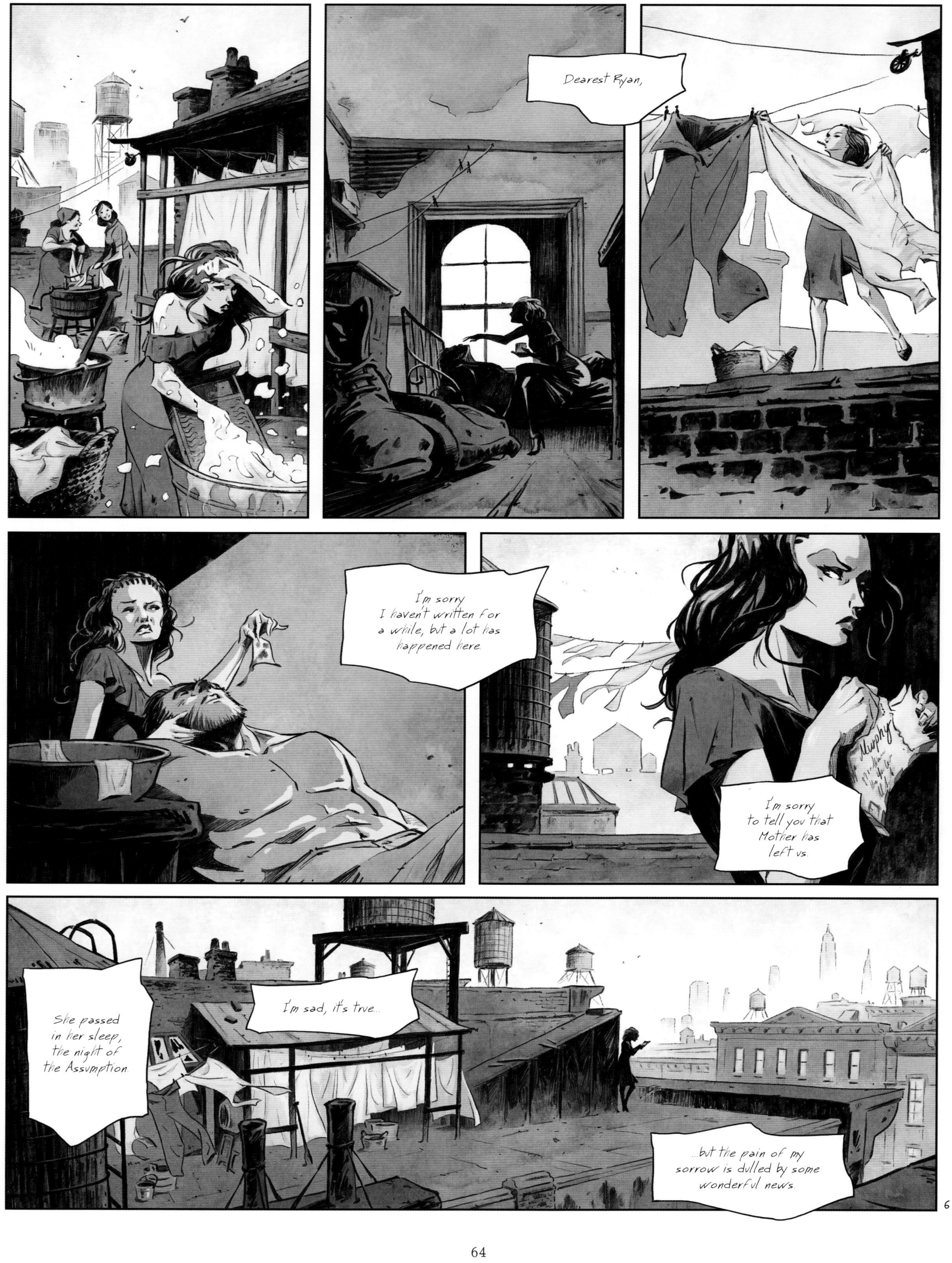
Dearest Ryan,
I'm sorry I haven't written for a while, but a lot has happened here.
I'm sorry to tell you that Mother has left us.
She passed in her sleep, the night of the Assumption.
I'm sad, it's true...
...but the pain of my sorrow is dulled by some wonderful news.

6

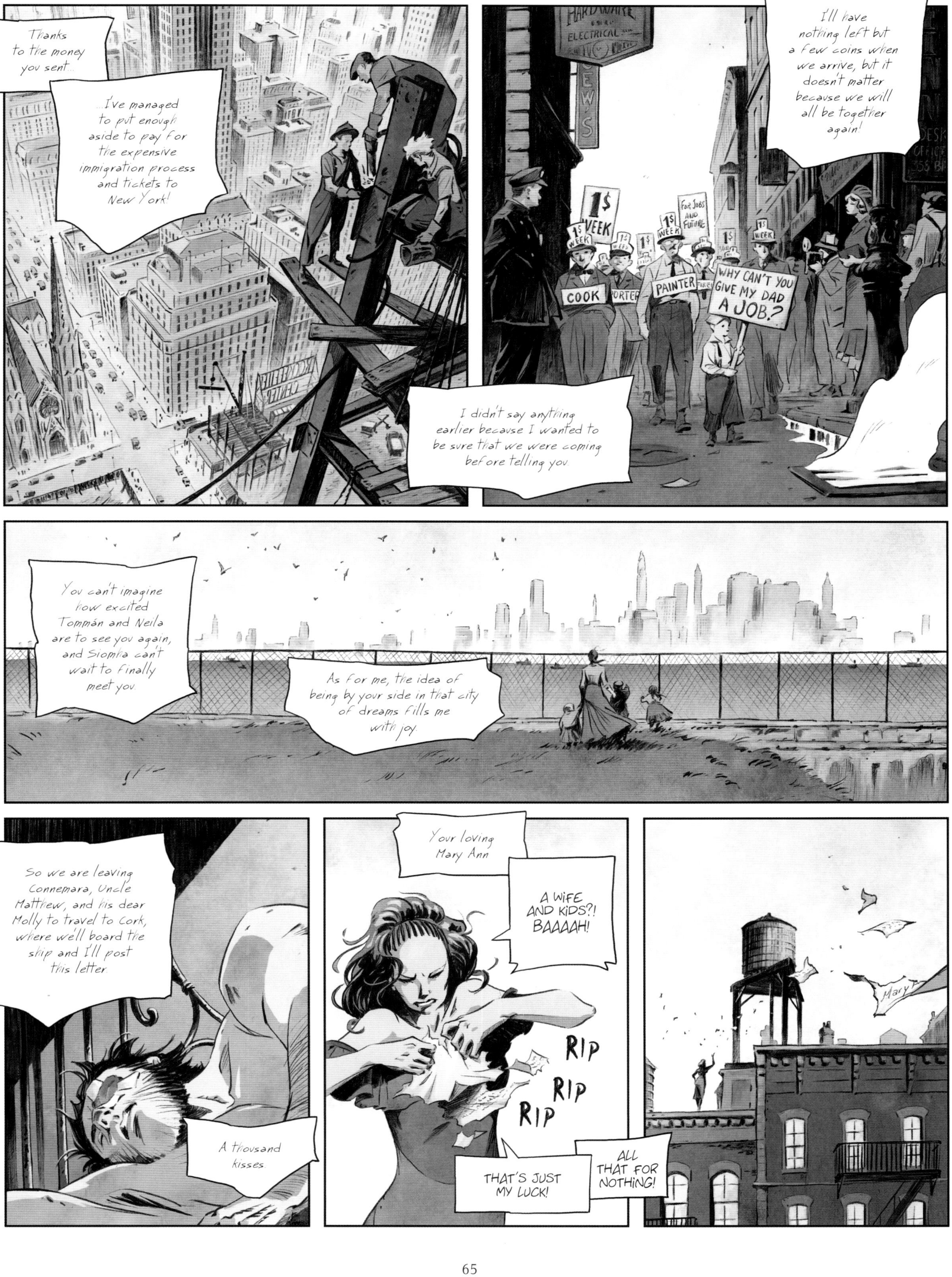
Thanks to the money you sent...
...I've managed to put enough aside to pay for the expensive immigration process and tickets to New York!
I'll have nothing left but a few coins when we arrive, but it doesn't matter because we will all be together again!
HARDWARE
ELECTRICAL
1$ WEEK
FOR JOBS AND FUTURE
COOK
PORTER
PAINTER
WHY CAN'T YOU GIVE MY DAD A JOB?
I didn't say anything earlier because I wanted to be sure that we were coming before telling you.
You can't imagine how excited Tommán and Neila are to see you again, and Siomha can't wait to finally meet you.
As for me, the idea of being by your side in that city of dreams fills me with joy.
So we are leaving Connemara, Uncle Matthew, and his dear Molly to travel to Cork, where we'll board the ship and I'll post this letter.
A thousand kisses.
Your loving Mary Ann
A WIFE AND KIDS?! BAAAAH!
RIP
RIP
RIP
THAT'S JUST MY LUCK!
ALL THAT FOR NOTHING!

7

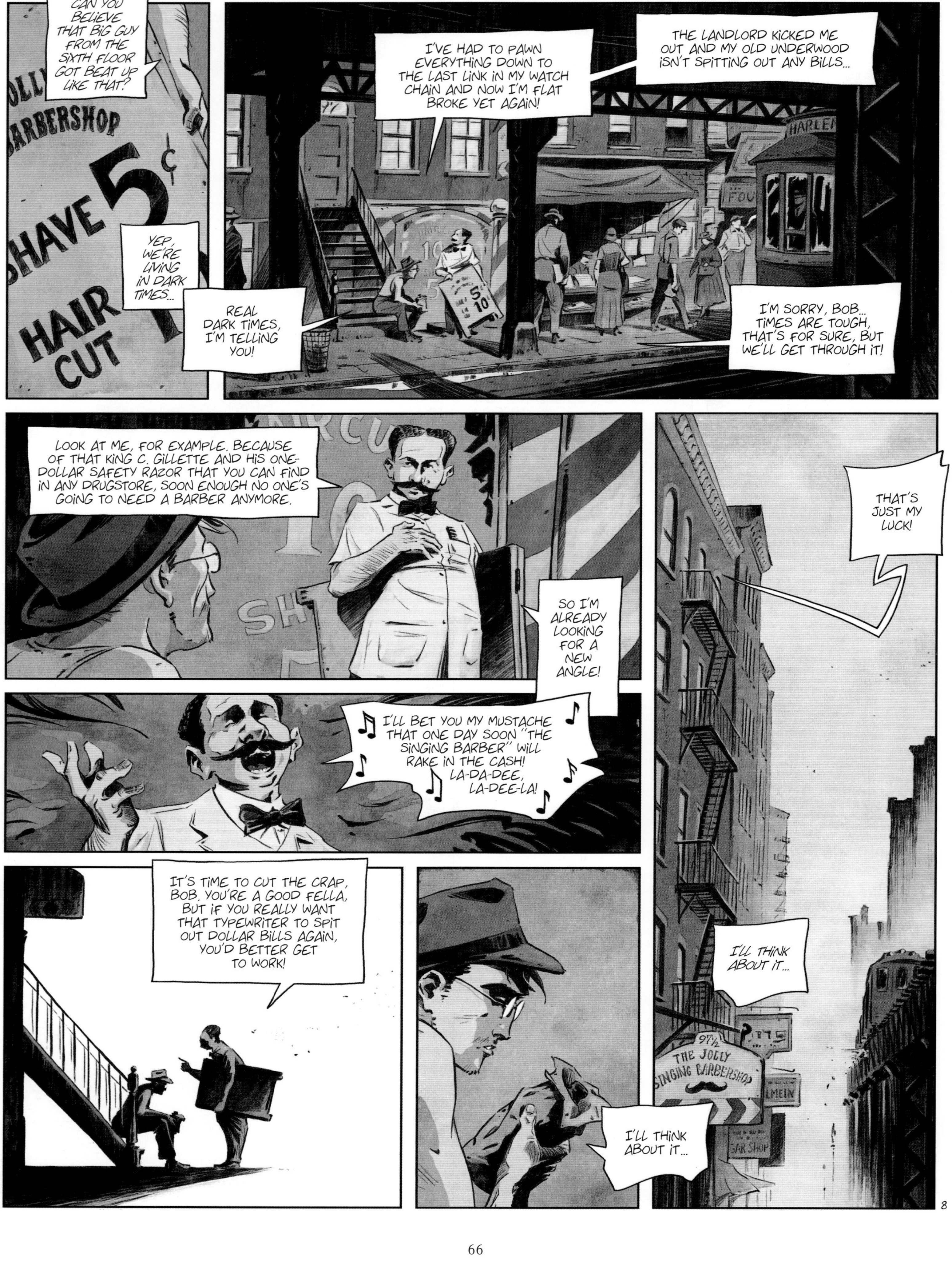
CAN YOU BELIEVE THAT BIG GUY FROM THE SIXTH FLOOR GOT BEAT UP LIKE THAT?
BARBERSHOP
SHAVE 5¢
HAIR CUT
YEP, WE'RE LIVING IN DARK TIMES...
REAL DARK TIMES, I'M TELLING YOU!
I'VE HAD TO PAWN EVERYTHING DOWN TO THE LAST LINK IN MY WATCH CHAIN AND NOW I'M FLAT BROKE YET AGAIN!
THE LANDLORD KICKED ME OUT AND MY OLD UNDERWOOD ISN'T SPITTING OUT ANY BILLS...
HARLEM
I'M SORRY, BOB... TIMES ARE TOUGH, THAT'S FOR SURE, BUT WE'LL GET THROUGH IT!
LOOK AT ME, FOR EXAMPLE. BECAUSE OF THAT KING C. GILLETTE AND HIS ONE-DOLLAR SAFETY RAZOR THAT YOU CAN FIND IN ANY DRUGSTORE, SOON ENOUGH NO ONE'S GOING TO NEED A BARBER ANYMORE.
SO I'M ALREADY LOOKING FOR A NEW ANGLE!
I'LL BET YOU MY MUSTACHE THAT ONE DAY SOON "THE SINGING BARBER" WILL RAKE IN THE CASH! LA-DA-DEE, LA-DEE-LA!
THAT'S JUST MY LUCK!
IT'S TIME TO CUT THE CRAP, BOB. YOU'RE A GOOD FELLA, BUT IF YOU REALLY WANT THAT TYPEWRITER TO SPIT OUT DOLLAR BILLS AGAIN, YOU'D BETTER GET TO WORK!
I'LL THINK ABOUT IT...
97½
THE JOLLY SINGING BARBERSHOP
I'LL THINK ABOUT IT...
8

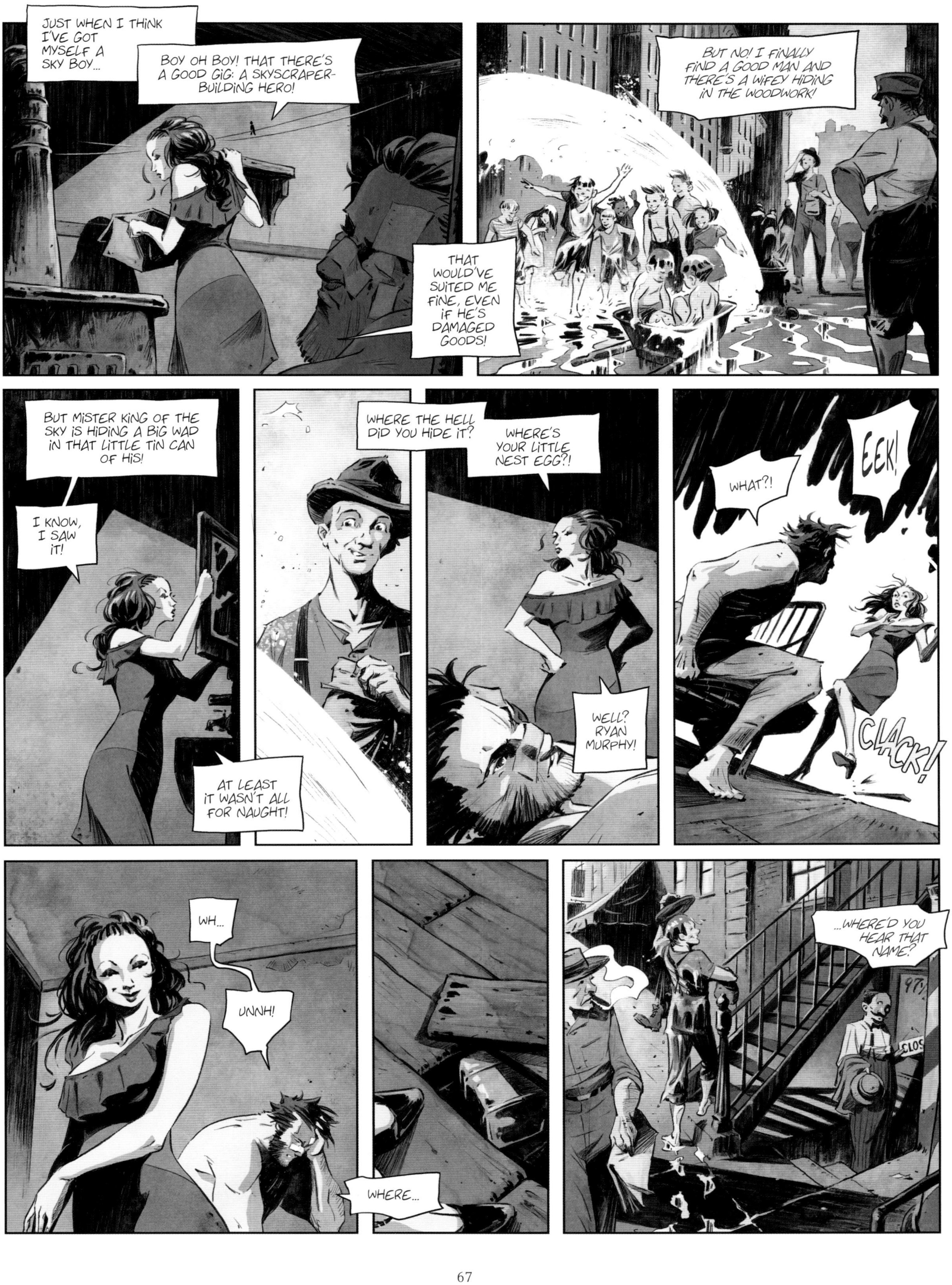
JUST WHEN I THINK I'VE GOT MYSELF A SKY BOY...
BOY OH BOY! THAT THERE'S A GOOD GIG: A SKYSCRAPER-BUILDING HERO!
THAT WOULD'VE SUITED ME FINE, EVEN IF HE'S DAMAGED GOODS!
BUT NO! I FINALLY FIND A GOOD MAN AND THERE'S A WIFEY HIDING IN THE WOODWORK!
BUT MISTER KING OF THE SKY IS HIDING A BIG WAD IN THAT LITTLE TIN CAN OF HIS!
I KNOW, I SAW IT!
AT LEAST IT WASN'T ALL FOR NAUGHT!
WHERE THE HELL DID YOU HIDE IT?
WHERE'S YOUR LITTLE NEST EGG?!
WELL? RYAN MURPHY!
WHAT?!
EEK!
CLACK!
WH...
UNNH!
WHERE...
...WHERE'D YOU HEAR THAT NAME?

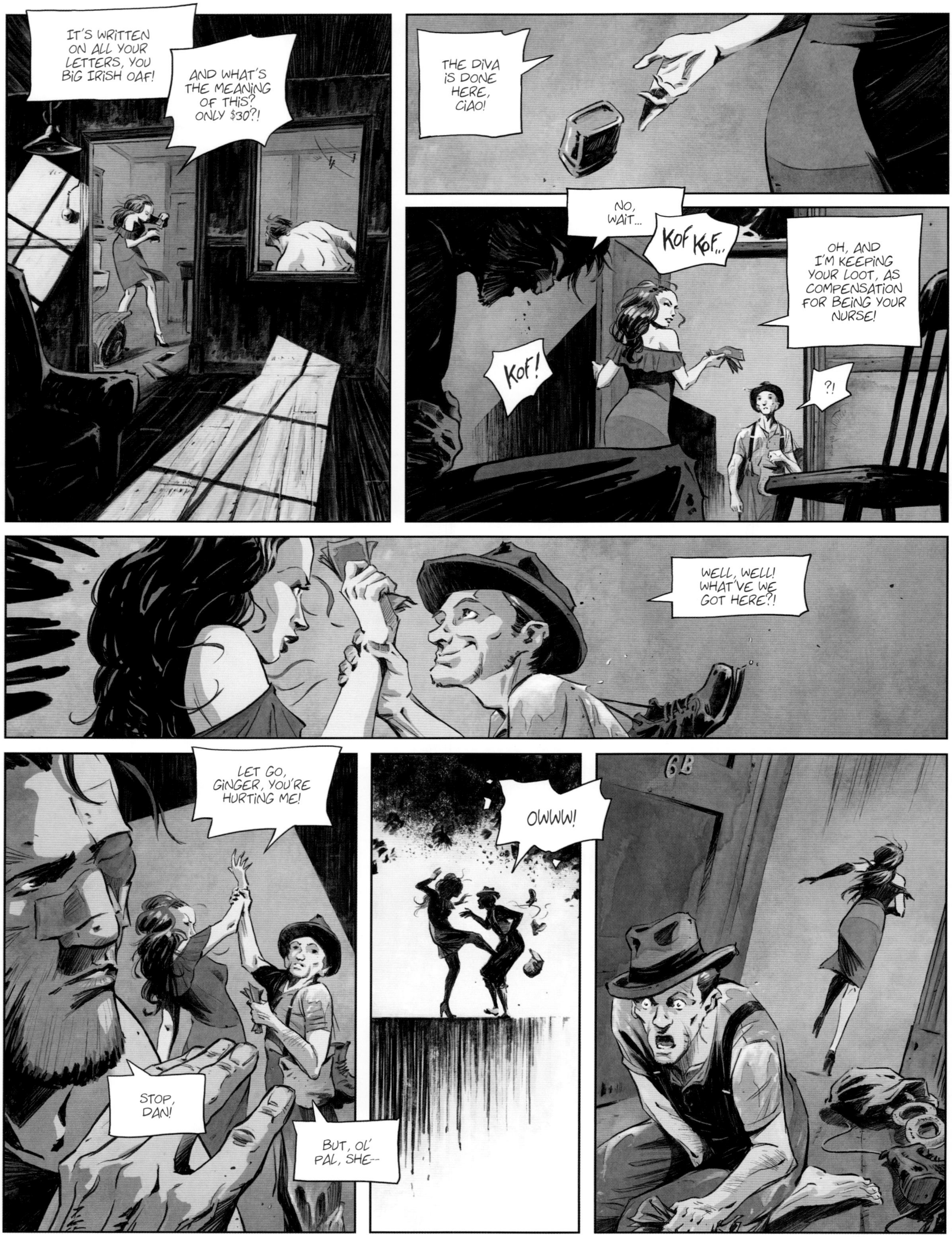

IT'S WRITTEN ON ALL YOUR LETTERS, YOU BIG IRISH OAF!
AND WHAT'S THE MEANING OF THIS? ONLY $30?!
THE DIVA IS DONE HERE, CIAO!
NO, WAIT...
KOF KOF...
KOF!
OH, AND I'M KEEPING YOUR LOOT, AS COMPENSATION FOR BEING YOUR NURSE!
?!
WELL, WELL! WHAT'VE WE GOT HERE?!
LET GO, GINGER, YOU'RE HURTING ME!
STOP, DAN!
BUT, OL' PAL, SHE--
OWWW!
6B
10

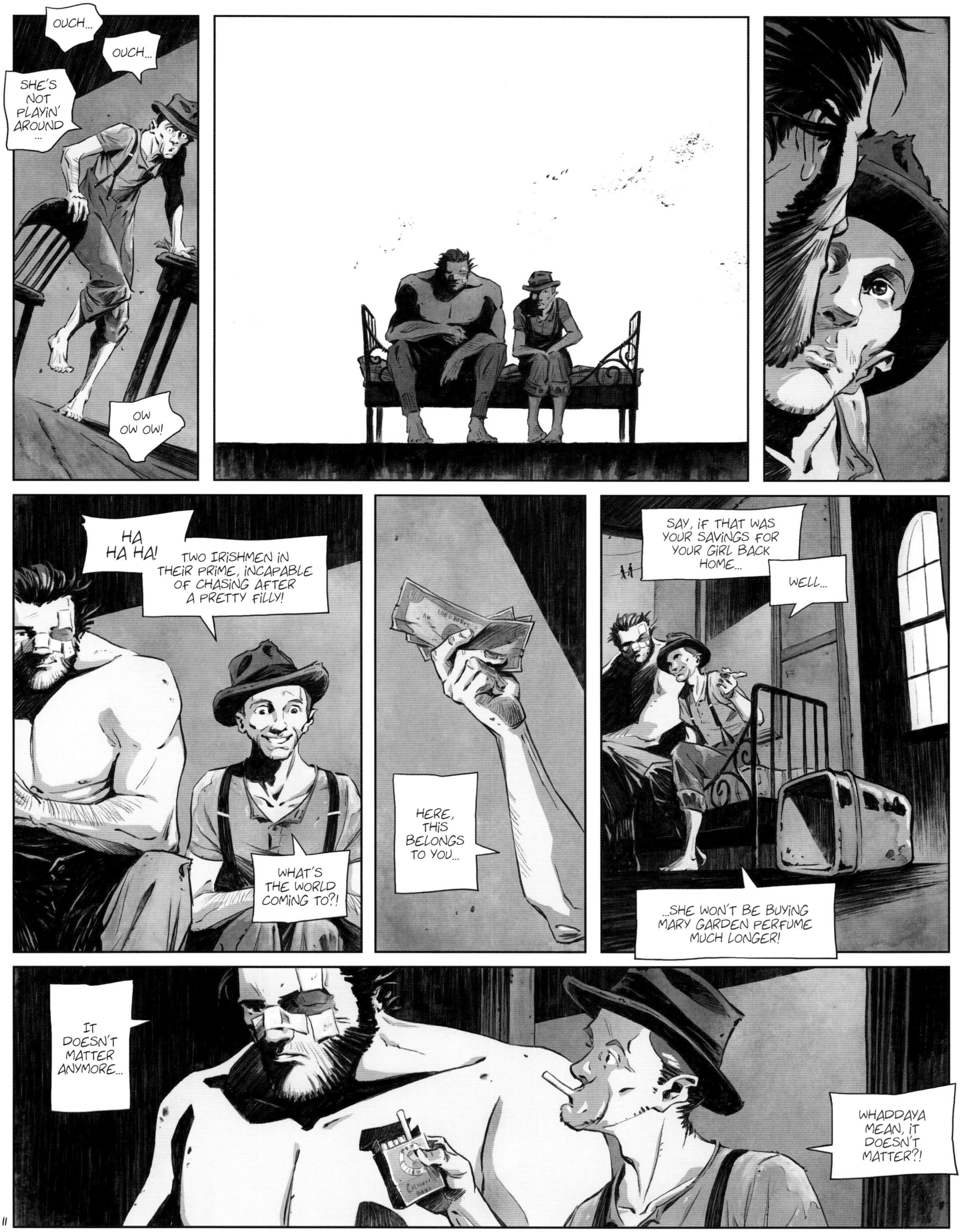
OUCH...
OUCH...
SHE'S NOT PLAYIN' AROUND ...
OW OW OW!
HA HA HA!
TWO IRISHMEN IN THEIR PRIME, INCAPABLE OF CHASING AFTER A PRETTY FILLY!
WHAT'S THE WORLD COMING TO?!
HERE, THIS BELONGS TO YOU...
SAY, IF THAT WAS YOUR SAVINGS FOR YOUR GIRL BACK HOME...
WELL...
...SHE WON'T BE BUYING MARY GARDEN PERFUME MUCH LONGER!
IT DOESN'T MATTER ANYMORE...
WHADDAYA MEAN, IT DOESN'T MATTER?!
11

OF COURSE IT MATTERS!

ARE YOU STILL BENT OUTTA SHAPE BECAUSE YOU HAVEN'T GOTTEN ANY NEW LETTERS?

DAN.

BECAUSE YOU KNOW...

...IF MY SUZY, SHE--

DANIEL!

DAN!

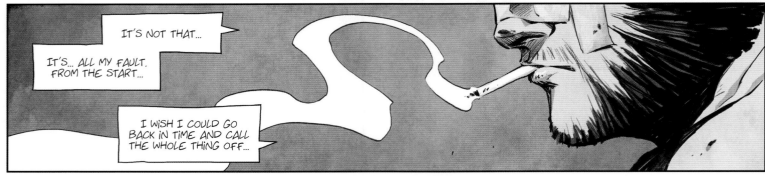

IT'S NOT THAT...

IT'S... ALL MY FAULT. FROM THE START...

I WISH I COULD GO BACK IN TIME AND CALL THE WHOLE THING OFF...

GO BACK IN TIME?!

SO YOU CAN GO ON BEING A GLOOMY GUS WHO CAN HARDLY STRING THREE WORDS TOGETHER, ROTTING AWAY LIKE SOME DEAD RAT?

NO WAY, NEVER! GODDAMN IT!

A BLASPHEMOUS IRISHMAN?!

AND HERE I THOUGHT YOU WERE ALL PIOUS TO A FAULT!

12

70

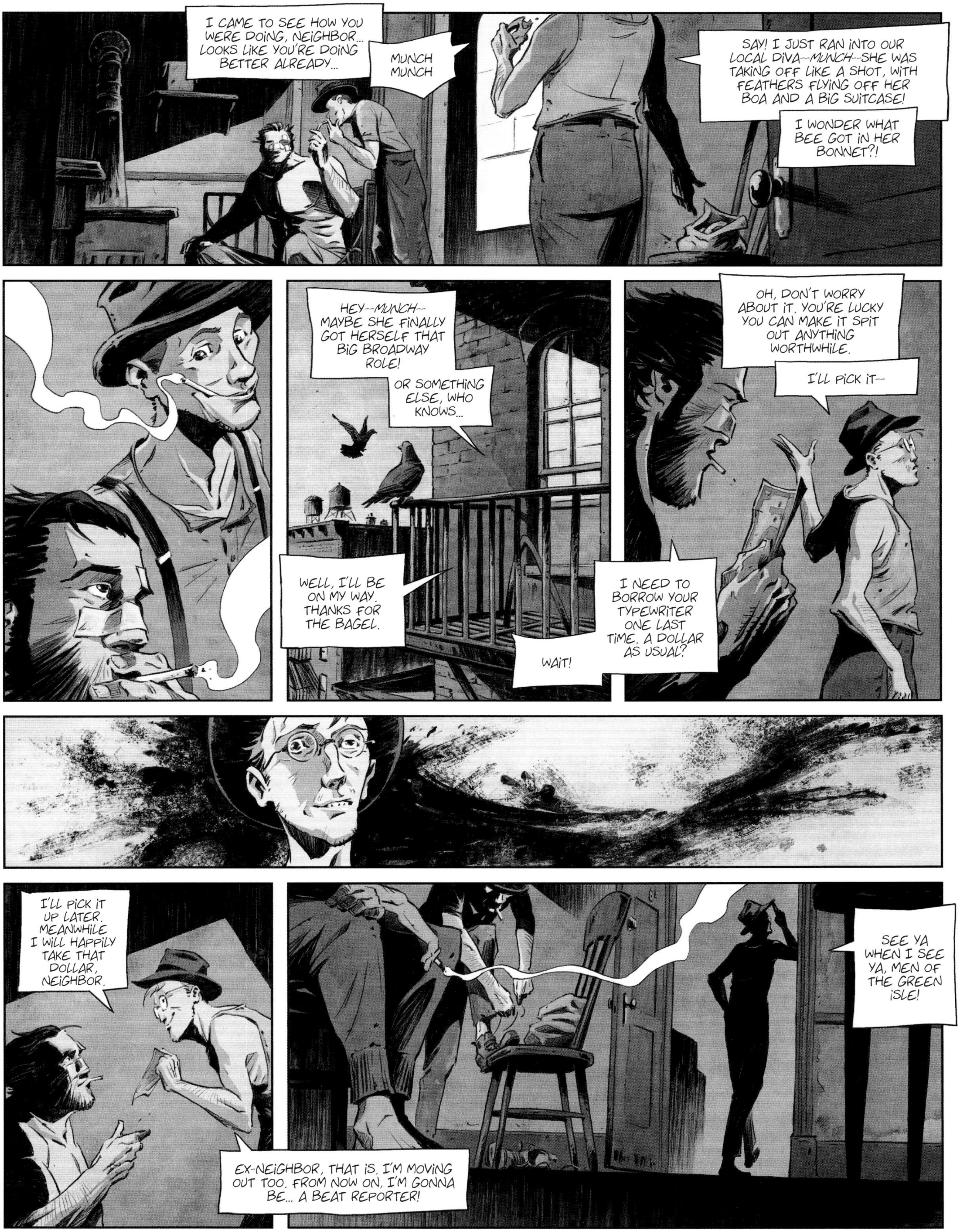
I CAME TO SEE HOW YOU WERE DOING, NEIGHBOR... LOOKS LIKE YOU'RE DOING BETTER ALREADY...
MUNCH MUNCH
SAY! I JUST RAN INTO OUR LOCAL DIVA--MUNCH--SHE WAS TAKING OFF LIKE A SHOT, WITH FEATHERS FLYING OFF HER BOA AND A BIG SUITCASE!
I WONDER WHAT BEE GOT IN HER BONNET?!
HEY--MUNCH--MAYBE SHE FINALLY GOT HERSELF THAT BIG BROADWAY ROLE!
OR SOMETHING ELSE, WHO KNOWS...
WELL, I'LL BE ON MY WAY. THANKS FOR THE BAGEL.
WAIT!
I NEED TO BORROW YOUR TYPEWRITER ONE LAST TIME. A DOLLAR AS USUAL?
OH, DON'T WORRY ABOUT IT. YOU'RE LUCKY YOU CAN MAKE IT SPIT OUT ANYTHING WORTHWHILE.
I'LL PICK IT--
I'LL PICK IT UP LATER. MEANWHILE I WILL HAPPILY TAKE THAT DOLLAR, NEIGHBOR.
EX-NEIGHBOR, THAT IS. I'M MOVING OUT TOO. FROM NOW ON, I'M GONNA BE... A BEAT REPORTER!
SEE YA WHEN I SEE YA, MEN OF THE GREEN ISLE!
13

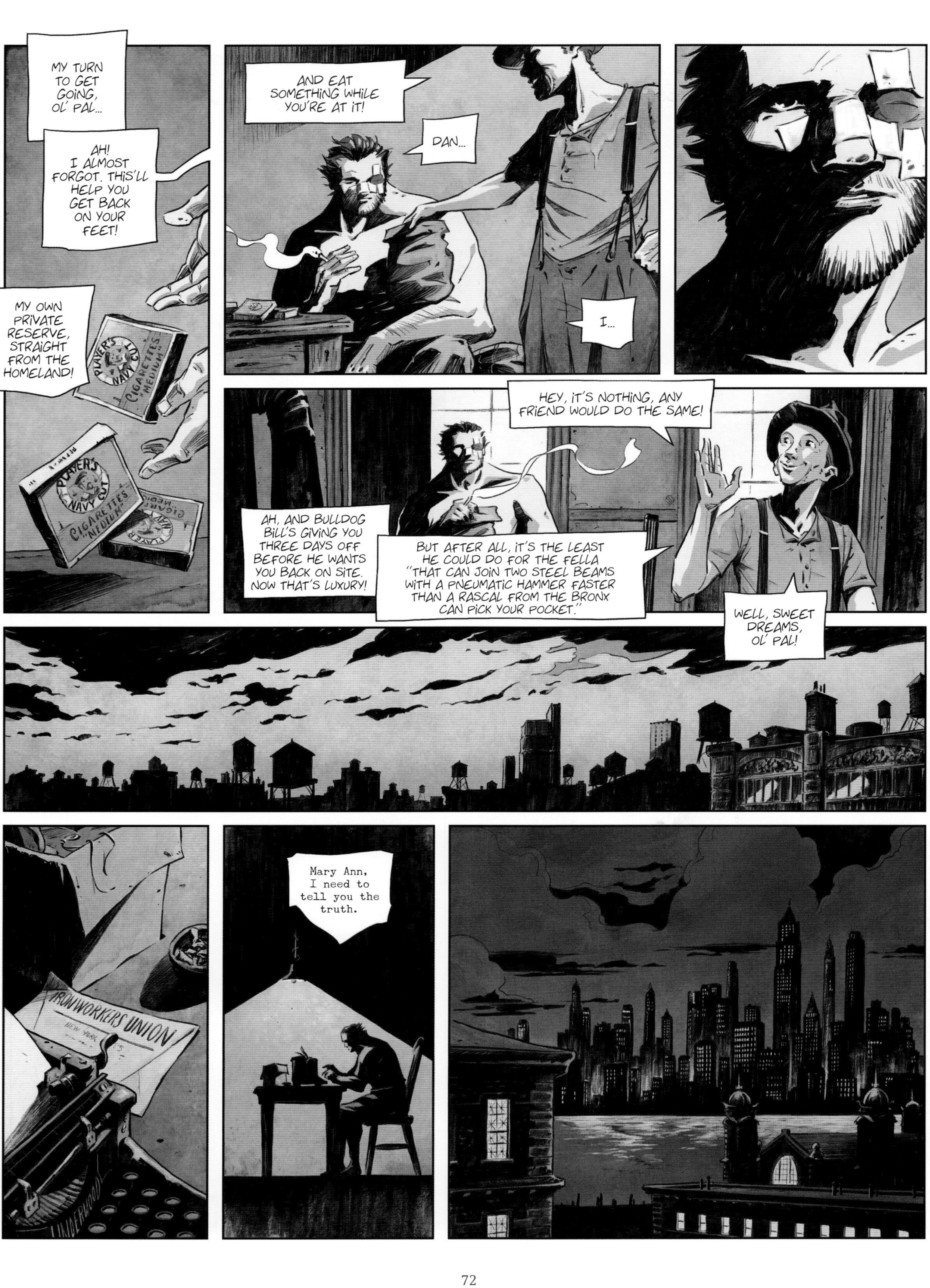
MY TURN TO GET GOING, OL' PAL...
AH! I ALMOST FORGOT. THIS'LL HELP YOU GET BACK ON YOUR FEET!
MY OWN PRIVATE RESERVE, STRAIGHT FROM THE HOMELAND!
PLAYER'S NAVY CUT CIGARETTES MEDIUM
AND EAT SOMETHING WHILE YOU'RE AT IT!
DAN...
I...
HEY, IT'S NOTHING, ANY FRIEND WOULD DO THE SAME!
AH, AND BULLDOG BILL'S GIVING YOU THREE DAYS OFF BEFORE HE WANTS YOU BACK ON SITE. NOW THAT'S LUXURY!
BUT AFTER ALL, IT'S THE LEAST HE COULD DO FOR THE FELLA "THAT CAN JOIN TWO STEEL BEAMS WITH A PNEUMATIC HAMMER FASTER THAN A RASCAL FROM THE BRONX CAN PICK YOUR POCKET."
WELL, SWEET DREAMS, OL' PAL!
IRONWORKERS UNION
NEW YORK
UNDERWOOD
Mary Ann, I need to tell you the truth.
14

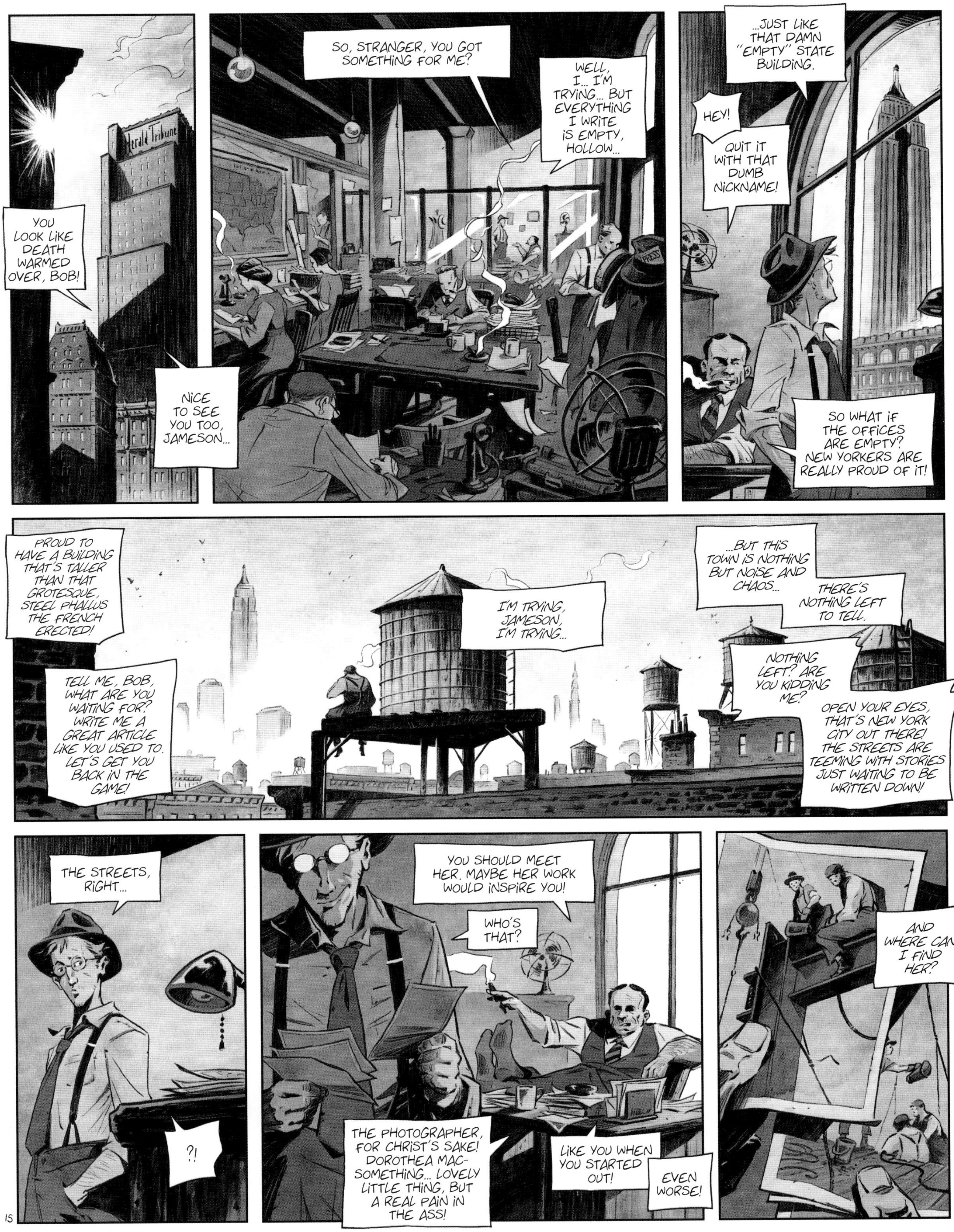
YOU LOOK LIKE DEATH WARMED OVER, BOB!
NICE TO SEE YOU TOO, JAMESON...
SO, STRANGER, YOU GOT SOMETHING FOR ME?
WELL, I... I'M TRYING... BUT EVERYTHING I WRITE IS EMPTY, HOLLOW...
...JUST LIKE THAT DAMN "EMPTY" STATE BUILDING.
HEY!
QUIT IT WITH THAT DUMB NICKNAME!
SO WHAT IF THE OFFICES ARE EMPTY? NEW YORKERS ARE REALLY PROUD OF IT!
PROUD TO HAVE A BUILDING THAT'S TALLER THAN THAT GROTESQUE, STEEL PHALLUS THE FRENCH ERECTED!
TELL ME, BOB, WHAT ARE YOU WAITING FOR? WRITE ME A GREAT ARTICLE LIKE YOU USED TO. LET'S GET YOU BACK IN THE GAME!
I'M TRYING, JAMESON, I'M TRYING...
...BUT THIS TOWN IS NOTHING BUT NOISE AND CHAOS...
THERE'S NOTHING LEFT TO TELL.
NOTHING LEFT? ARE YOU KIDDING ME?
OPEN YOUR EYES, THAT'S NEW YORK CITY OUT THERE! THE STREETS ARE TEEMING WITH STORIES JUST WAITING TO BE WRITTEN DOWN!
THE STREETS, RIGHT...
?!
YOU SHOULD MEET HER. MAYBE HER WORK WOULD INSPIRE YOU!
WHO'S THAT?
THE PHOTOGRAPHER, FOR CHRIST'S SAKE! DOROTHEA MAC-SOMETHING... LOVELY LITTLE THING, BUT A REAL PAIN IN THE ASS!
LIKE YOU WHEN YOU STARTED OUT!
EVEN WORSE!
AND WHERE CAN I FIND HER?
15

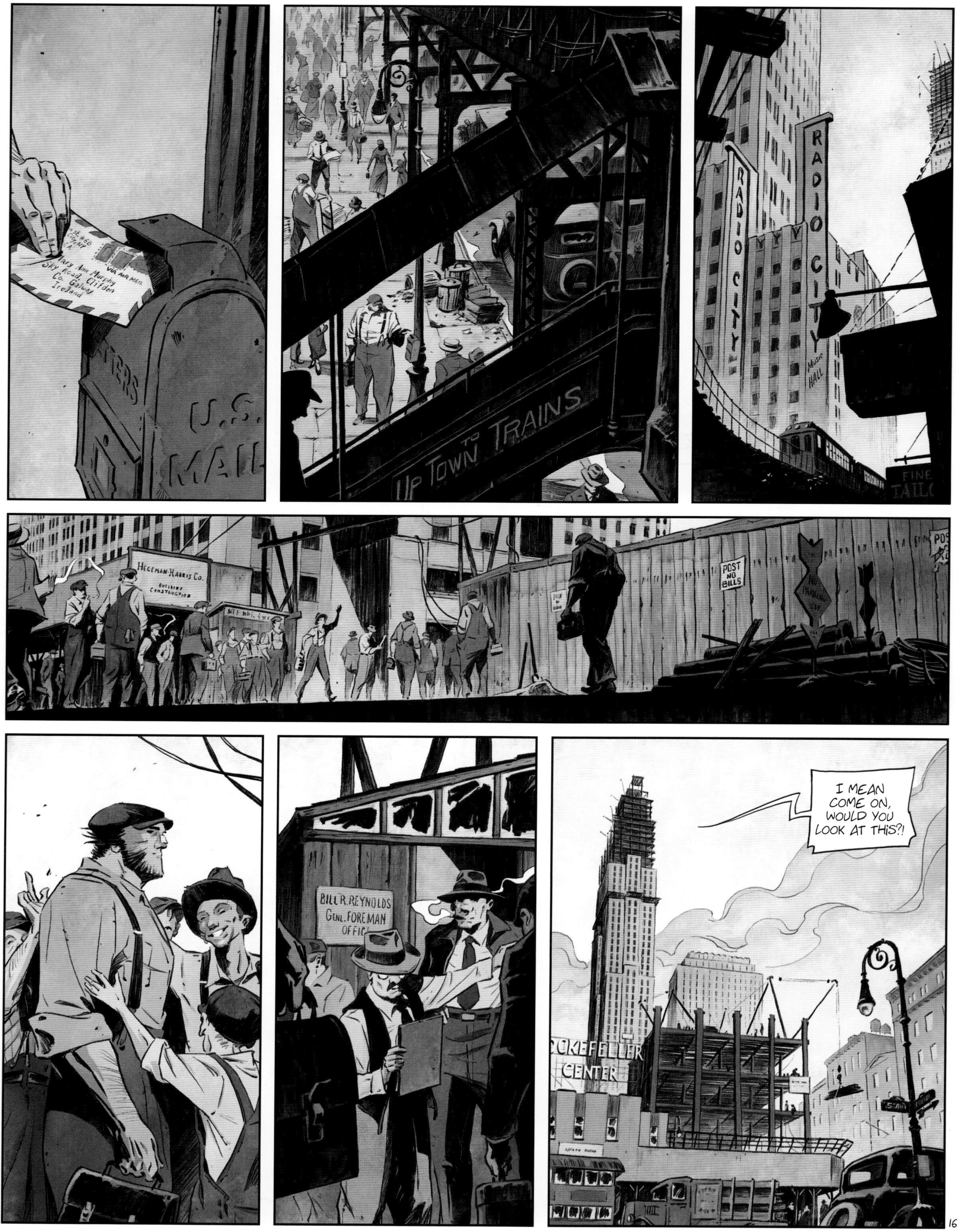
Mary Ann Murphy
Sky Road, Clifden
Co. Galway
Ireland
VIA AIR MAIL
U.S. MAI
UP TOWN TRAINS
TO
RADIO CITY
RADIO CITY
Music HALL
FINE
TAILO
HEGEMAN-HARRIS CO.
BUILDING CONSTRUCTION
POST NO BILLS
BILL R. REYNOLDS
GENL. FOREMAN
OFFIC
CKEFELLER
CENTER
I MEAN COME ON, WOULD YOU LOOK AT THIS?!
16

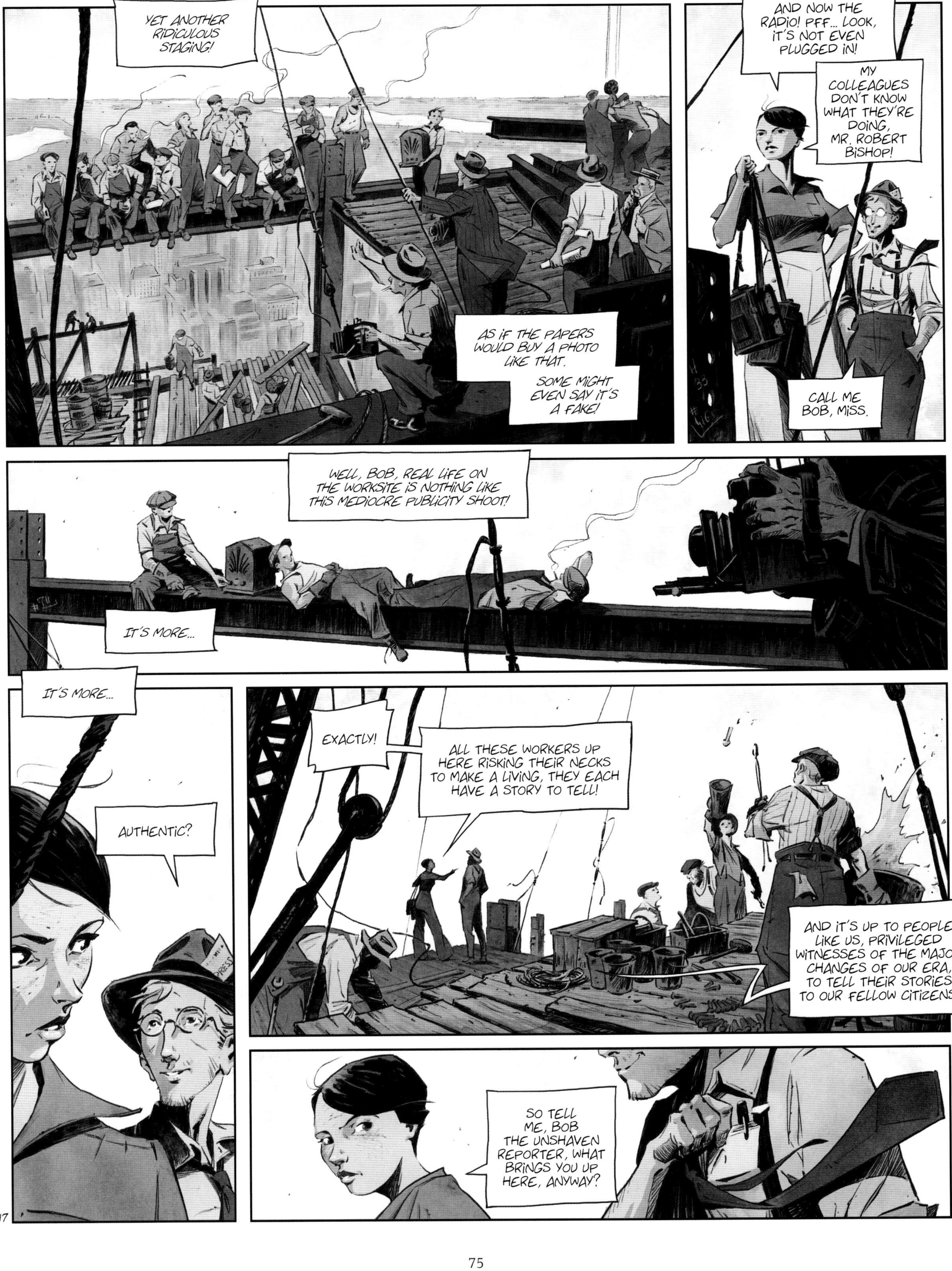

YET ANOTHER RIDICULOUS STAGING!
AS IF THE PAPERS WOULD BUY A PHOTO LIKE THAT.
SOME MIGHT EVEN SAY IT'S A FAKE!
AND NOW THE RADIO! PFF... LOOK, IT'S NOT EVEN PLUGGED IN!
MY COLLEAGUES DON'T KNOW WHAT THEY'RE DOING, MR. ROBERT BISHOP!
CALL ME BOB, MISS.
WELL, BOB, REAL LIFE ON THE WORKSITE IS NOTHING LIKE THIS MEDIOCRE PUBLICITY SHOOT!
IT'S MORE...
IT'S MORE...
AUTHENTIC?
EXACTLY!
ALL THESE WORKERS UP HERE RISKING THEIR NECKS TO MAKE A LIVING, THEY EACH HAVE A STORY TO TELL!
AND IT'S UP TO PEOPLE LIKE US, PRIVILEGED WITNESSES OF THE MAJOR CHANGES OF OUR ERA, TO TELL THEIR STORIES TO OUR FELLOW CITIZENS!
SO TELL ME, BOB THE UNSHAVEN REPORTER, WHAT BRINGS YOU UP HERE, ANYWAY?
17

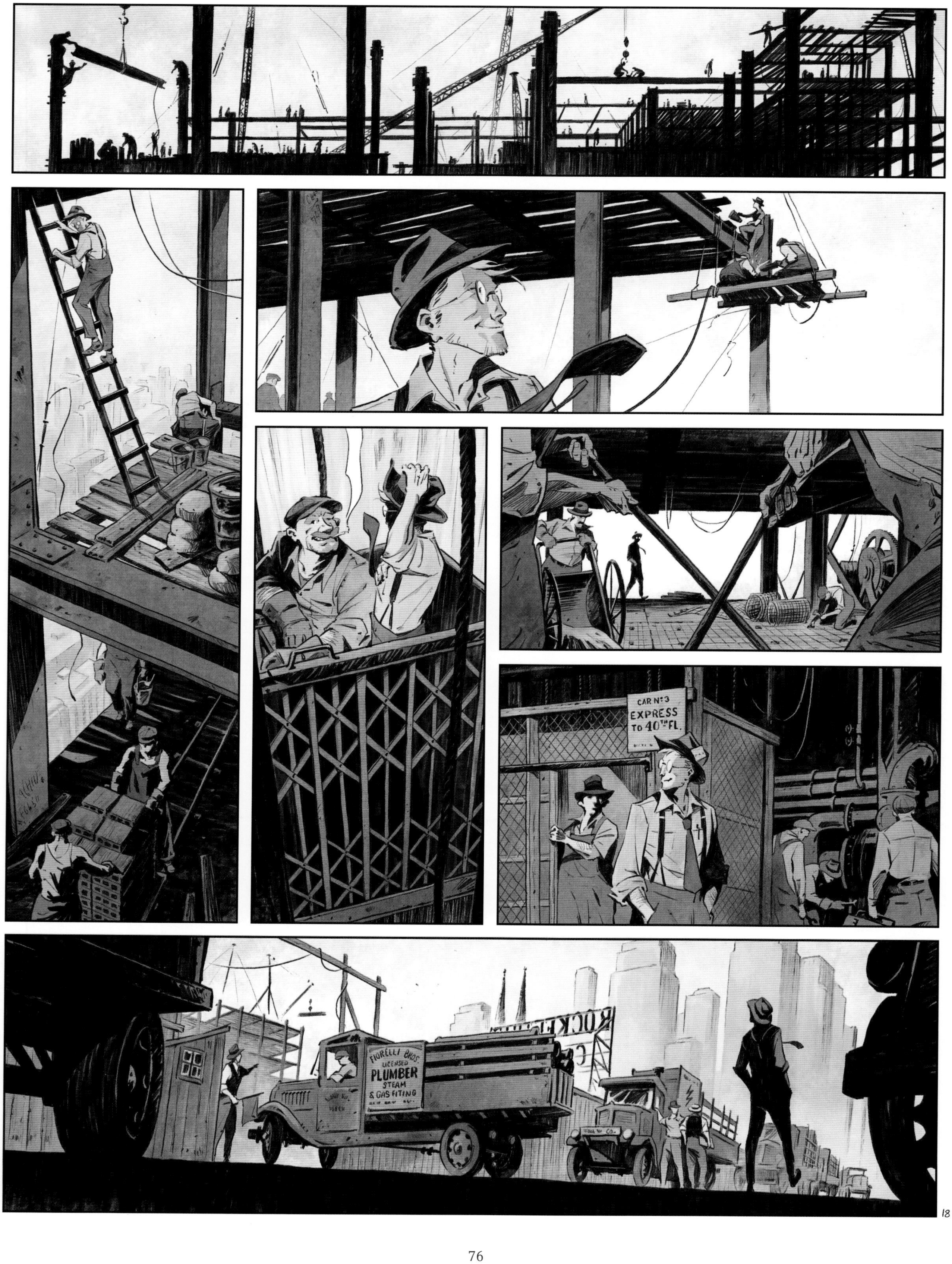
CAR Nº3
EXPRESS
TO 40TH FL.
FIORELLI BROS.
LICENSED
PLUMBER
STEAM
& GAS FITTING

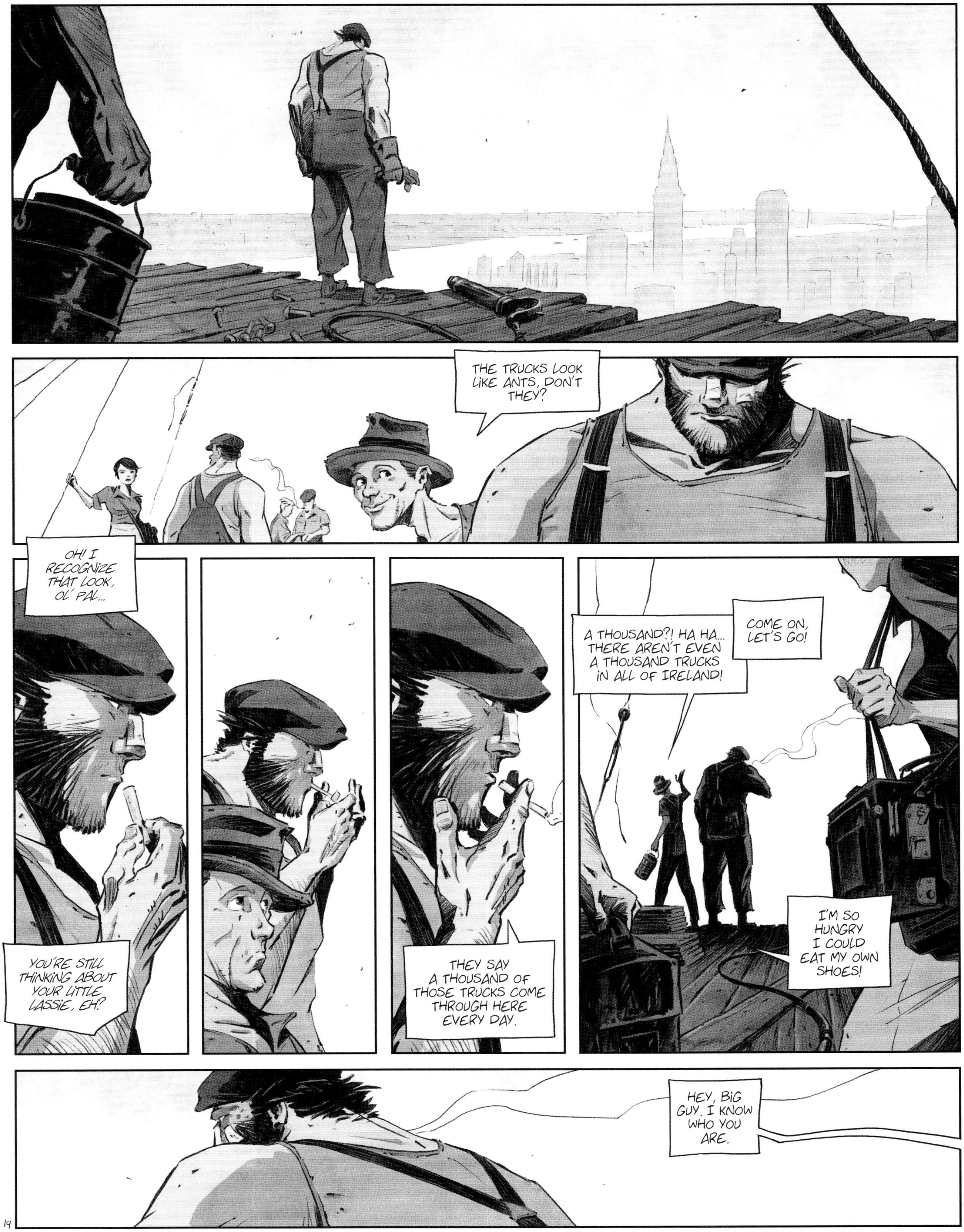

THE TRUCKS LOOK LIKE ANTS, DON'T THEY?
OH! I RECOGNIZE THAT LOOK, OL' PAL...
YOU'RE STILL THINKING ABOUT YOUR LITTLE LASSIE, EH?
THEY SAY A THOUSAND OF THOSE TRUCKS COME THROUGH HERE EVERY DAY.
A THOUSAND?! HA HA... THERE AREN'T EVEN A THOUSAND TRUCKS IN ALL OF IRELAND!
COME ON, LET'S GO!
I'M SO HUNGRY I COULD EAT MY OWN SHOES!
HEY, BIG GUY. I KNOW WHO YOU ARE.
19

JACK JORDAN, KNOWN AS GIANT. BORN AROUND 1900. NO KNOWN FAMILY. ACTIVE IRA MEMBER...

...KNOWN TO HAVE BLOWN UP RAILWAY BRIDGES, KILLED SOLDIERS ON GUARD DUTY, STOLEN WEAPONS, ROBBED A BANK...

TO SUM UP, A SERVICE RECORD TO MATCH HIS NICKNAME...

...AND THAT'S NOT ALL.

MY CONTACT AT THE IRISH INDEPENDENT IN DUBLIN GAVE ME THE CHERRY ON THE CAKE: JACK JORDAN DIED IN A FIRE DURING THE CIVIL WAR!

WELL, I'M NOT ONE TO BELIEVE IN GHOST STORIES, MISTER JORDAN.

WHAT WOULD THE FOREMAN OR YOUR WORKMATES SAY IF THEY FOUND OUT THEY WERE WORKING WITH A CRIMINAL?

NOT TO MENTION THE IMMIGRATION OFFICE. I'D BE SURPRISED IF THEY LET A GHOST SIGN THE REGISTRY AT ELLIS ISLAND...

SO WHAT'S YOUR STORY?

!!

IN ANOTHER TIME...

...IN ANOTHER PLACE...

...I WOULDN'T HAVE HESITATED TO SHOW YOU HOW DANGEROUS IT IS TO THREATEN A MAN LIKE THAT...

VIOLENCE DOESN'T FIX ANYTHING.

YOU CAN BE SURE...

...I KNOW THAT ONLY TOO WELL.

20

WELL, ARE YOU COMING OR NOT?

THE OTHERS ARE WAITING, WE'RE ALL GONNA HAVE LUNCH TOGETHER TO CELEBRATE YOUR RETURN!

COME, ON, OL' PAL!

THAT'S RIGHT, "OL' PAL," ISN'T THAT A GOOD IDEA?

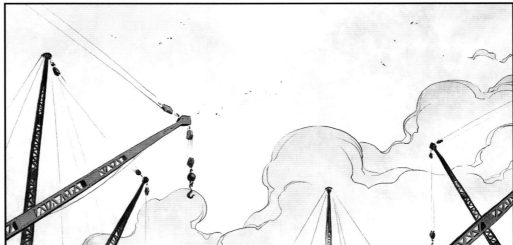

OK.

AMAZING!

HEY!

DOES THE PHOTOGRAPHER LADY WANNA COME BREAK BREAD WITH US?!

THANKS, BUT THE "PHOTOGRAPHER LADY" HAS A NAME! DOROTHEA MACPHAIL.

AND "SHE" DIDN'T BRING LUNCH.

BAH, DON'T WORRY! COME ON OVER, WE'LL GET YOU SORTED OUT!

21

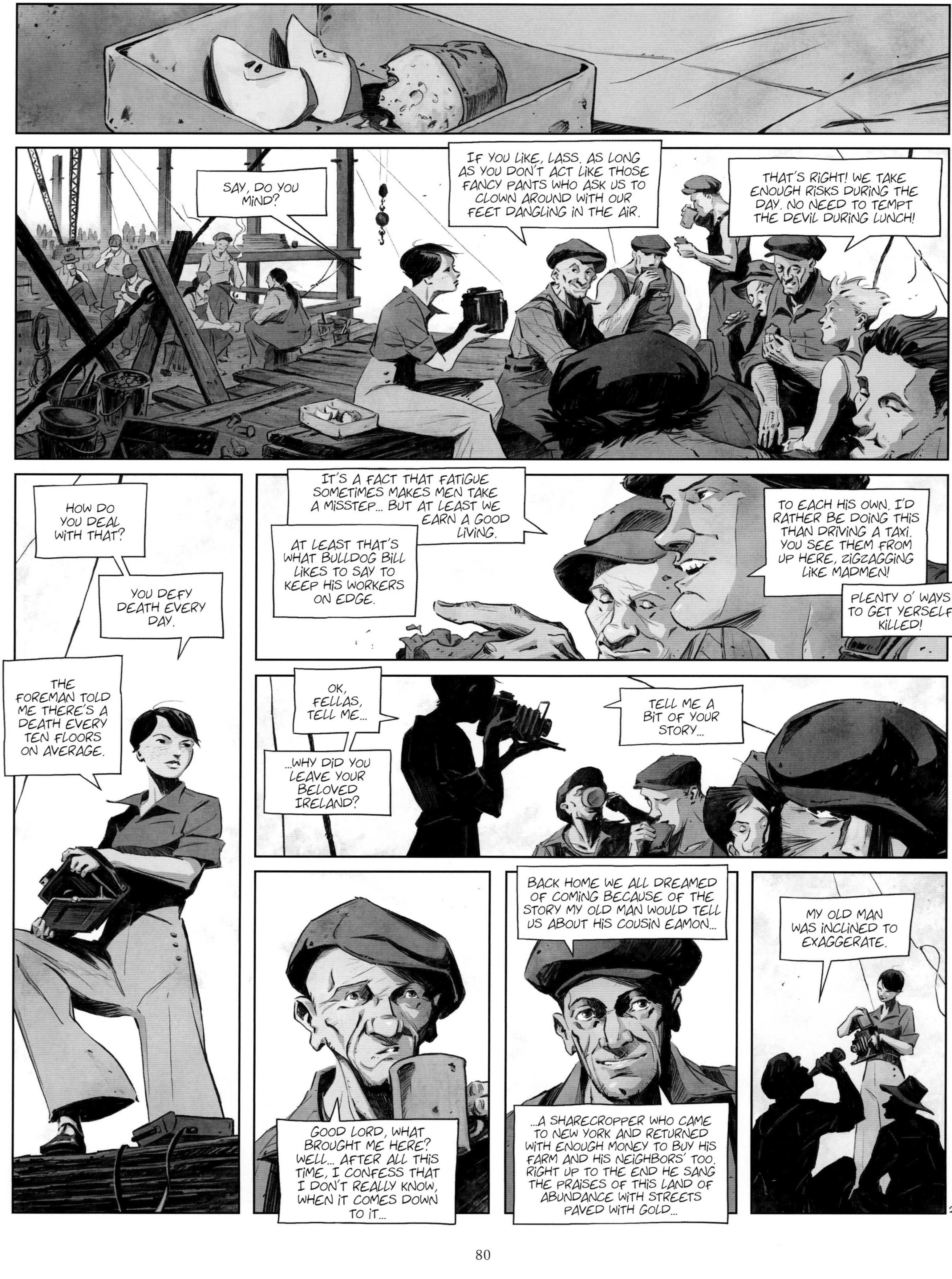
SAY, DO YOU MIND?
IF YOU LIKE, LASS. AS LONG AS YOU DON'T ACT LIKE THOSE FANCY PANTS WHO ASK US TO CLOWN AROUND WITH OUR FEET DANGLING IN THE AIR.
THAT'S RIGHT! WE TAKE ENOUGH RISKS DURING THE DAY. NO NEED TO TEMPT THE DEVIL DURING LUNCH!
HOW DO YOU DEAL WITH THAT?
YOU DEFY DEATH EVERY DAY.
THE FOREMAN TOLD ME THERE'S A DEATH EVERY TEN FLOORS ON AVERAGE.
IT'S A FACT THAT FATIGUE SOMETIMES MAKES MEN TAKE A MISSTEP... BUT AT LEAST WE EARN A GOOD LIVING.
AT LEAST THAT'S WHAT BULLDOG BILL LIKES TO SAY TO KEEP HIS WORKERS ON EDGE.
TO EACH HIS OWN. I'D RATHER BE DOING THIS THAN DRIVING A TAXI. YOU SEE THEM FROM UP HERE, ZIGZAGGING LIKE MADMEN!
PLENTY O' WAYS TO GET YERSELF KILLED!
OK, FELLAS, TELL ME...
...WHY DID YOU LEAVE YOUR BELOVED IRELAND?
TELL ME A BIT OF YOUR STORY...
GOOD LORD, WHAT BROUGHT ME HERE? WELL... AFTER ALL THIS TIME, I CONFESS THAT I DON'T REALLY KNOW, WHEN IT COMES DOWN TO IT...
BACK HOME WE ALL DREAMED OF COMING BECAUSE OF THE STORY MY OLD MAN WOULD TELL US ABOUT HIS COUSIN EAMON...
...A SHARECROPPER WHO CAME TO NEW YORK AND RETURNED WITH ENOUGH MONEY TO BUY HIS FARM AND HIS NEIGHBORS' TOO. RIGHT UP TO THE END HE SANG THE PRAISES OF THIS LAND OF ABUNDANCE WITH STREETS PAVED WITH GOLD...
MY OLD MAN WAS INCLINED TO EXAGGERATE.
22

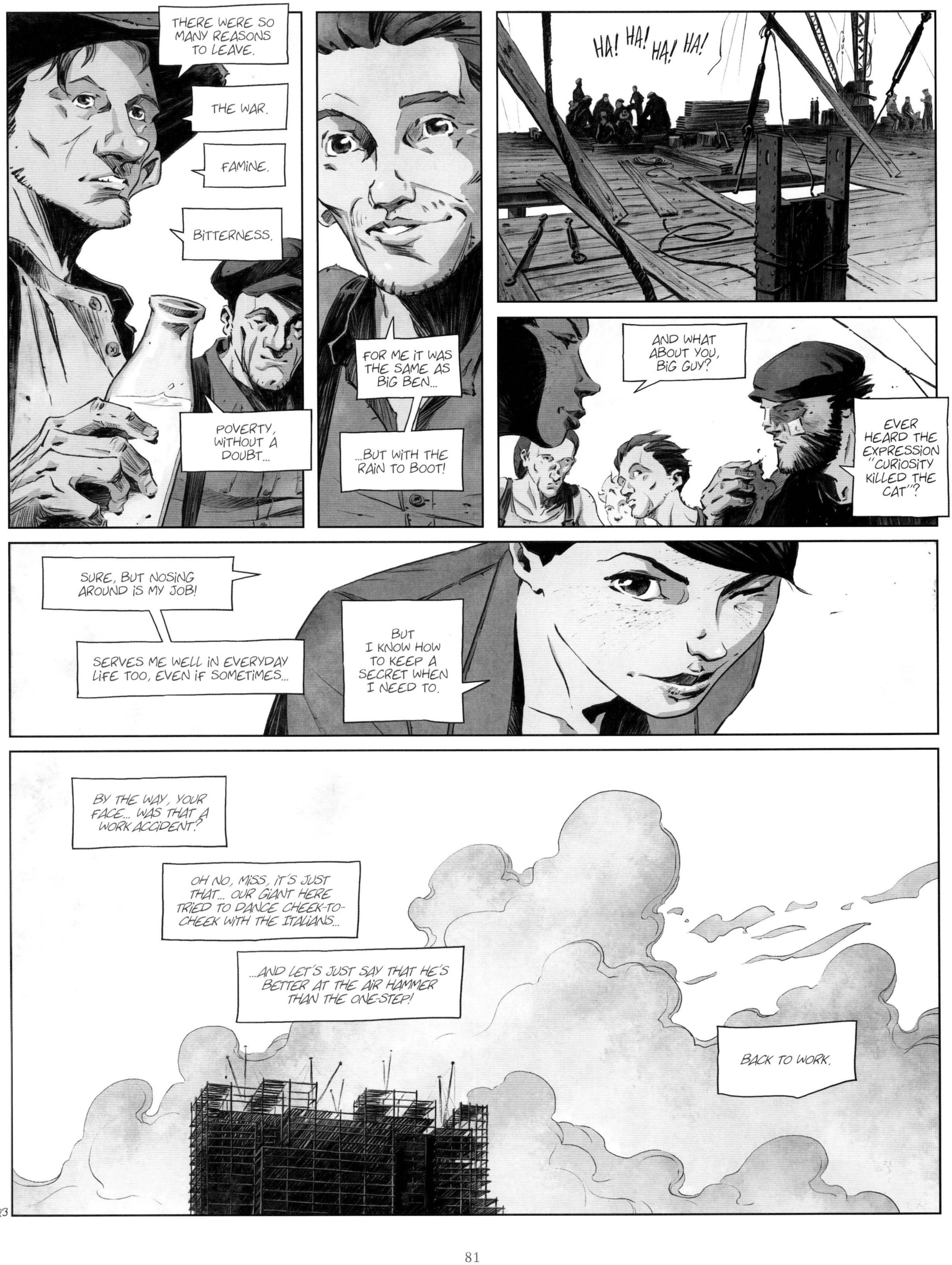
THERE WERE SO MANY REASONS TO LEAVE.
THE WAR.
FAMINE.
BITTERNESS.
POVERTY, WITHOUT A DOUBT...
FOR ME IT WAS THE SAME AS BIG BEN...
...BUT WITH THE RAIN TO BOOT!
HA! HA! HA! HA!
AND WHAT ABOUT YOU, BIG GUY?
EVER HEARD THE EXPRESSION "CURIOSITY KILLED THE CAT"?
SURE, BUT NOSING AROUND IS MY JOB!
SERVES ME WELL IN EVERYDAY LIFE TOO, EVEN IF SOMETIMES...
BUT I KNOW HOW TO KEEP A SECRET WHEN I NEED TO.
BY THE WAY, YOUR FACE... WAS THAT A WORK ACCIDENT?
OH NO, MISS, IT'S JUST THAT... OUR GIANT HERE TRIED TO DANCE CHEEK-TO-CHEEK WITH THE ITALIANS...
...AND LET'S JUST SAY THAT HE'S BETTER AT THE AIR HAMMER THAN THE ONE-STEP!
BACK TO WORK.
23

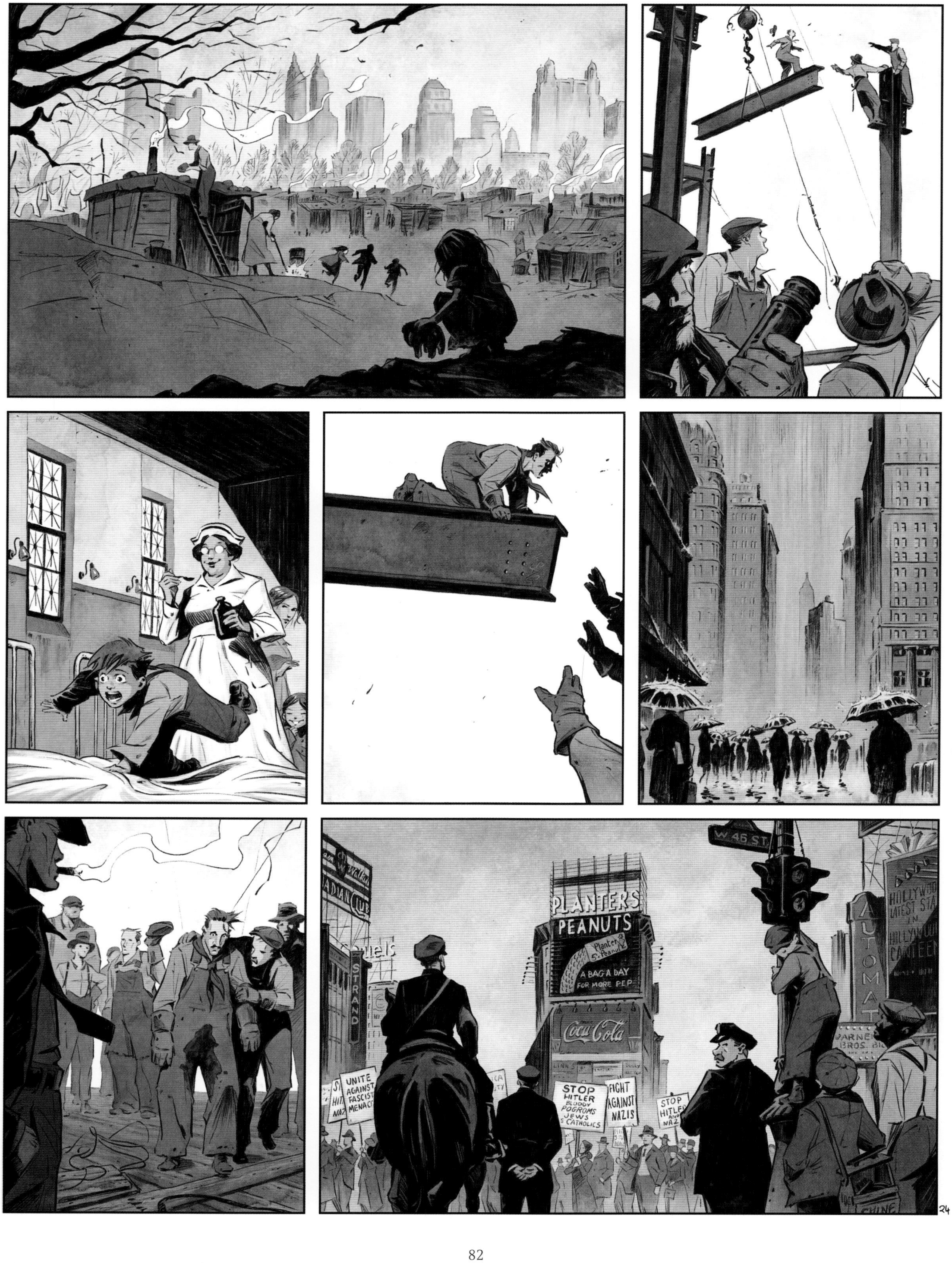
W 46 ST
PLANTERS
PEANUTS
A BAG A DAY FOR MORE PEP
STRAND
Coca-Cola
AUTOMAT
UNITE AGAINST FASCIST
STOP HITLER BLOODY POGROMS JEWS & CATHOLICS
FIGHT AGAINST NAZIS
24

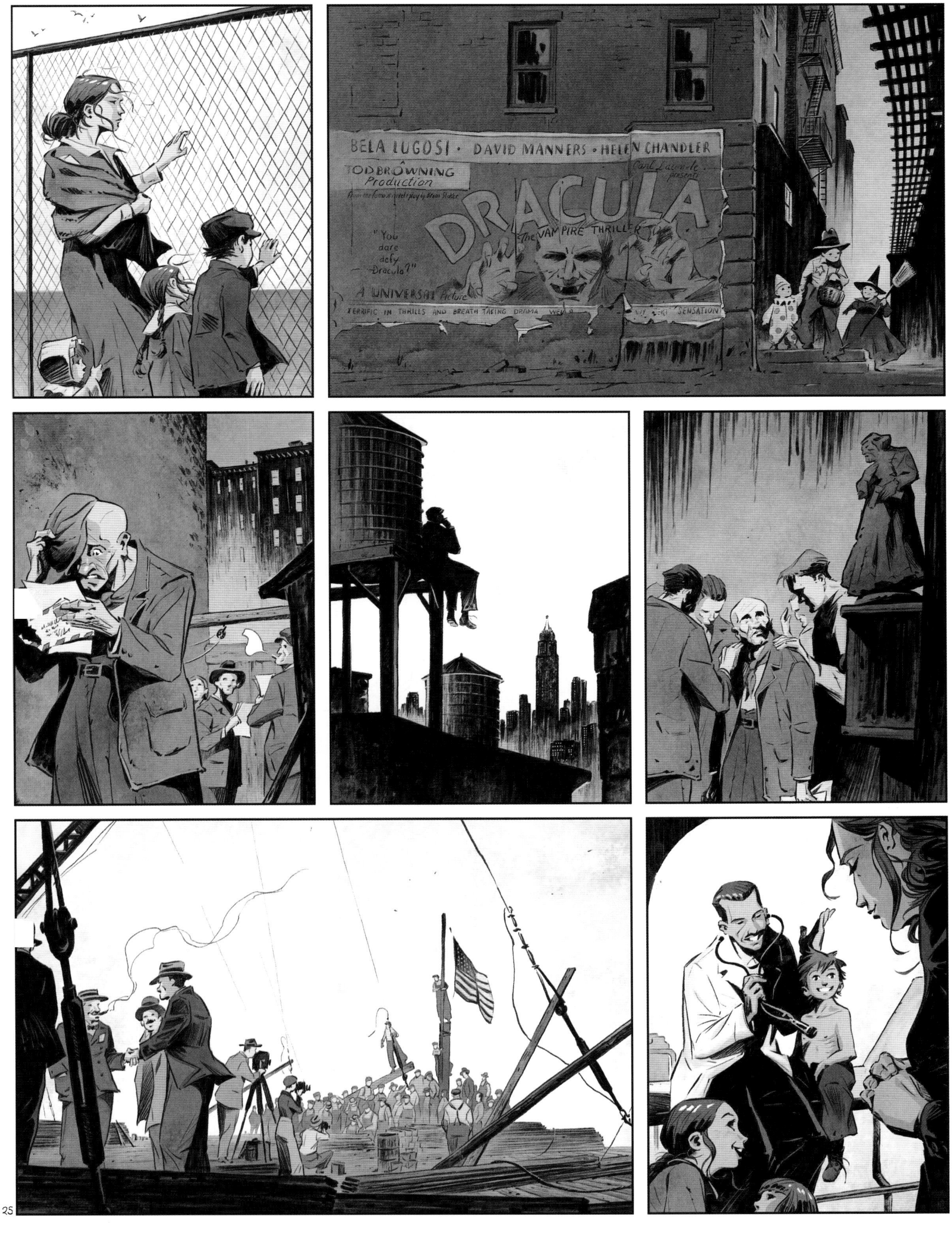
BELA LUGOSI • DAVID MANNERS • HELEN CHANDLER
A TOD BROWNING Production
DRACULA
"You dare defy Dracula?"
A UNIVERSAL Picture
TERRIFIC IN THRILLS AND BREATH TAKING DRAMA
SENSATION

WE HAVEN'T FINISHED STACKIN' STEEL!

RIGHT, OL' PAL?

THE MAIN BUILDING WAS BARELY FINISHED BEFORE BULLDOG BILL SENT US TO THE ONE NEXT DOOR!

HEY, YOU LITTLE FIENDS! GO PLAY SOMEWHERE ELSE!

BASEBALL... WHAT A NUISANCE, IT'S WORSE THAN CRICKET!

HURLING, NOW THERE'S A NOBLE, GAELIC SPORT. A GAME WORTHY OF THE NAME. BUT BASEBALL... IT'S BORING AS ALL HELL!

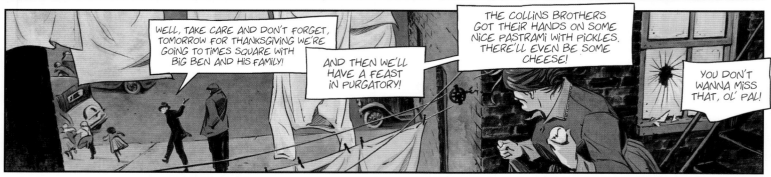

WELL, TAKE CARE AND DON'T FORGET, TOMORROW FOR THANKSGIVING WE'RE GOING TO TIMES SQUARE WITH BIG BEN AND HIS FAMILY!

AND THEN WE'LL HAVE A FEAST IN PURGATORY!

THE COLLINS BROTHERS GOT THEIR HANDS ON SOME NICE PASTRAMI WITH PICKLES. THERE'LL EVEN BE SOME CHEESE!

YOU DON'T WANNA MISS THAT, OL' PAL!

SAY, BIG FELLA FROM 6-B, I'VE GOT SOMETHING FOR YOU HERE.

BEEN A WHILE, HASN'T IT?

THIS LETTER OF YOURS GOT SENT BACK FROM IRELAND. THE CORRESPONDENT NO LONGER RESIDES AT THIS ADDRESS...

26

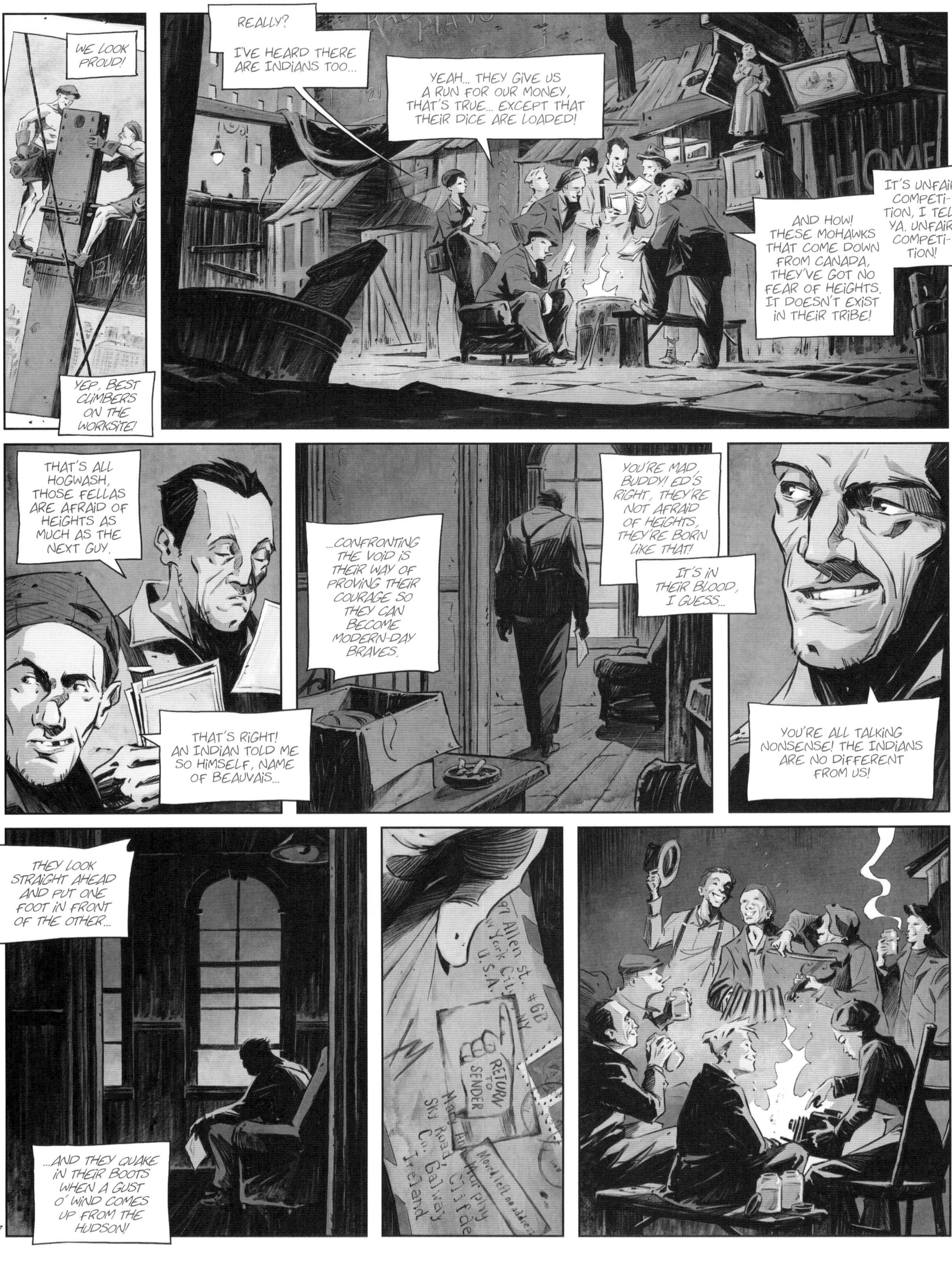
WE LOOK PROUD!
YEP. BEST CLIMBERS ON THE WORKSITE!
REALLY?
I'VE HEARD THERE ARE INDIANS TOO...
YEAH... THEY GIVE US A RUN FOR OUR MONEY, THAT'S TRUE... EXCEPT THAT THEIR DICE ARE LOADED!
AND HOW! THESE MOHAWKS THAT COME DOWN FROM CANADA, THEY'VE GOT NO FEAR OF HEIGHTS. IT DOESN'T EXIST IN THEIR TRIBE!
IT'S UNFAIR COMPETITION, I TELL YA. UNFAIR COMPETITION!
HOME
THAT'S ALL HOGWASH, THOSE FELLAS ARE AFRAID OF HEIGHTS AS MUCH AS THE NEXT GUY.
THAT'S RIGHT! AN INDIAN TOLD ME SO HIMSELF, NAME OF BEAUVAIS...
...CONFRONTING THE VOID IS THEIR WAY OF PROVING THEIR COURAGE SO THEY CAN BECOME MODERN-DAY BRAVES.
YOU'RE MAD, BUDDY! ED'S RIGHT, THEY'RE NOT AFRAID OF HEIGHTS, THEY'RE BORN LIKE THAT!
IT'S IN THEIR BLOOD, I GUESS...
YOU'RE ALL TALKING NONSENSE! THE INDIANS ARE NO DIFFERENT FROM US!
THEY LOOK STRAIGHT AHEAD AND PUT ONE FOOT IN FRONT OF THE OTHER...
...AND THEY QUAKE IN THEIR BOOTS WHEN A GUST O' WIND COMES UP FROM THE HUDSON!
Allen st.
U.S.A.
RETURN TO SENDER
Sky Road
Co. Galway
Ireland

27

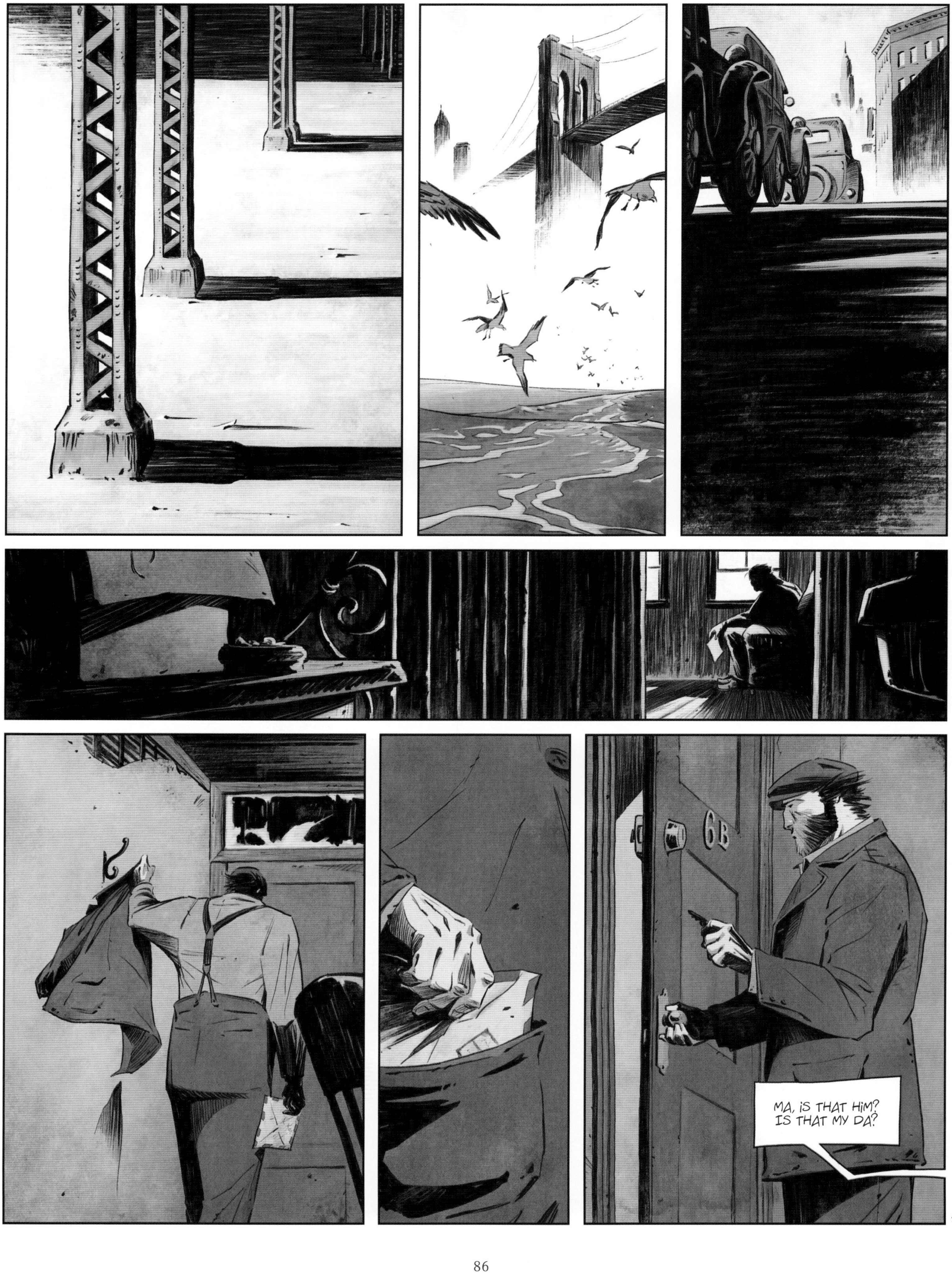
MA, IS THAT HIM?
IS THAT MY DA?
28

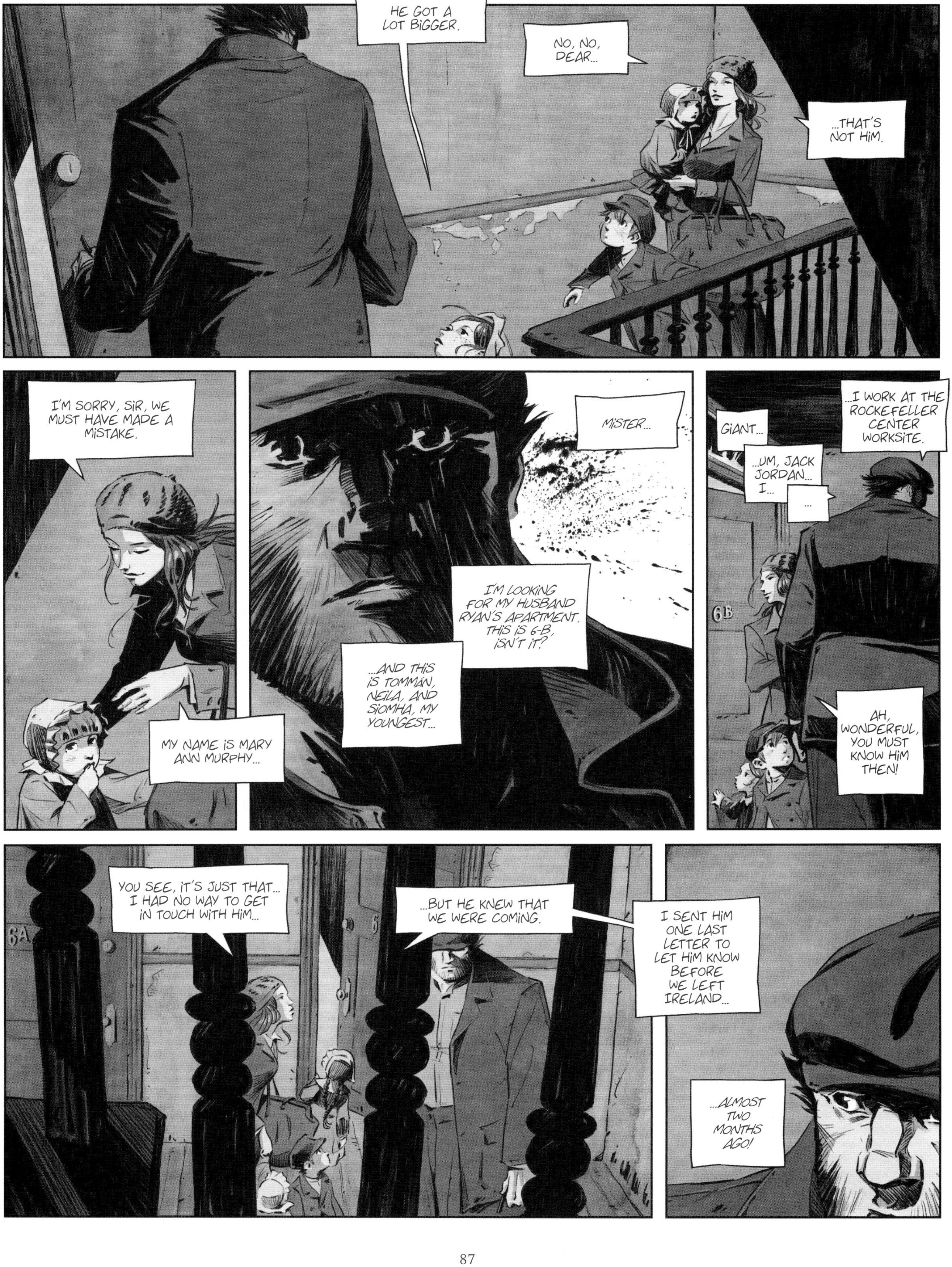

HE GOT A LOT BIGGER.
NO, NO, DEAR...
...THAT'S NOT HIM.
I'M SORRY, SIR, WE MUST HAVE MADE A MISTAKE.
MY NAME IS MARY ANN MURPHY...
...AND THIS IS TOMMAN, NEILA, AND SIOMHA, MY YOUNGEST...
I'M LOOKING FOR MY HUSBAND RYAN'S APARTMENT. THIS IS 6-B, ISN'T IT?
MISTER...
GIANT...
...UM, JACK JORDAN... I...
...
...I WORK AT THE ROCKEFELLER CENTER WORKSITE.
6B
AH, WONDERFUL, YOU MUST KNOW HIM THEN!
YOU SEE, IT'S JUST THAT... I HAD NO WAY TO GET IN TOUCH WITH HIM...
...BUT HE KNEW THAT WE WERE COMING.
I SENT HIM ONE LAST LETTER TO LET HIM KNOW BEFORE WE LEFT IRELAND...
...ALMOST TWO MONTHS AGO!
6A

29

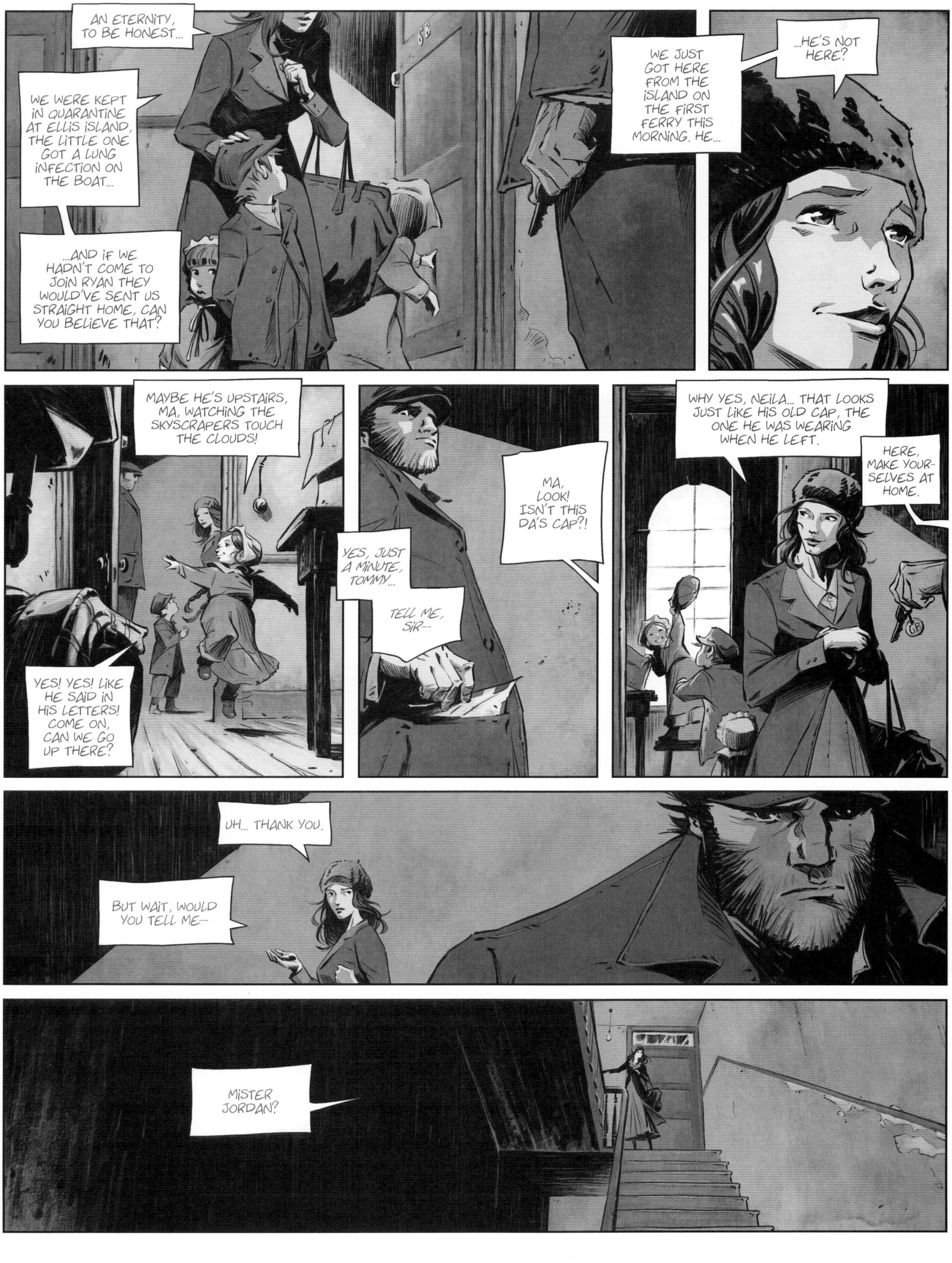
AN ETERNITY, TO BE HONEST...
WE WERE KEPT IN QUARANTINE AT ELLIS ISLAND, THE LITTLE ONE GOT A LUNG INFECTION ON THE BOAT...
...AND IF WE HADN'T COME TO JOIN RYAN THEY WOULD'VE SENT US STRAIGHT HOME, CAN YOU BELIEVE THAT?
WE JUST GOT HERE FROM THE ISLAND ON THE FIRST FERRY THIS MORNING. HE...
...HE'S NOT HERE?
MAYBE HE'S UPSTAIRS, MA, WATCHING THE SKYSCRAPERS TOUCH THE CLOUDS!
YES! YES! LIKE HE SAID IN HIS LETTERS! COME ON, CAN WE GO UP THERE?
MA, LOOK! ISN'T THIS DA'S CAP?!
YES, JUST A MINUTE, TOMMY...
TELL ME, SIR--
WHY YES, NEILA... THAT LOOKS JUST LIKE HIS OLD CAP, THE ONE HE WAS WEARING WHEN HE LEFT.
HERE, MAKE YOURSELVES AT HOME.
UH... THANK YOU.
BUT WAIT, WOULD YOU TELL ME--
MISTER JORDAN?
30

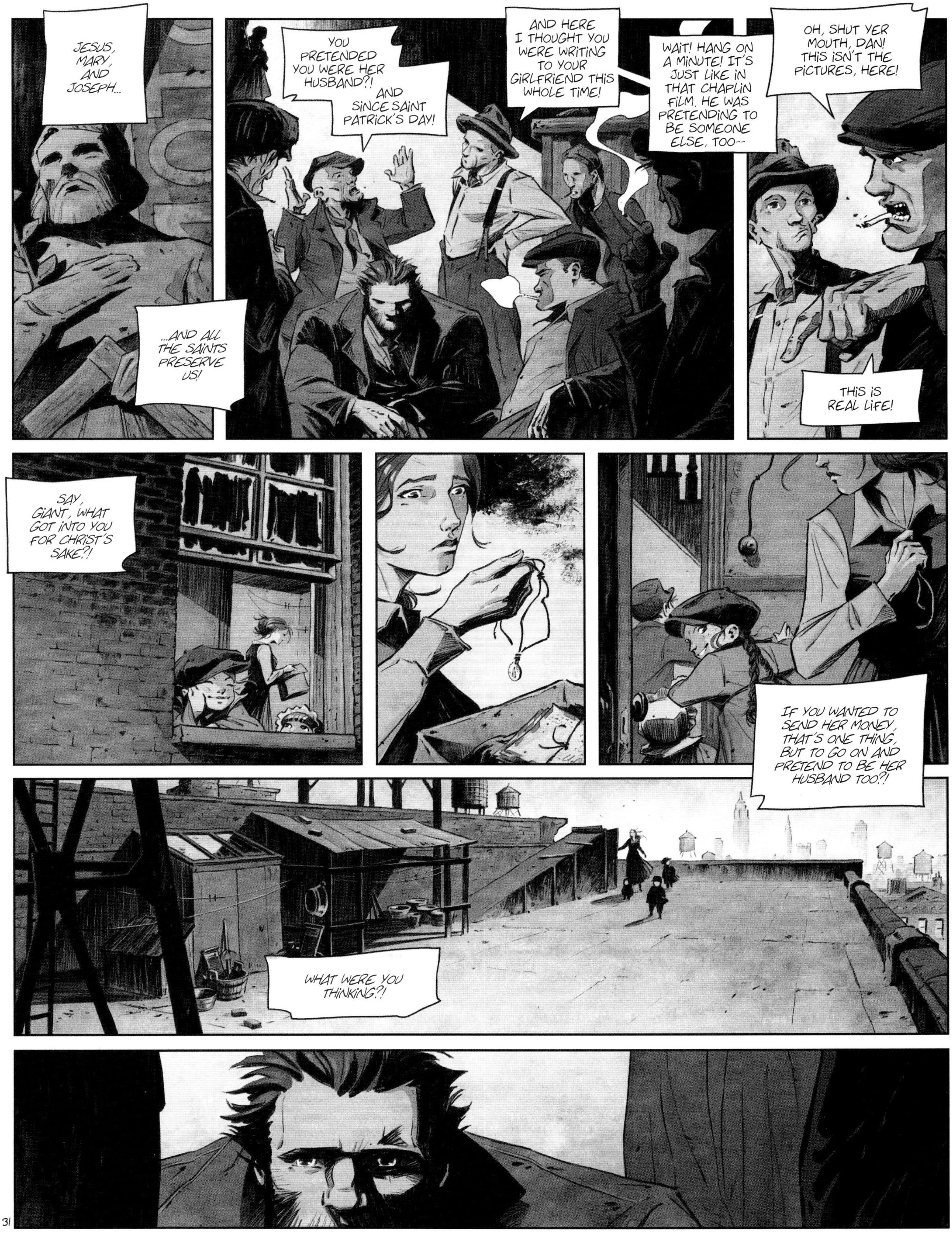
JESUS, MARY, AND JOSEPH...
...AND ALL THE SAINTS PRESERVE US!
YOU PRETENDED YOU WERE HER HUSBAND?!
AND SINCE SAINT PATRICK'S DAY!
AND HERE I THOUGHT YOU WERE WRITING TO YOUR GIRLFRIEND THIS WHOLE TIME!
WAIT! HANG ON A MINUTE! IT'S JUST LIKE IN THAT CHAPLIN FILM. HE WAS PRETENDING TO BE SOMEONE ELSE, TOO--
OH, SHUT YER MOUTH, DAN! THIS ISN'T THE PICTURES, HERE!
THIS IS REAL LIFE!
SAY, GIANT, WHAT GOT INTO YOU FOR CHRIST'S SAKE?!
IF YOU WANTED TO SEND HER MONEY, THAT'S ONE THING, BUT TO GO ON AND PRETEND TO BE HER HUSBAND TOO?!
WHAT WERE YOU THINKING?!
31

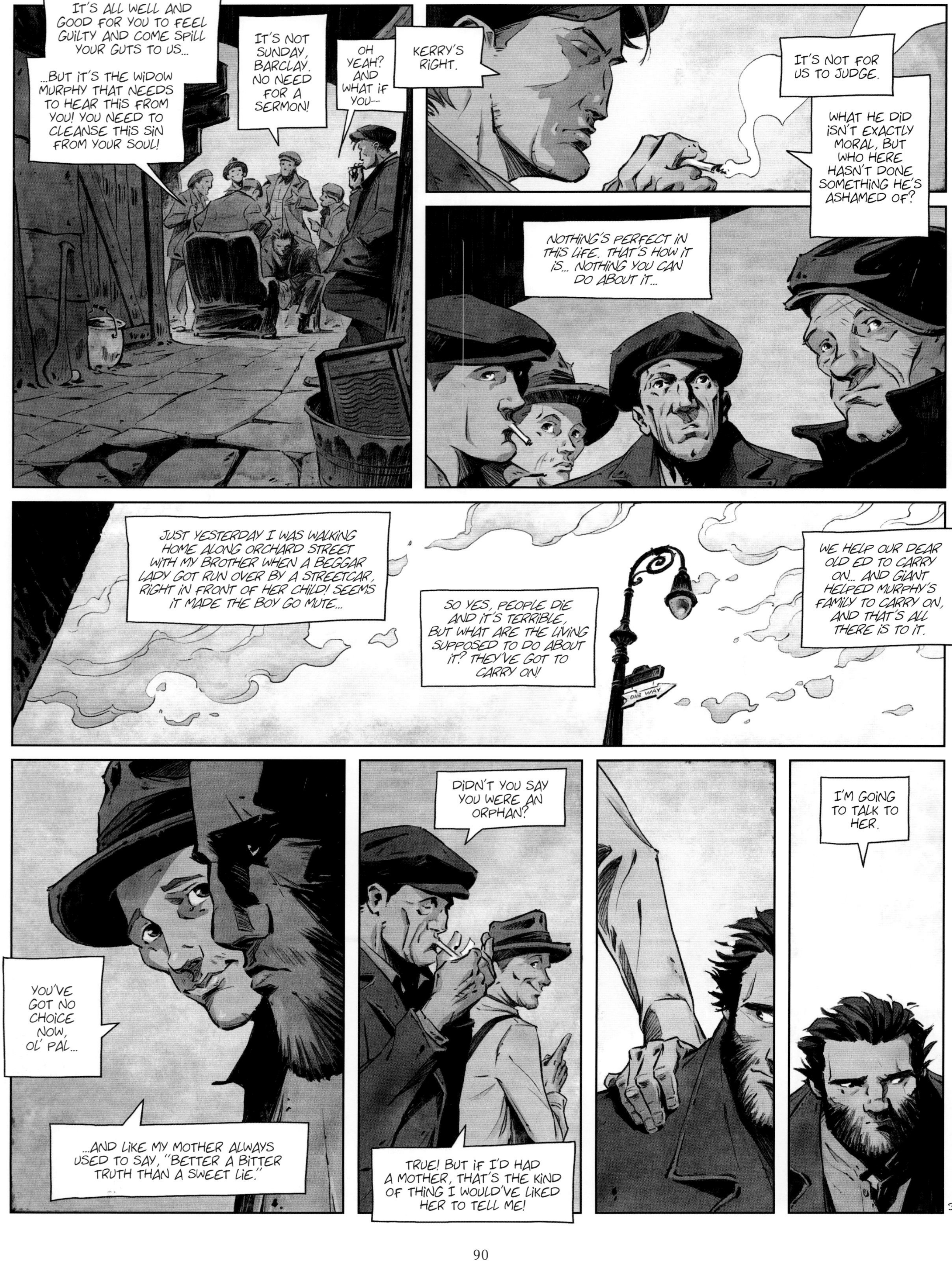
IT'S ALL WELL AND GOOD FOR YOU TO FEEL GUILTY AND COME SPILL YOUR GUTS TO US...
...BUT IT'S THE WIDOW MURPHY THAT NEEDS TO HEAR THIS FROM YOU! YOU NEED TO CLEANSE THIS SIN FROM YOUR SOUL!
IT'S NOT SUNDAY, BARCLAY. NO NEED FOR A SERMON!
OH YEAH? AND WHAT IF YOU--
KERRY'S RIGHT.
IT'S NOT FOR US TO JUDGE.
WHAT HE DID ISN'T EXACTLY MORAL, BUT WHO HERE HASN'T DONE SOMETHING HE'S ASHAMED OF?
NOTHING'S PERFECT IN THIS LIFE. THAT'S HOW IT IS... NOTHING YOU CAN DO ABOUT IT...
JUST YESTERDAY I WAS WALKING HOME ALONG ORCHARD STREET WITH MY BROTHER WHEN A BEGGAR LADY GOT RUN OVER BY A STREETCAR, RIGHT IN FRONT OF HER CHILD! SEEMS IT MADE THE BOY GO MUTE...
SO YES, PEOPLE DIE AND IT'S TERRIBLE, BUT WHAT ARE THE LIVING SUPPOSED TO DO ABOUT IT? THEY'VE GOT TO CARRY ON!
ONE WAY
WE HELP OUR DEAR OLD ED TO CARRY ON... AND GIANT HELPED MURPHY'S FAMILY TO CARRY ON, AND THAT'S ALL THERE IS TO IT.
YOU'VE GOT NO CHOICE NOW, OL' PAL...
...AND LIKE MY MOTHER ALWAYS USED TO SAY, "BETTER A BITTER TRUTH THAN A SWEET LIE."
DIDN'T YOU SAY YOU WERE AN ORPHAN?
TRUE! BUT IF I'D HAD A MOTHER, THAT'S THE KIND OF THING I WOULD'VE LIKED HER TO TELL ME!
I'M GOING TO TALK TO HER.
32

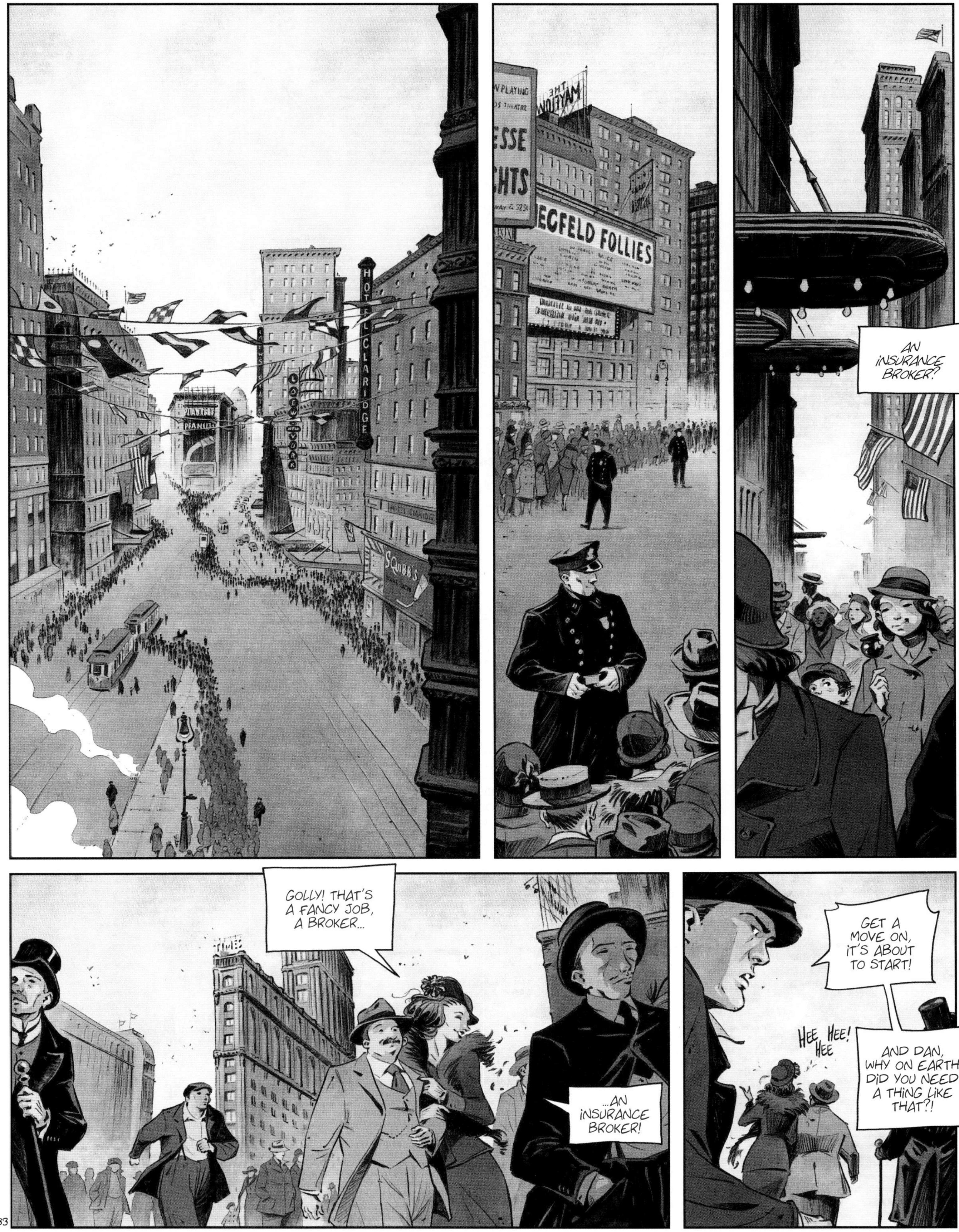
HOTEL CLARIDGE
SQUIBB'S
EGFELD FOLLIES
AN INSURANCE BROKER?
GOLLY! THAT'S A FANCY JOB, A BROKER...
...AN INSURANCE BROKER!
GET A MOVE ON, IT'S ABOUT TO START!
HEE HEE! HEE
AND DAN, WHY ON EARTH DID YOU NEED A THING LIKE THAT?!

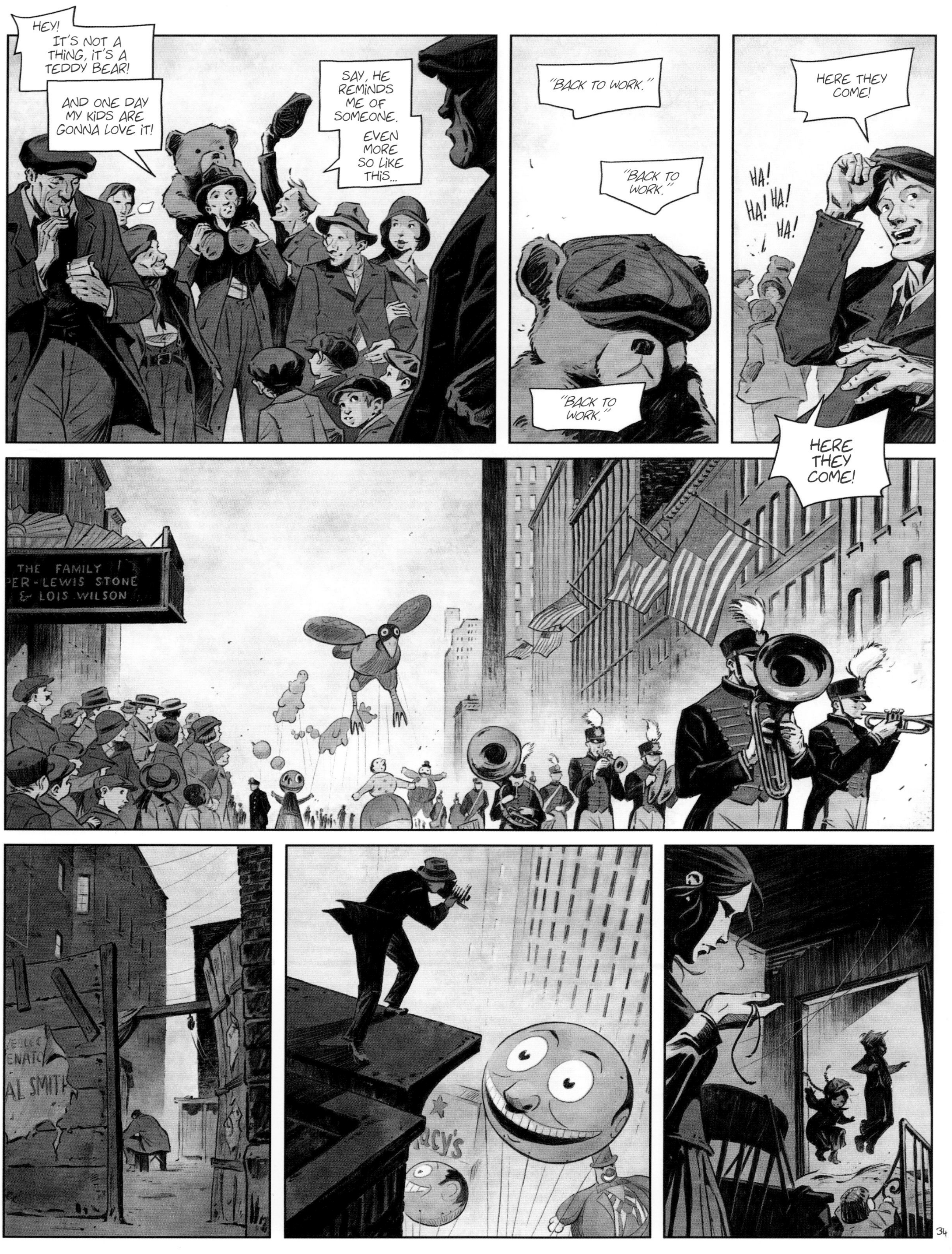
HEY!
IT'S NOT A THING, IT'S A TEDDY BEAR!
AND ONE DAY MY KIDS ARE GONNA LOVE IT!
SAY, HE REMINDS ME OF SOMEONE.
EVEN MORE SO LIKE THIS...
"BACK TO WORK."
"BACK TO WORK."
"BACK TO WORK."
HERE THEY COME!
HA! HA! HA! HA!
HERE THEY COME!
THE FAMILY
PER-LEWIS STONE
& LOIS WILSON
AL SMITH
34

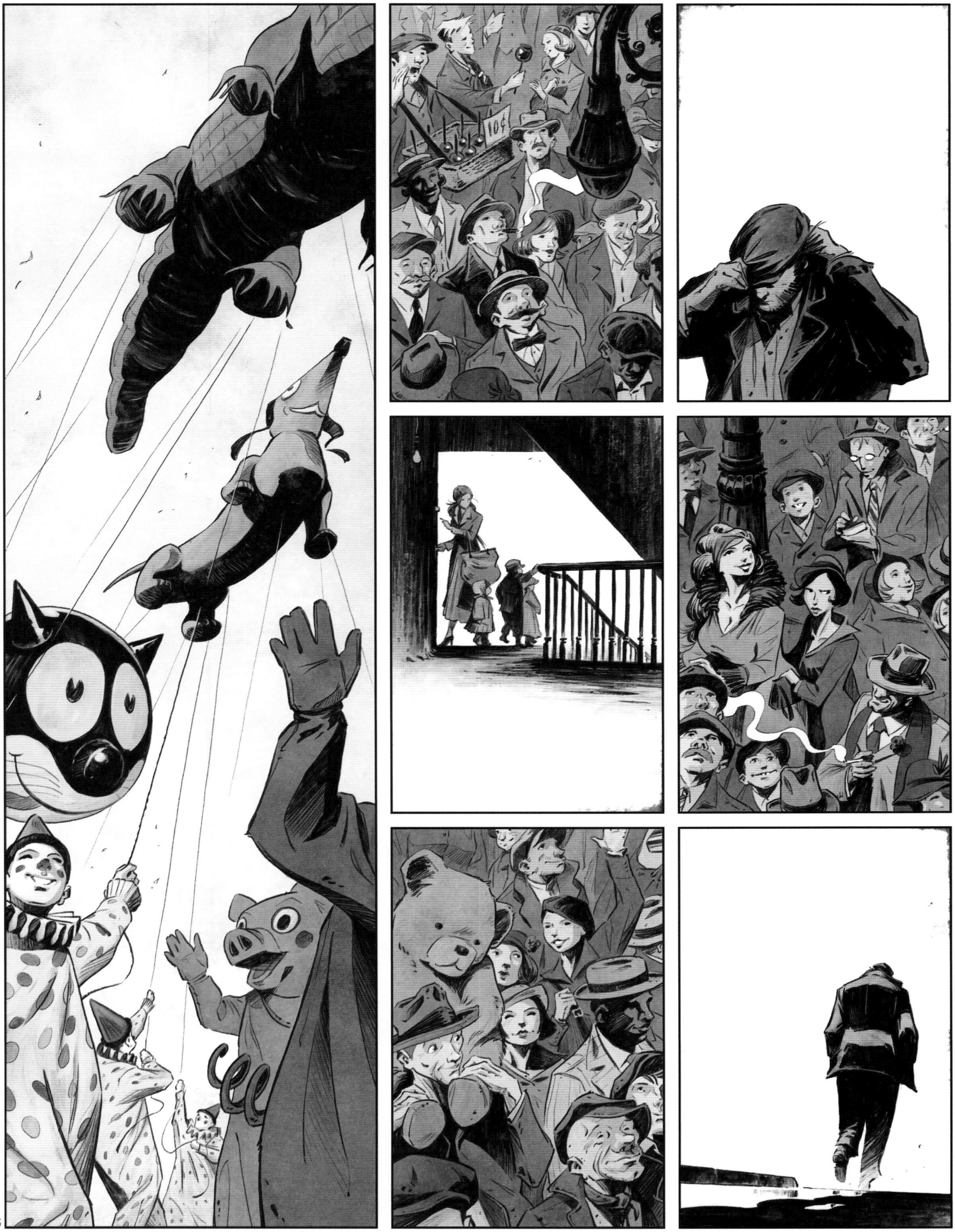
10¢

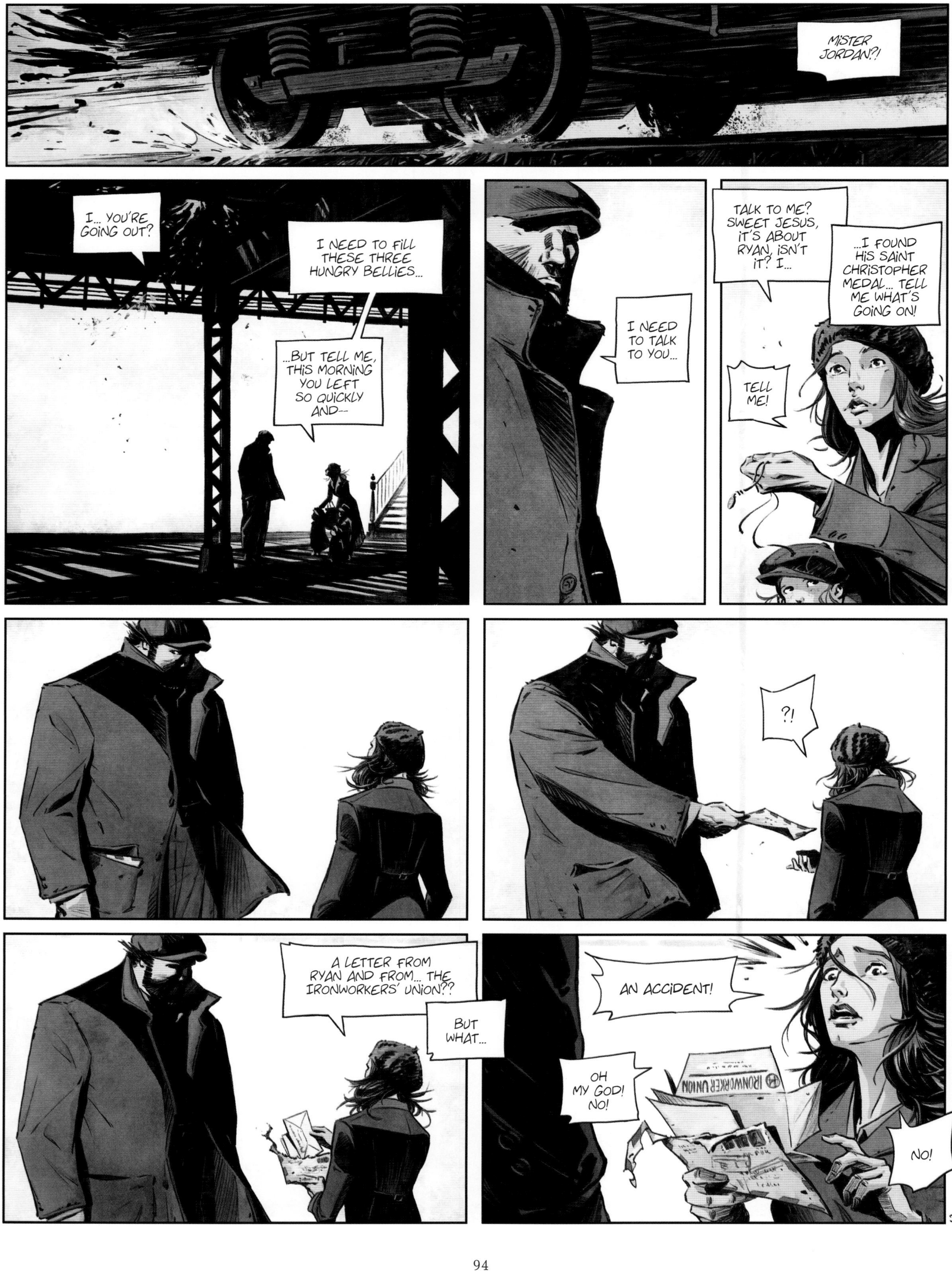

MISTER JORDAN?!
I... YOU'RE GOING OUT?
I NEED TO FILL THESE THREE HUNGRY BELLIES...
...BUT TELL ME, THIS MORNING YOU LEFT SO QUICKLY AND--
I NEED TO TALK TO YOU...
TALK TO ME? SWEET JESUS, IT'S ABOUT RYAN, ISN'T IT? I...
...I FOUND HIS SAINT CHRISTOPHER MEDAL... TELL ME WHAT'S GOING ON!
TELL ME!
?!
A LETTER FROM RYAN AND FROM... THE IRONWORKERS' UNION??
BUT WHAT...
AN ACCIDENT!
IRONWORKER UNION
OH MY GOD! NO!
NO!
36

HE LOST HIS BALANCE... HE WAS FAR TOO HIGH UP... I'M SORRY.

MA... DID DA HAVE AN ACCIDENT? IS HE HURT?

DOES THAT MEAN HE CAN'T COME SEE US?

OH, MY DARLINGS...

THAT'S RIGHT, HE CAN'T COME...

HE'S NOT COMING BACK...

MAY THE LORD HAVE PITY ON HIS SOUL...

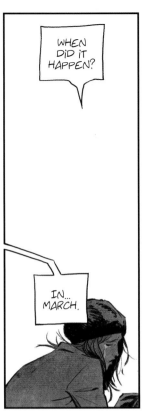

WHEN DID IT HAPPEN?

IN... MARCH.

IN MARCH?! BUT THE LETTER...?

THE LETTERS?!

WHO--?!

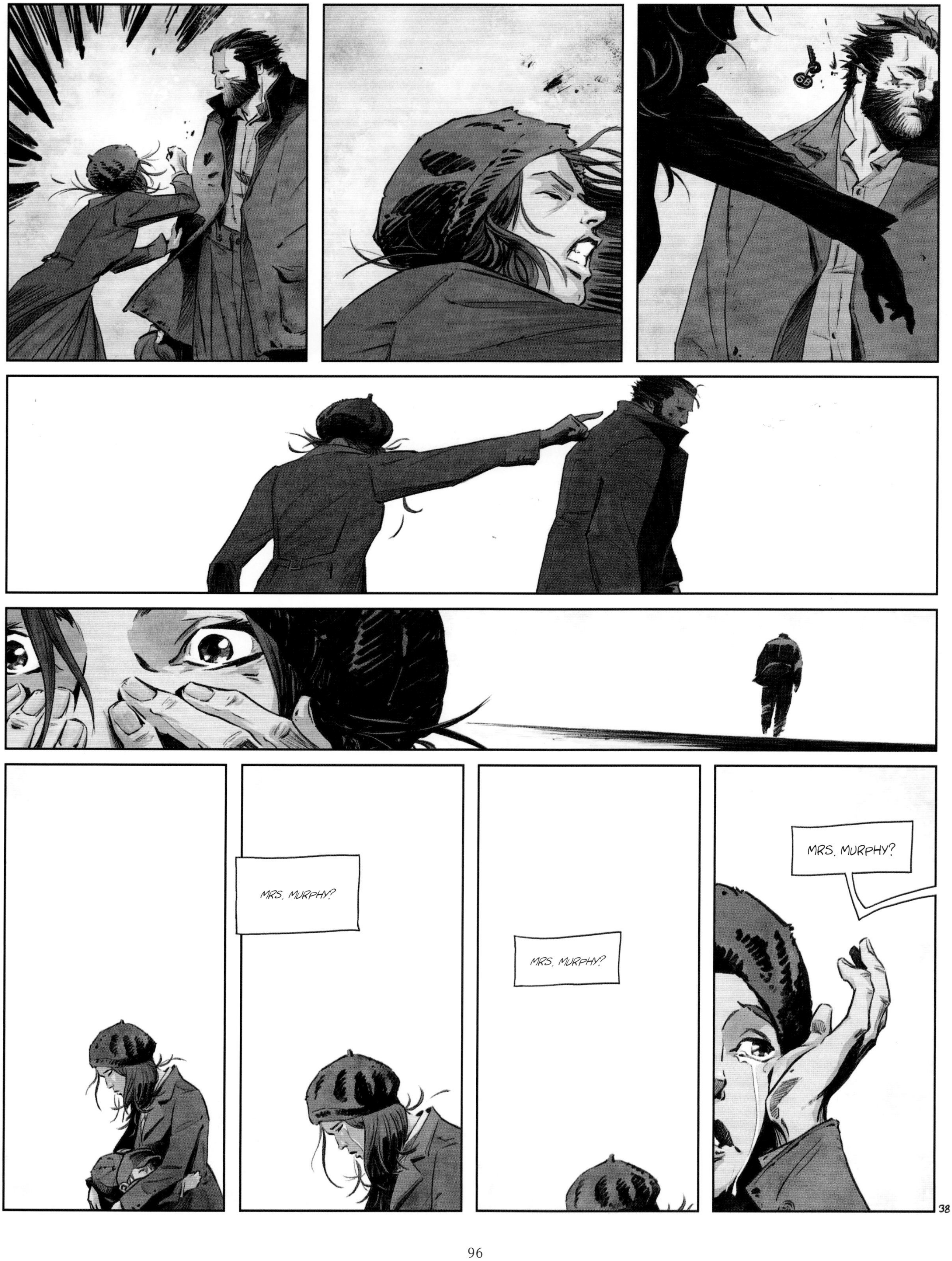
6B
MRS. MURPHY?
MRS. MURPHY?
MRS. MURPHY?
38

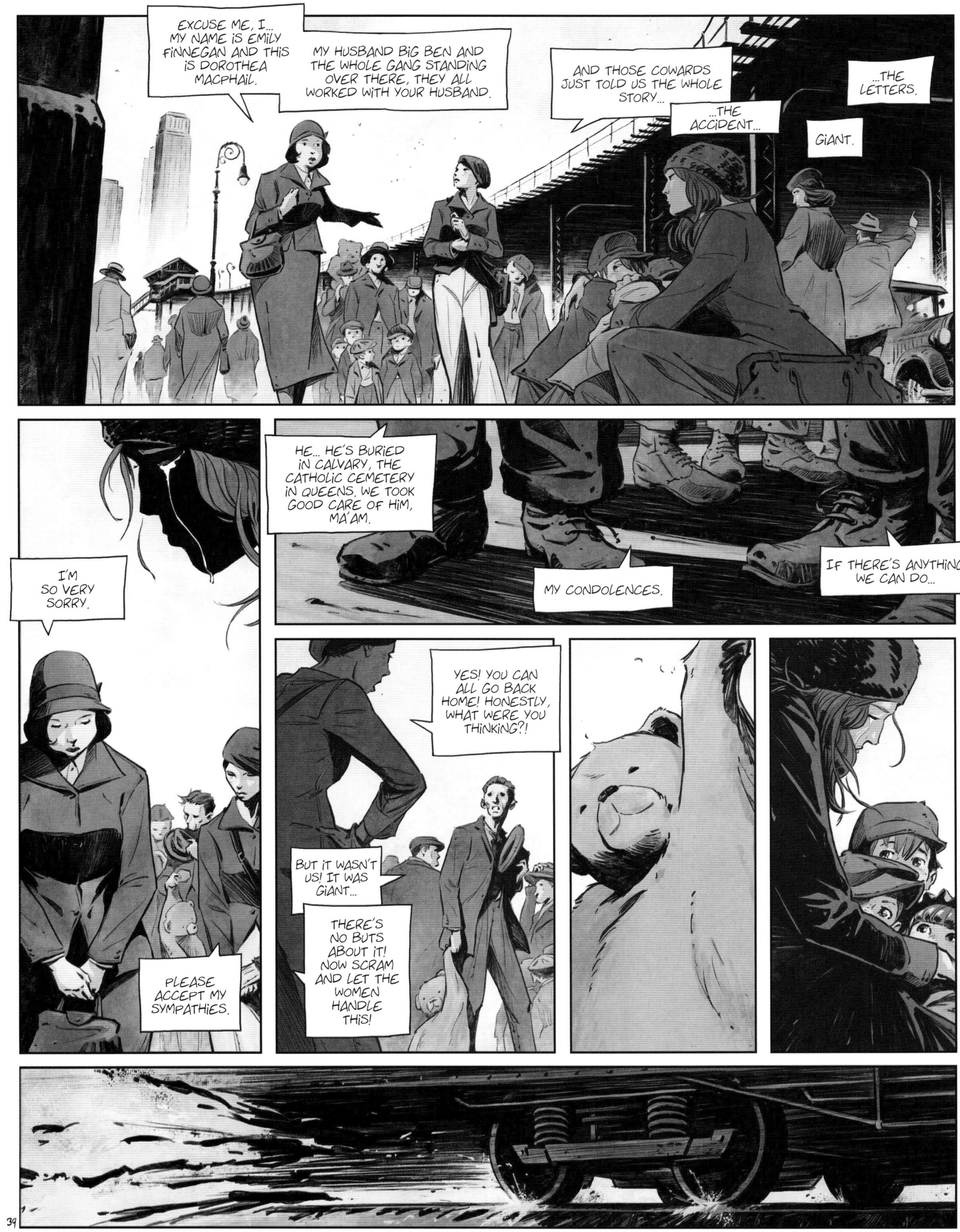
EXCUSE ME, I... MY NAME IS EMILY FINNEGAN AND THIS IS DOROTHEA MACPHAIL.
MY HUSBAND BIG BEN AND THE WHOLE GANG STANDING OVER THERE, THEY ALL WORKED WITH YOUR HUSBAND.
AND THOSE COWARDS JUST TOLD US THE WHOLE STORY...
...THE ACCIDENT...
GIANT.
...THE LETTERS.
I'M SO VERY SORRY.
PLEASE ACCEPT MY SYMPATHIES.
HE... HE'S BURIED IN CALVARY, THE CATHOLIC CEMETERY IN QUEENS. WE TOOK GOOD CARE OF HIM, MA'AM.
MY CONDOLENCES.
IF THERE'S ANYTHING WE CAN DO...
YES! YOU CAN ALL GO BACK HOME! HONESTLY, WHAT WERE YOU THINKING?!
BUT IT WASN'T US! IT WAS GIANT...
THERE'S NO BUTS ABOUT IT! NOW SCRAM AND LET THE WOMEN HANDLE THIS!
39

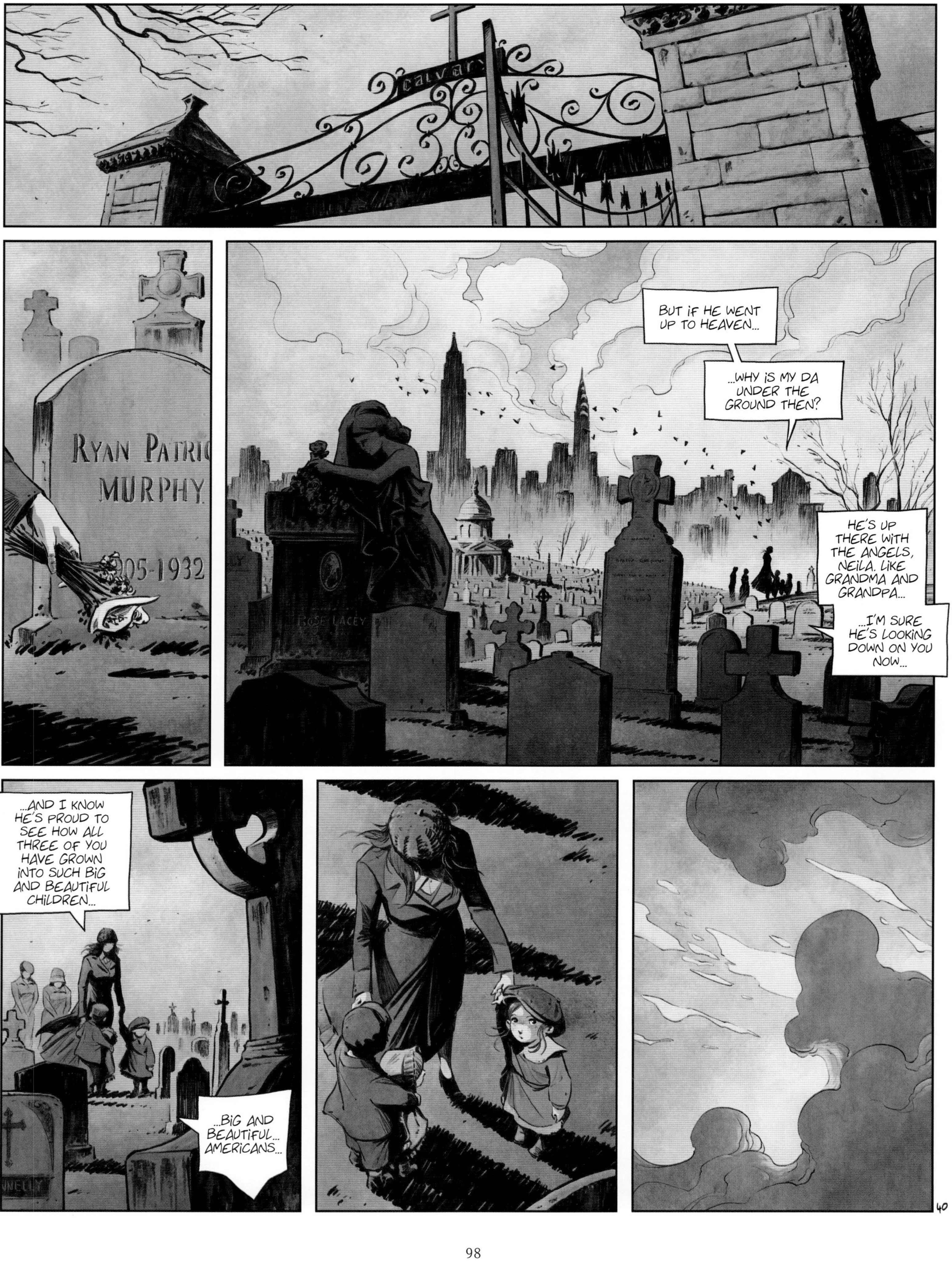
calvary
RYAN PATRIC
MURPHY
905-1932
BUT IF HE WENT UP TO HEAVEN...
...WHY IS MY DA UNDER THE GROUND THEN?
ROSE LACEY
HE'S UP THERE WITH THE ANGELS, NEILA. LIKE GRANDMA AND GRANDPA...
...I'M SURE HE'S LOOKING DOWN ON YOU NOW...
...AND I KNOW HE'S PROUD TO SEE HOW ALL THREE OF YOU HAVE GROWN INTO SUCH BIG AND BEAUTIFUL CHILDREN...
...BIG AND BEAUTIFUL... AMERICANS...
NNELLY
40

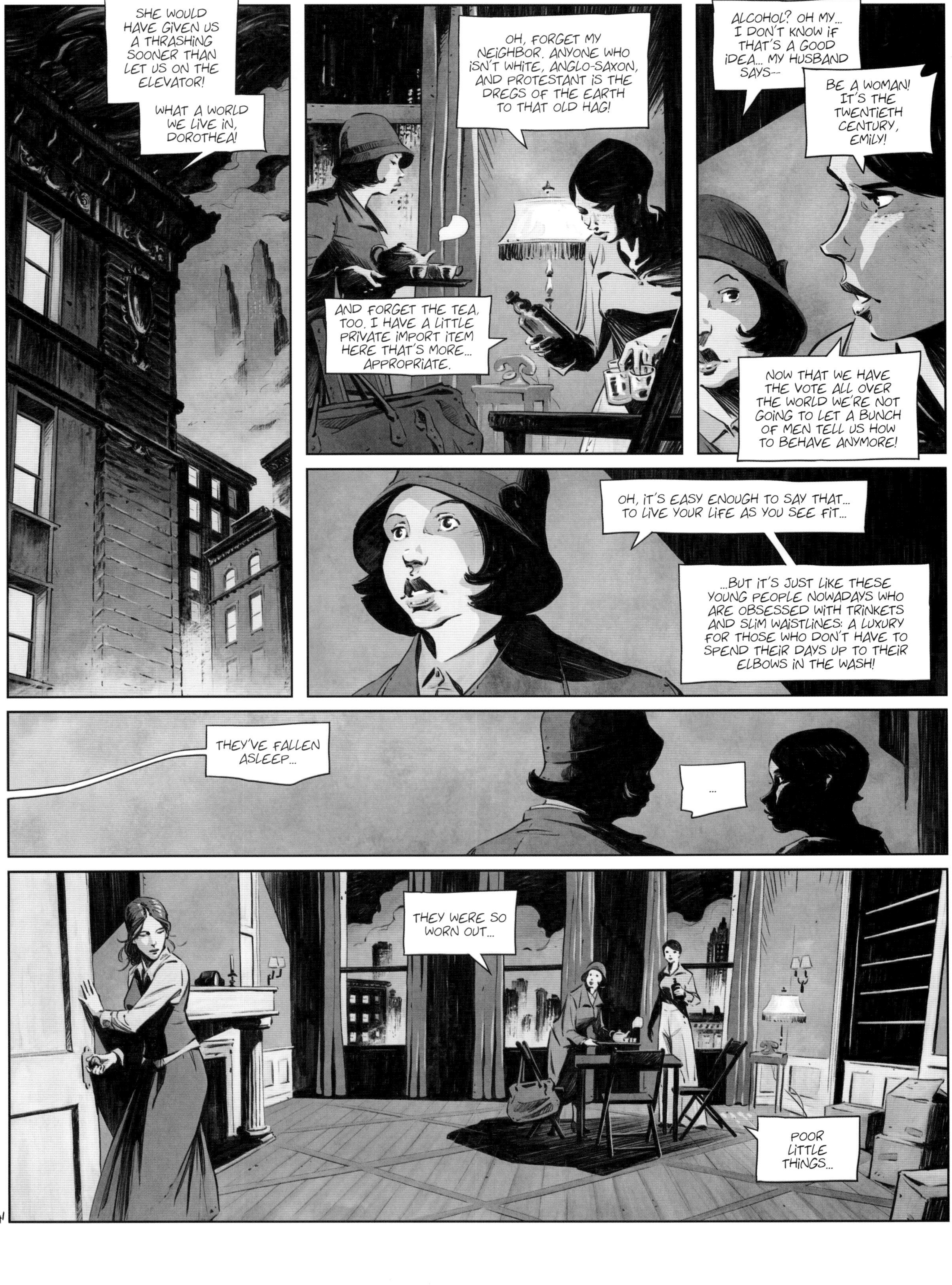
SHE WOULD HAVE GIVEN US A THRASHING SOONER THAN LET US ON THE ELEVATOR!
WHAT A WORLD WE LIVE IN, DOROTHEA!
OH, FORGET MY NEIGHBOR. ANYONE WHO ISN'T WHITE, ANGLO-SAXON, AND PROTESTANT IS THE DREGS OF THE EARTH TO THAT OLD HAG!
AND FORGET THE TEA, TOO. I HAVE A LITTLE PRIVATE IMPORT ITEM HERE THAT'S MORE... APPROPRIATE.
ALCOHOL? OH MY... I DON'T KNOW IF THAT'S A GOOD IDEA... MY HUSBAND SAYS--
BE A WOMAN! IT'S THE TWENTIETH CENTURY, EMILY!
NOW THAT WE HAVE THE VOTE ALL OVER THE WORLD WE'RE NOT GOING TO LET A BUNCH OF MEN TELL US HOW TO BEHAVE ANYMORE!
OH, IT'S EASY ENOUGH TO SAY THAT... TO LIVE YOUR LIFE AS YOU SEE FIT...
...BUT IT'S JUST LIKE THESE YOUNG PEOPLE NOWADAYS WHO ARE OBSESSED WITH TRINKETS AND SLIM WAISTLINES: A LUXURY FOR THOSE WHO DON'T HAVE TO SPEND THEIR DAYS UP TO THEIR ELBOWS IN THE WASH!
THEY'VE FALLEN ASLEEP...
...
THEY WERE SO WORN OUT...
POOR LITTLE THINGS...

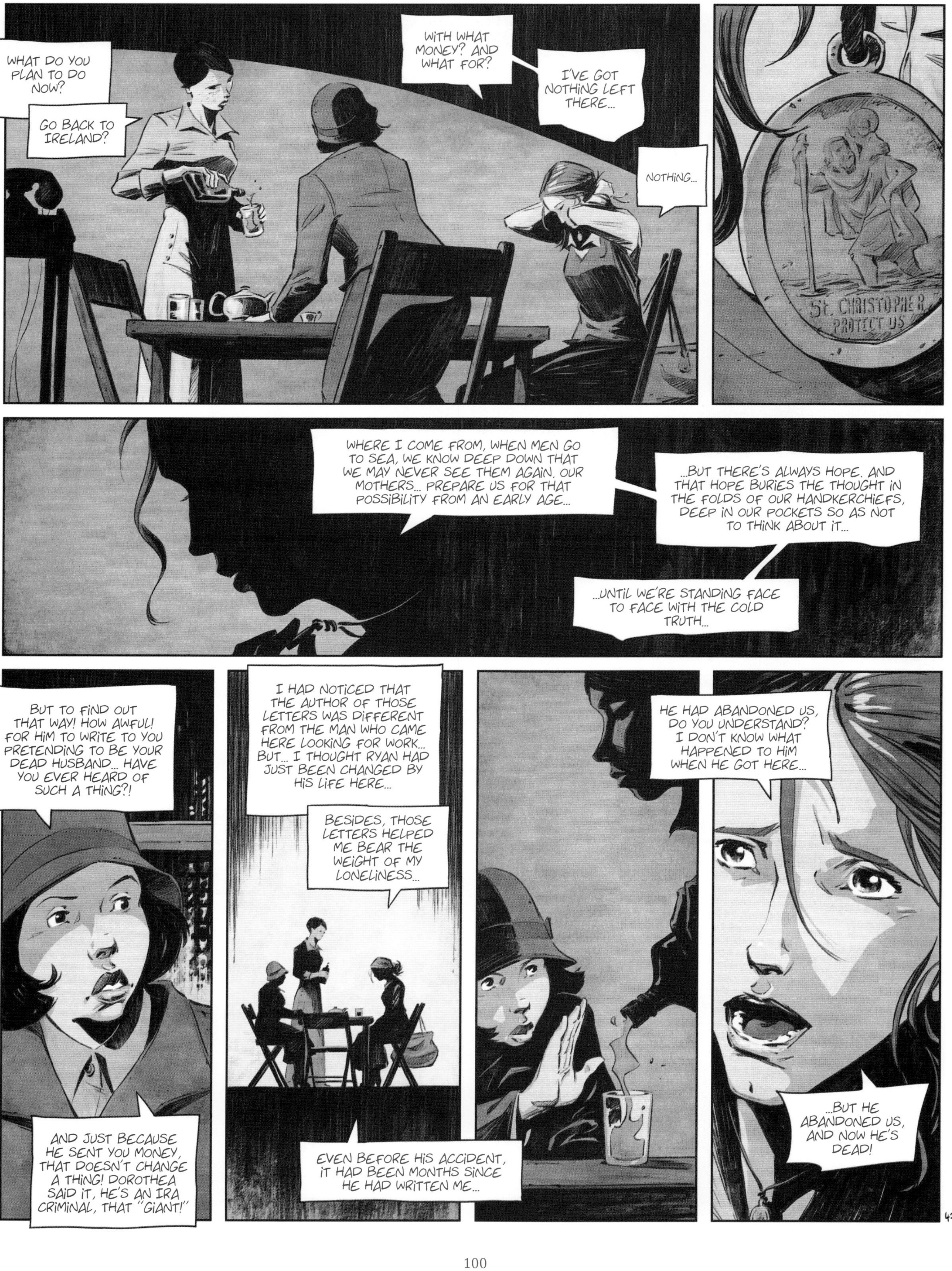

WHAT DO YOU PLAN TO DO NOW?
GO BACK TO IRELAND?
WITH WHAT MONEY? AND WHAT FOR?
I'VE GOT NOTHING LEFT THERE...
NOTHING...
St. CHRISTOPHER PROTECT US
WHERE I COME FROM, WHEN MEN GO TO SEA, WE KNOW DEEP DOWN THAT WE MAY NEVER SEE THEM AGAIN. OUR MOTHERS... PREPARE US FOR THAT POSSIBILITY FROM AN EARLY AGE...
...BUT THERE'S ALWAYS HOPE. AND THAT HOPE BURIES THE THOUGHT IN THE FOLDS OF OUR HANDKERCHIEFS, DEEP IN OUR POCKETS SO AS NOT TO THINK ABOUT IT...
...UNTIL WE'RE STANDING FACE TO FACE WITH THE COLD TRUTH...
BUT TO FIND OUT THAT WAY! HOW AWFUL! FOR HIM TO WRITE TO YOU PRETENDING TO BE YOUR DEAD HUSBAND... HAVE YOU EVER HEARD OF SUCH A THING?!
AND JUST BECAUSE HE SENT YOU MONEY, THAT DOESN'T CHANGE A THING! DOROTHEA SAID IT, HE'S AN IRA CRIMINAL, THAT "GIANT!"
I HAD NOTICED THAT THE AUTHOR OF THOSE LETTERS WAS DIFFERENT FROM THE MAN WHO CAME HERE LOOKING FOR WORK... BUT... I THOUGHT RYAN HAD JUST BEEN CHANGED BY HIS LIFE HERE...
BESIDES, THOSE LETTERS HELPED ME BEAR THE WEIGHT OF MY LONELINESS...
EVEN BEFORE HIS ACCIDENT, IT HAD BEEN MONTHS SINCE HE HAD WRITTEN ME...
HE HAD ABANDONED US, DO YOU UNDERSTAND? I DON'T KNOW WHAT HAPPENED TO HIM WHEN HE GOT HERE...
...BUT HE ABANDONED US, AND NOW HE'S DEAD!
42

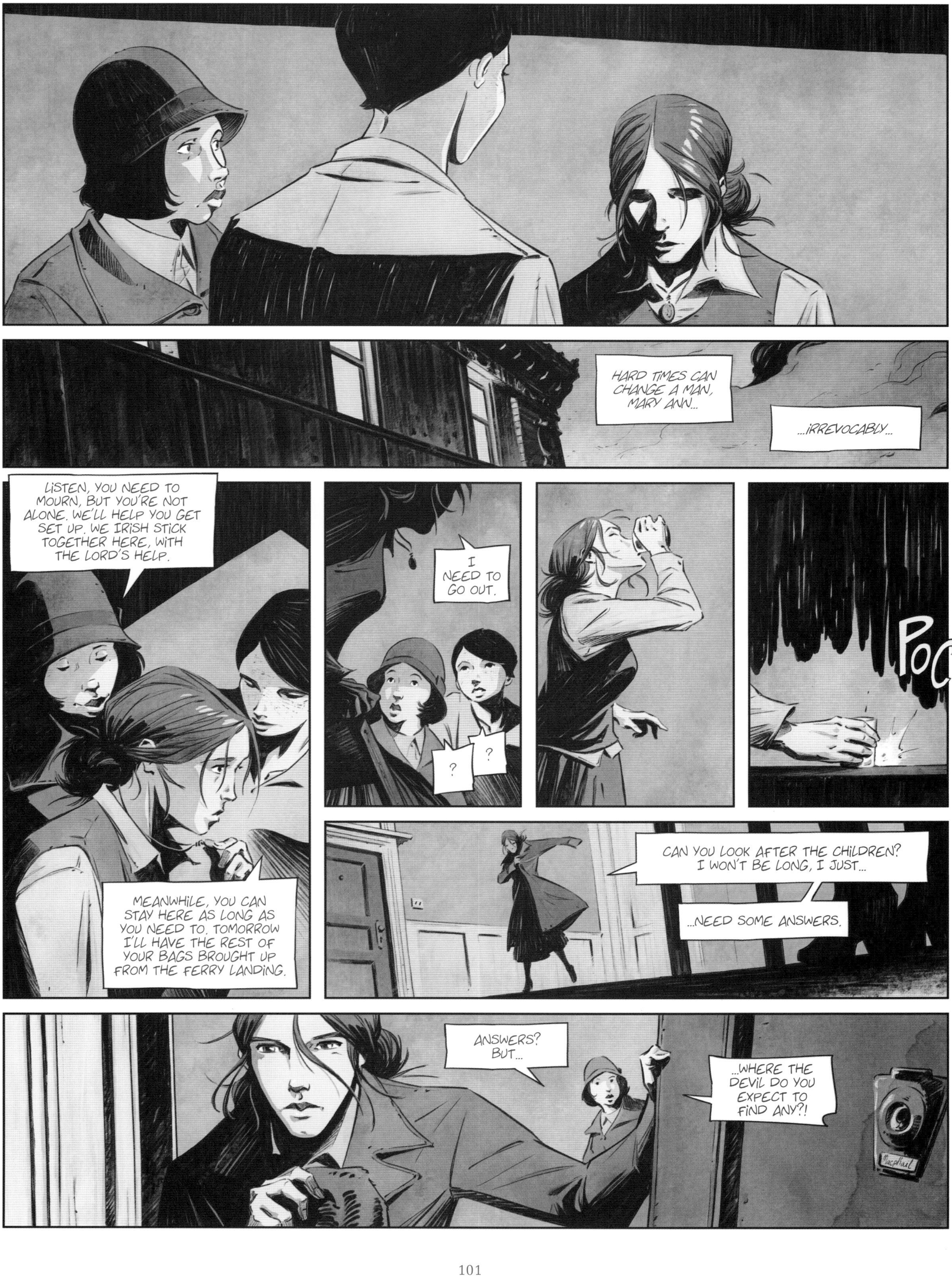
HARD TIMES CAN CHANGE A MAN, MARY ANN...
...IRREVOCABLY...
LISTEN, YOU NEED TO MOURN, BUT YOU'RE NOT ALONE. WE'LL HELP YOU GET SET UP. WE IRISH STICK TOGETHER HERE, WITH THE LORD'S HELP.
MEANWHILE, YOU CAN STAY HERE AS LONG AS YOU NEED TO. TOMORROW I'LL HAVE THE REST OF YOUR BAGS BROUGHT UP FROM THE FERRY LANDING.
I NEED TO GO OUT.
?
?
POC
CAN YOU LOOK AFTER THE CHILDREN? I WON'T BE LONG, I JUST...
...NEED SOME ANSWERS.
ANSWERS? BUT...
...WHERE THE DEVIL DO YOU EXPECT TO FIND ANY?!
43

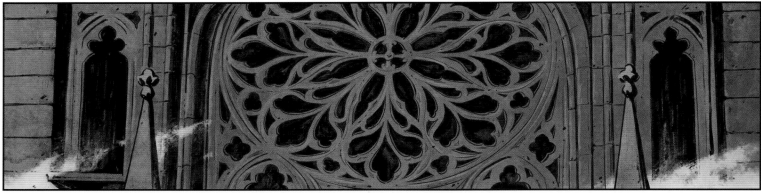

44

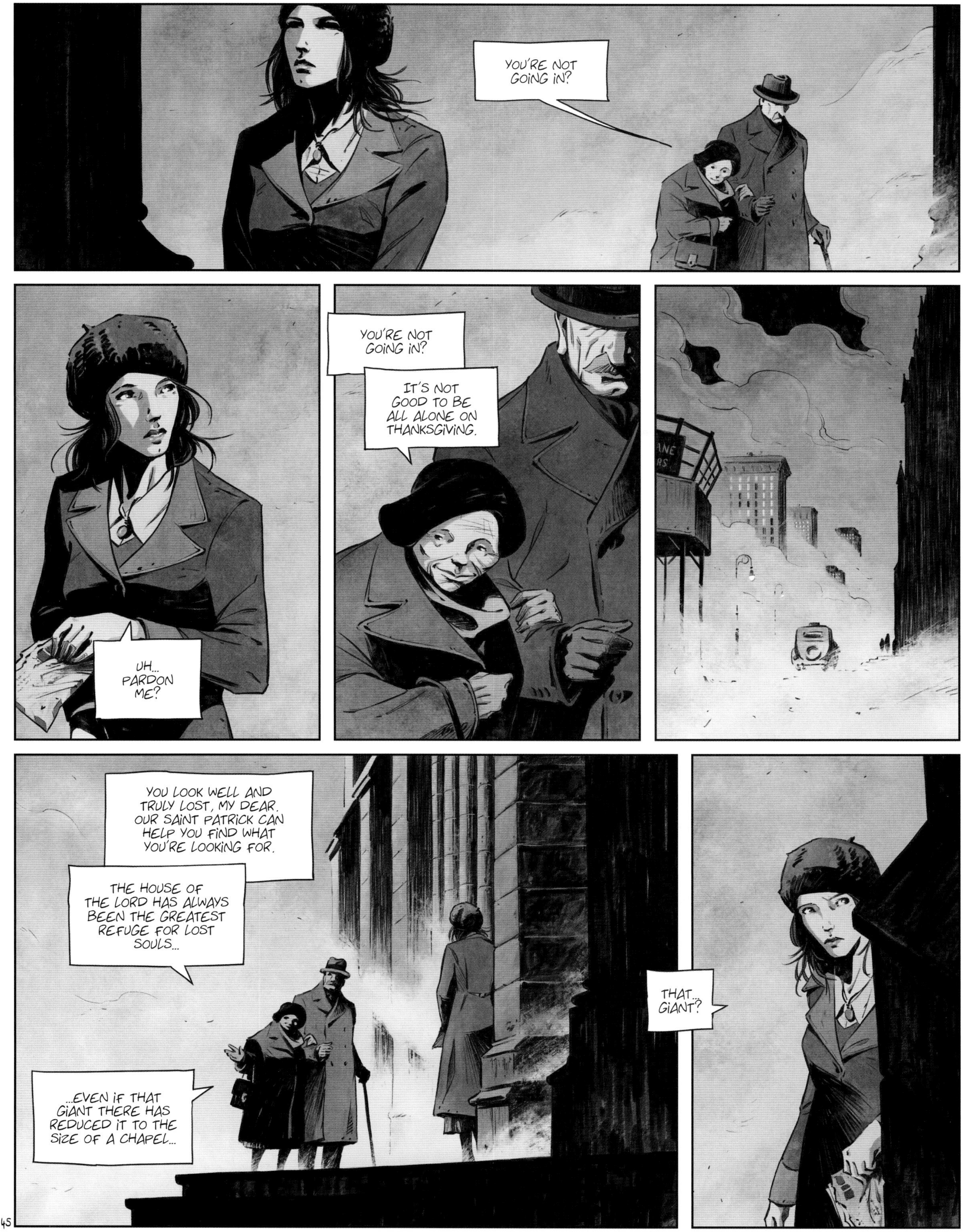
YOU'RE NOT GOING IN?
UH... PARDON ME?
YOU'RE NOT GOING IN?
IT'S NOT GOOD TO BE ALL ALONE ON THANKSGIVING.
YOU LOOK WELL AND TRULY LOST, MY DEAR. OUR SAINT PATRICK CAN HELP YOU FIND WHAT YOU'RE LOOKING FOR.
THE HOUSE OF THE LORD HAS ALWAYS BEEN THE GREATEST REFUGE FOR LOST SOULS...
...EVEN IF THAT GIANT THERE HAS REDUCED IT TO THE SIZE OF A CHAPEL...
THAT... GIANT?
45

THANK YOU, BUT...

...THIS ISN'T WHERE I NEED TO BE.

Mary Ann, I owe you the truth.

46

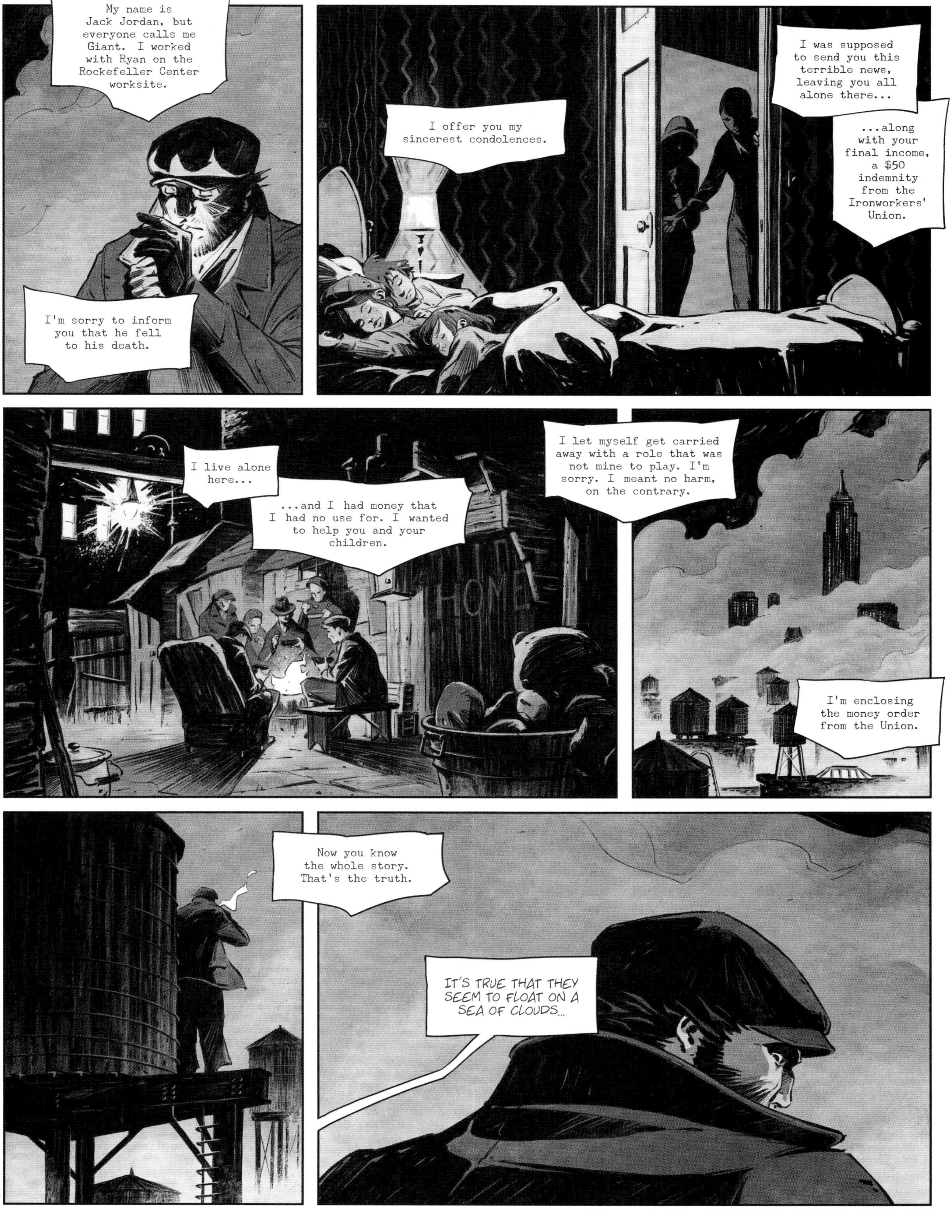
My name is Jack Jordan, but everyone calls me Giant. I worked with Ryan on the Rockefeller Center worksite.
I'm sorry to inform you that he fell to his death.
I offer you my sincerest condolences.
I was supposed to send you this terrible news, leaving you all alone there...
...along with your final income, a $50 indemnity from the Ironworkers' Union.
I live alone here...
...and I had money that I had no use for. I wanted to help you and your children.
HOME
I let myself get carried away with a role that was not mine to play. I'm sorry. I meant no harm, on the contrary.
I'm enclosing the money order from the Union.
Now you know the whole story. That's the truth.
IT'S TRUE THAT THEY SEEM TO FLOAT ON A SEA OF CLOUDS...
47

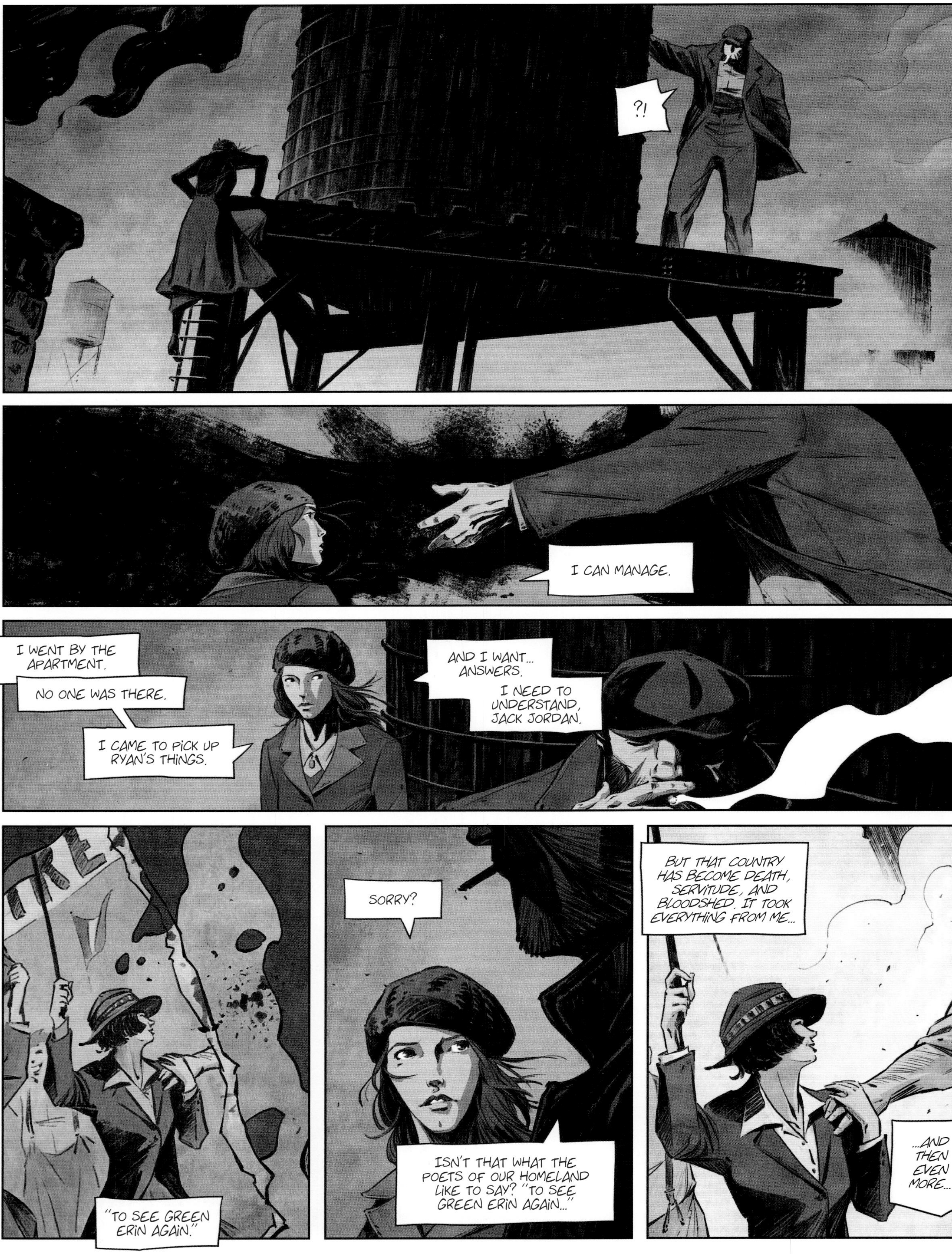
?!
I CAN MANAGE.
I WENT BY THE APARTMENT.
NO ONE WAS THERE.
I CAME TO PICK UP RYAN'S THINGS.
AND I WANT... ANSWERS.
I NEED TO UNDERSTAND, JACK JORDAN.
"TO SEE GREEN ERIN AGAIN."
SORRY?
ISN'T THAT WHAT THE POETS OF OUR HOMELAND LIKE TO SAY? "TO SEE GREEN ERIN AGAIN..."
BUT THAT COUNTRY HAS BECOME DEATH, SERVITUDE, AND BLOODSHED. IT TOOK EVERYTHING FROM ME...
...AND THEN EVEN MORE...
48

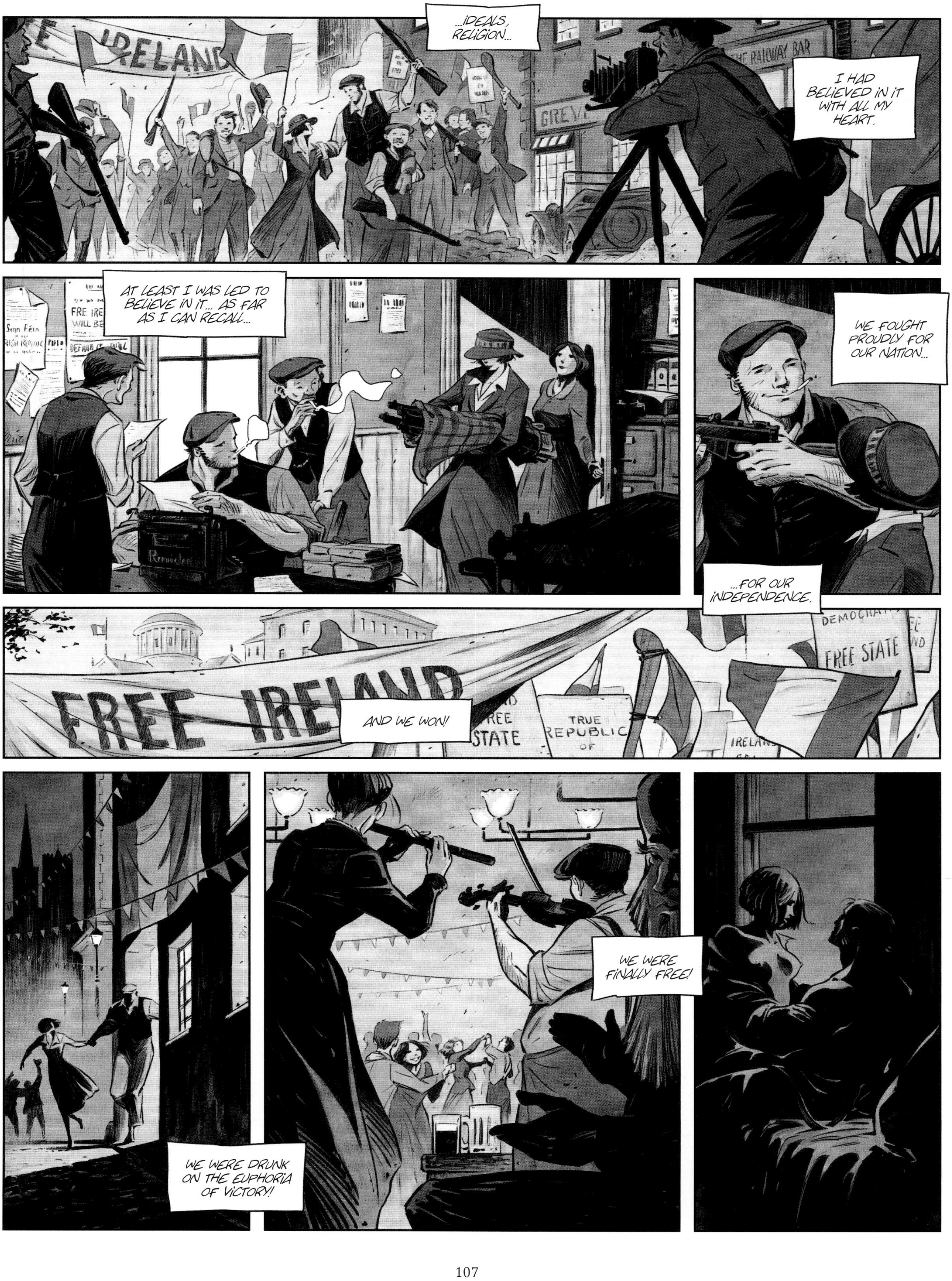
...IDEALS, RELIGION...
IRELAND
THE RAILWAY BAR
I HAD BELIEVED IN IT WITH ALL MY HEART.
AT LEAST I WAS LED TO BELIEVE IN IT... AS FAR AS I CAN RECALL...
WE FOUGHT PROUDLY FOR OUR NATION...
...FOR OUR INDEPENDENCE.
FREE STATE
FREE IRELAND
AND WE WON!
STATE
TRUE REPUBLIC OF
WE WERE FINALLY FREE!
WE WERE DRUNK ON THE EUPHORIA OF VICTORY!

49

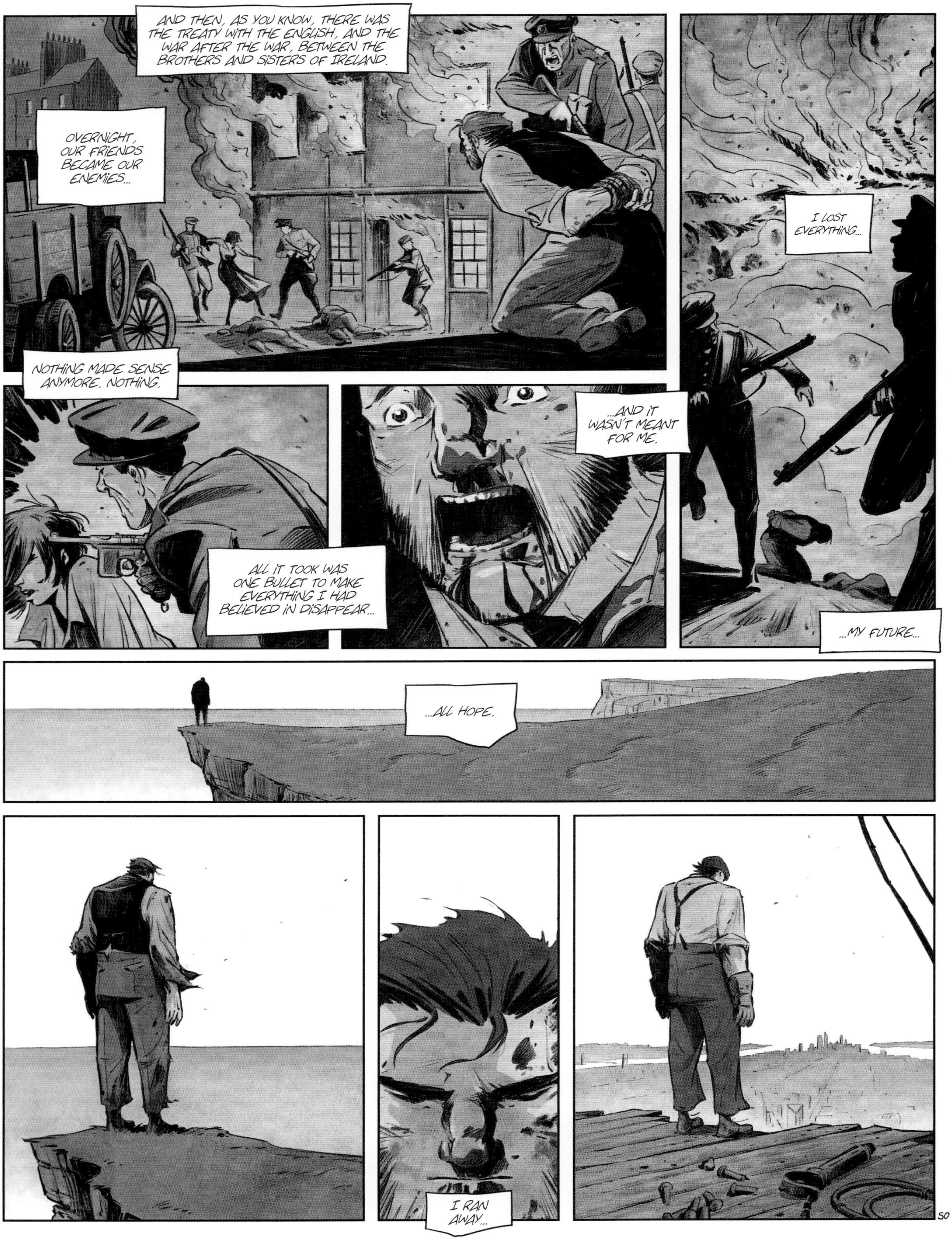
AND THEN, AS YOU KNOW, THERE WAS THE TREATY WITH THE ENGLISH, AND THE WAR AFTER THE WAR, BETWEEN THE BROTHERS AND SISTERS OF IRELAND.
OVERNIGHT, OUR FRIENDS BECAME OUR ENEMIES...
I LOST EVERYTHING...
NOTHING MADE SENSE ANYMORE. NOTHING.
...AND IT WASN'T MEANT FOR ME.
ALL IT TOOK WAS ONE BULLET TO MAKE EVERYTHING I HAD BELIEVED IN DISAPPEAR...
...MY FUTURE...
...ALL HOPE.
I RAN AWAY...
SO

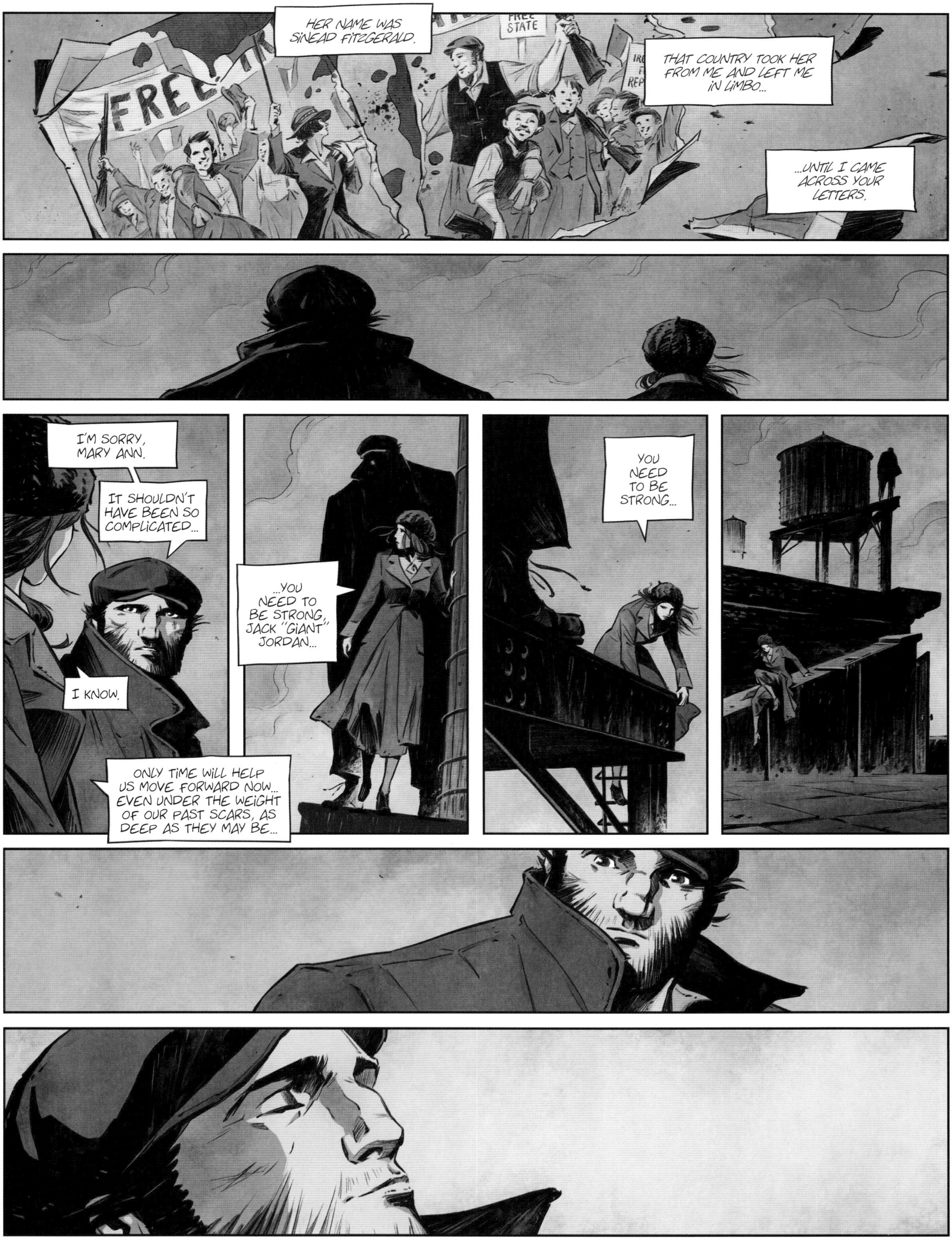
HER NAME WAS SINEAD FITZGERALD.
FREE
FREE STATE
THAT COUNTRY TOOK HER FROM ME AND LEFT ME IN LIMBO...
...UNTIL I CAME ACROSS YOUR LETTERS.
I'M SORRY, MARY ANN.
IT SHOULDN'T HAVE BEEN SO COMPLICATED...
I KNOW.
ONLY TIME WILL HELP US MOVE FORWARD NOW... EVEN UNDER THE WEIGHT OF OUR PAST SCARS, AS DEEP AS THEY MAY BE...
...YOU NEED TO BE STRONG, JACK "GIANT" JORDAN...
YOU NEED TO BE STRONG...

51

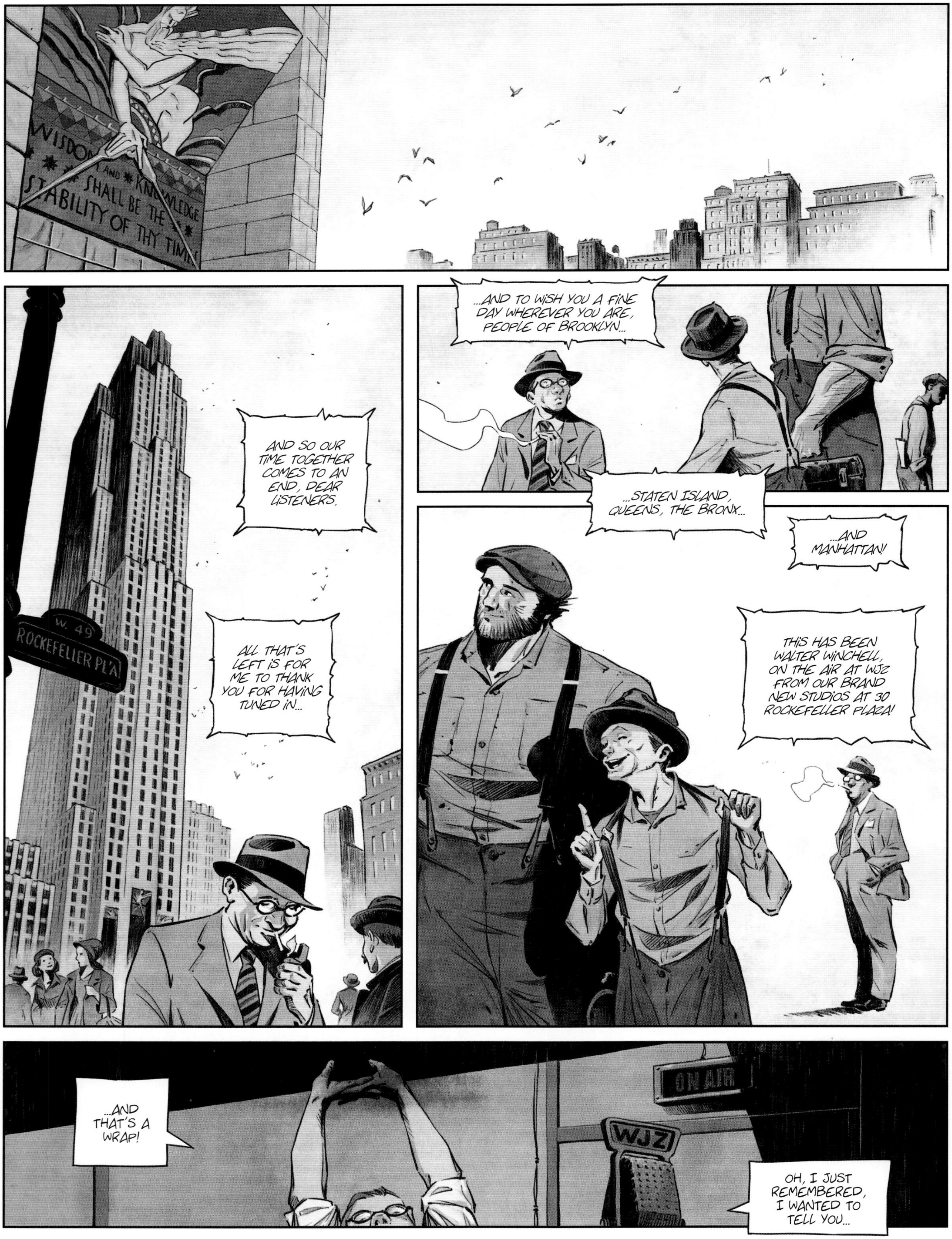
WISDOM AND KNOWLEDGE SHALL BE THE STABILITY OF THY TIMES
W. 49
ROCKEFELLER PL'A
AND SO OUR TIME TOGETHER COMES TO AN END, DEAR LISTENERS.
ALL THAT'S LEFT IS FOR ME TO THANK YOU FOR HAVING TUNED IN...
...AND TO WISH YOU A FINE DAY WHEREVER YOU ARE, PEOPLE OF BROOKLYN...
...STATEN ISLAND, QUEENS, THE BRONX...
...AND MANHATTAN!
THIS HAS BEEN WALTER WINCHELL, ON THE AIR AT WJZ FROM OUR BRAND NEW STUDIOS AT 30 ROCKEFELLER PLAZA!
ON AIR
WJZ
...AND THAT'S A WRAP!
OH, I JUST REMEMBERED, I WANTED TO TELL YOU...
52

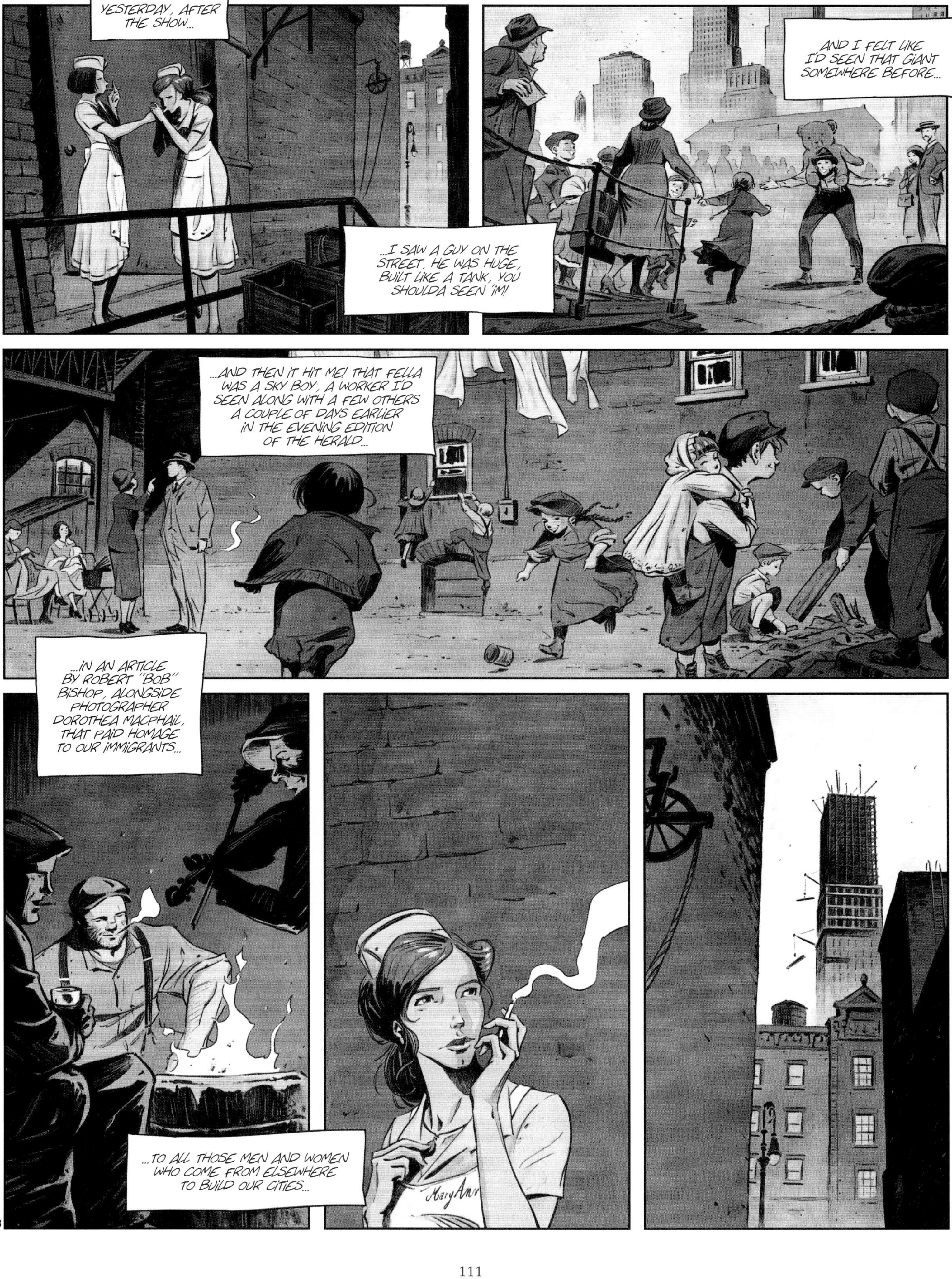
YESTERDAY, AFTER THE SHOW...
...I SAW A GUY ON THE STREET. HE WAS HUGE, BUILT LIKE A TANK, YOU SHOULDA SEEN 'IM!
AND I FELT LIKE I'D SEEN THAT GIANT SOMEWHERE BEFORE...
...AND THEN IT HIT ME! THAT FELLA WAS A SKY BOY, A WORKER I'D SEEN ALONG WITH A FEW OTHERS A COUPLE OF DAYS EARLIER IN THE EVENING EDITION OF THE HERALD...
...IN AN ARTICLE BY ROBERT "BOB" BISHOP, ALONGSIDE PHOTOGRAPHER DOROTHEA MACPHAIL, THAT PAID HOMAGE TO OUR IMMIGRANTS...
...TO ALL THOSE MEN AND WOMEN WHO COME FROM ELSEWHERE TO BUILD OUR CITIES...
Mary Ann
53

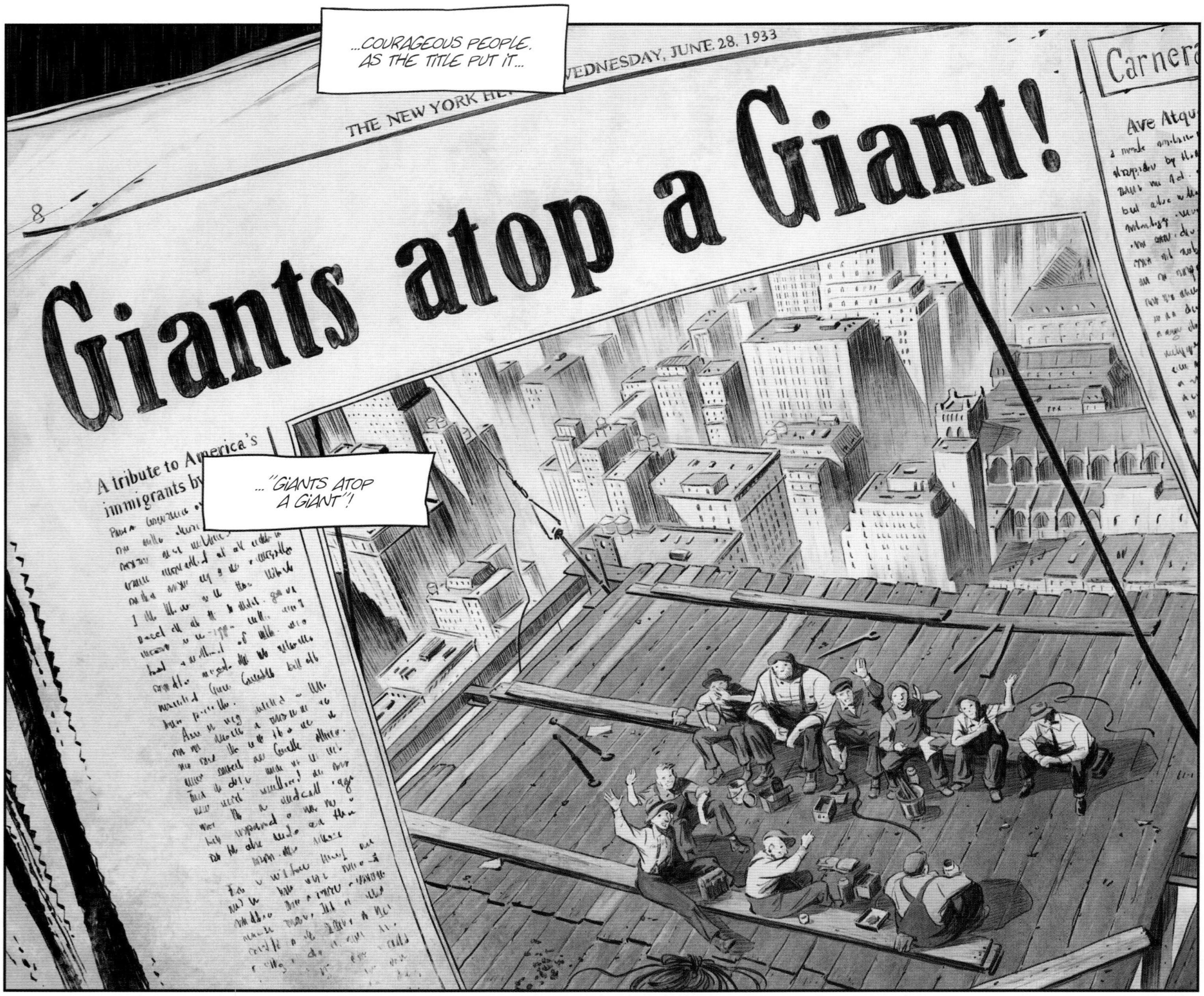
...COURAGEOUS PEOPLE, AS THE TITLE PUT IT...
THE NEW YORK HE... WEDNESDAY, JUNE 28, 1933
Giants atop a Giant!
8
Carnera
Ave Atqu
A tribute to America's immigrants by
..."GIANTS ATOP A GIANT"!

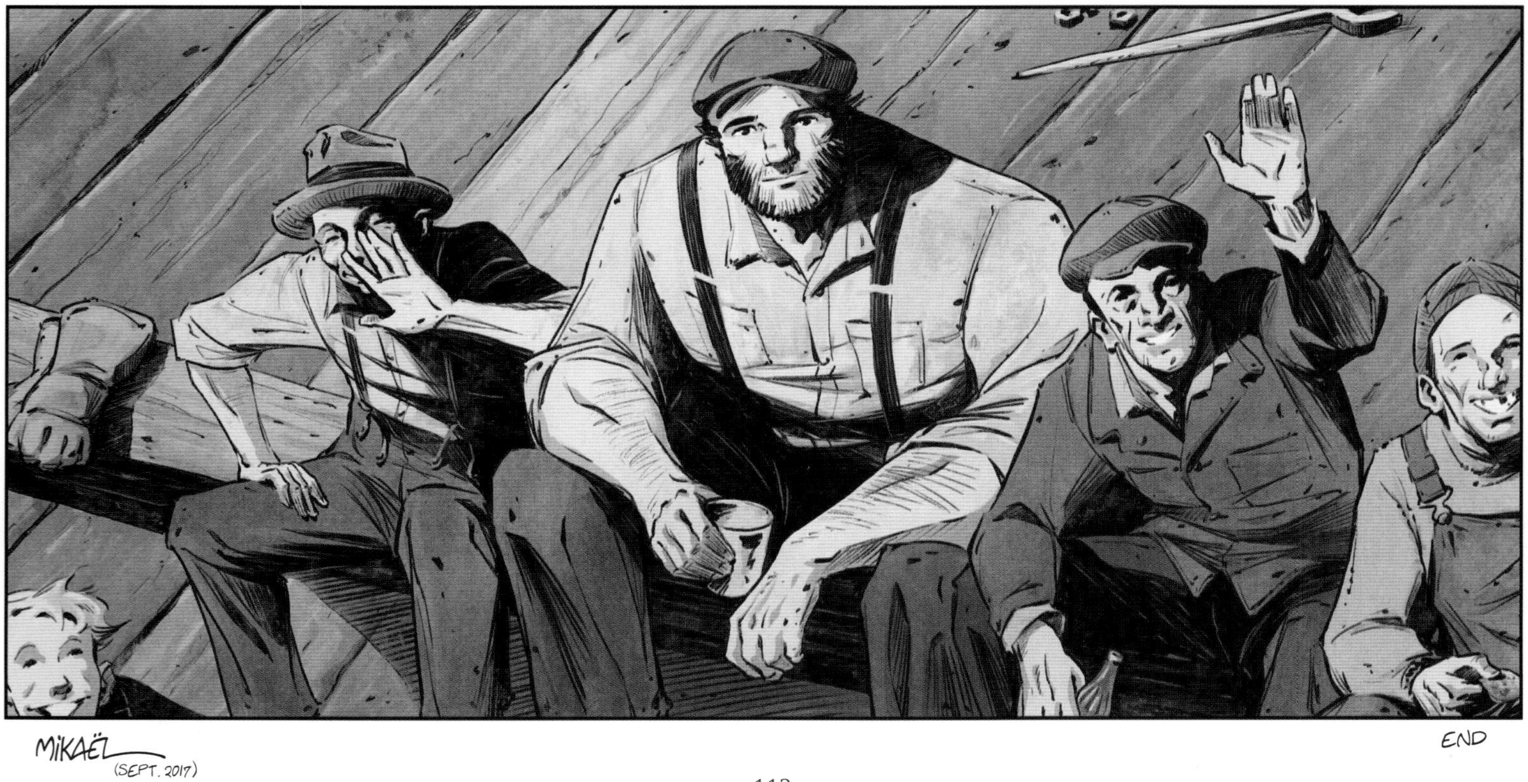

MIKAËL (SEPT. 2017)

END

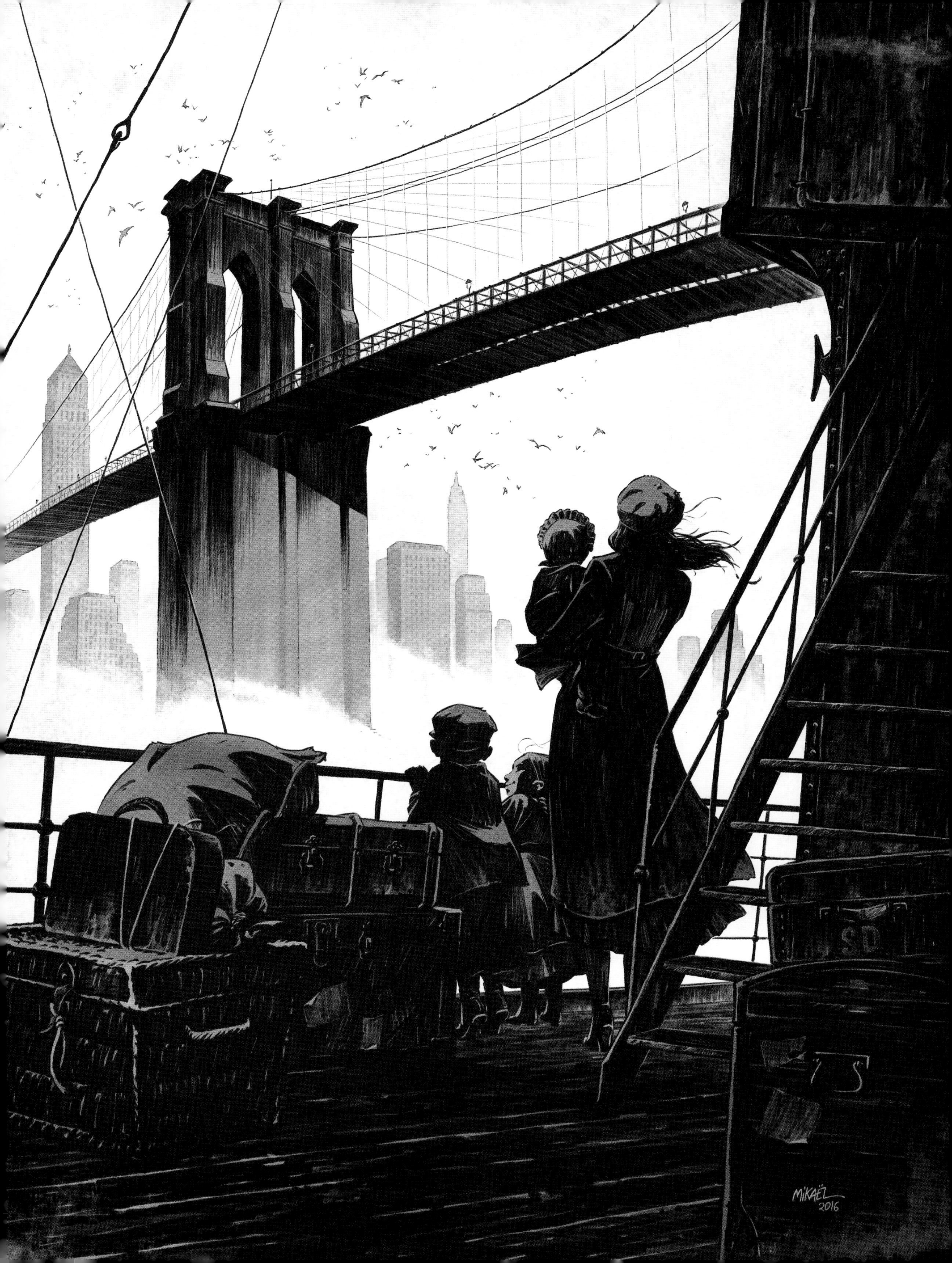
SD
MIKAËL
2016

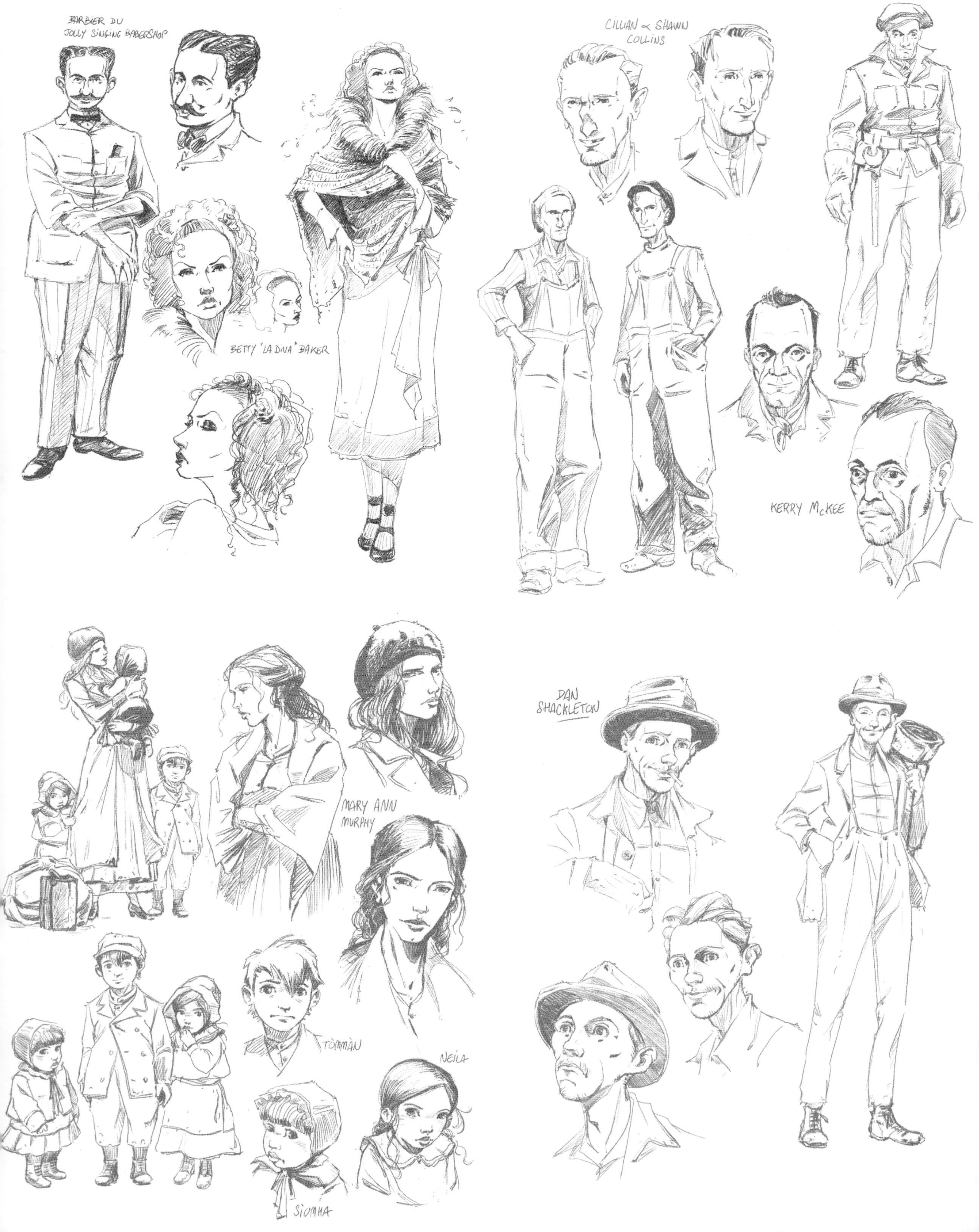

BARBIER DU
JOLLY SINGING BABERSHOP
BETTY "LA DIVA" BAKER
CILLIAN & SHAWN
COLLINS
KERRY McKEE
MARY ANN
MURPHY
TÒMMÀN
NEILA
SIOMHA
DAN
SHACKLETON

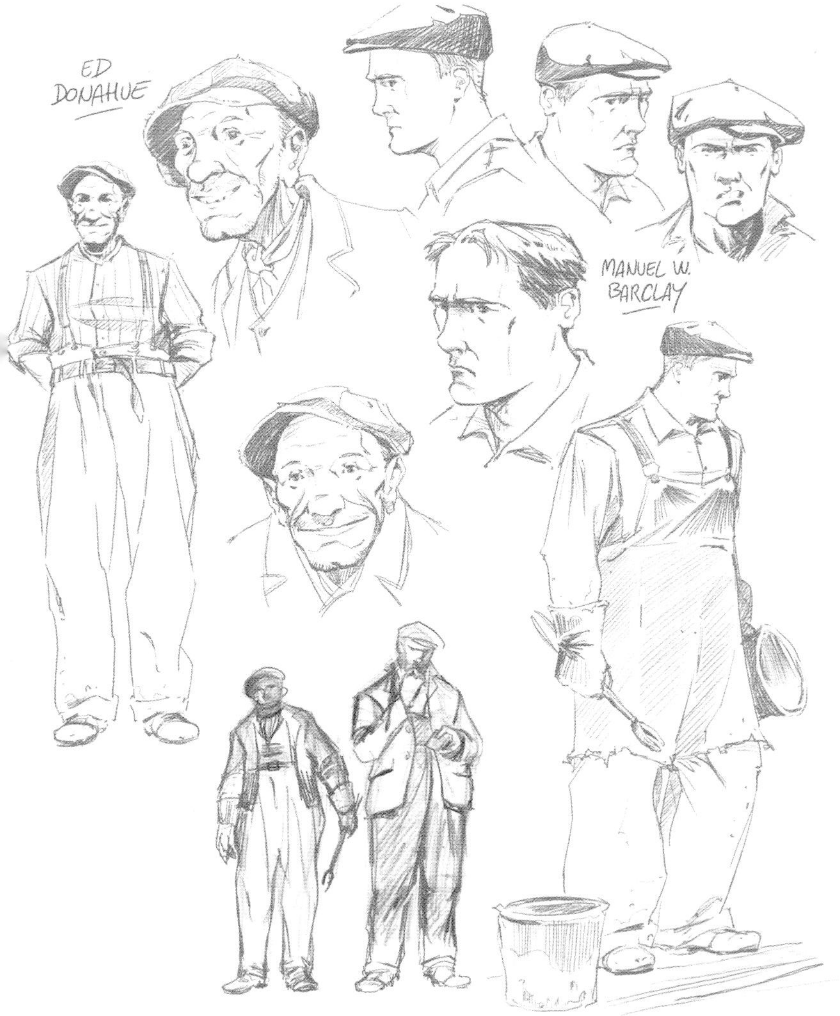
ED DONAHUE
MANUEL W. BARCLAY

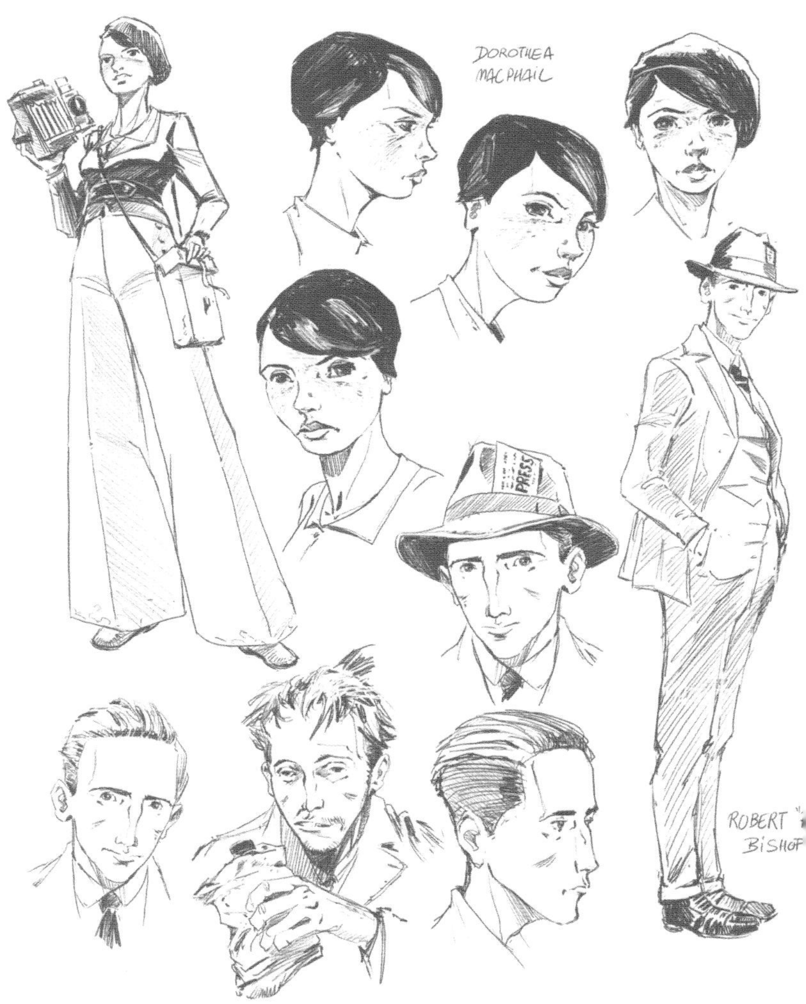
DOROTHEA MACPHAIL
PRESS
ROBERT " BISHOF

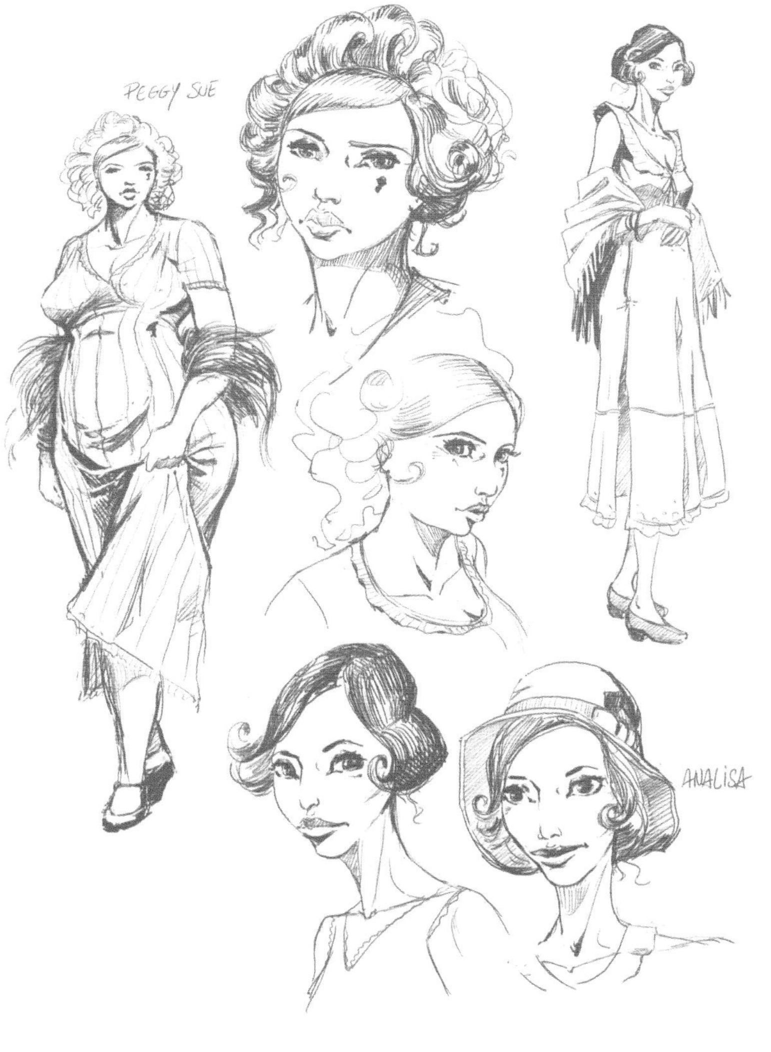
PEGGY SUE
ANALISA

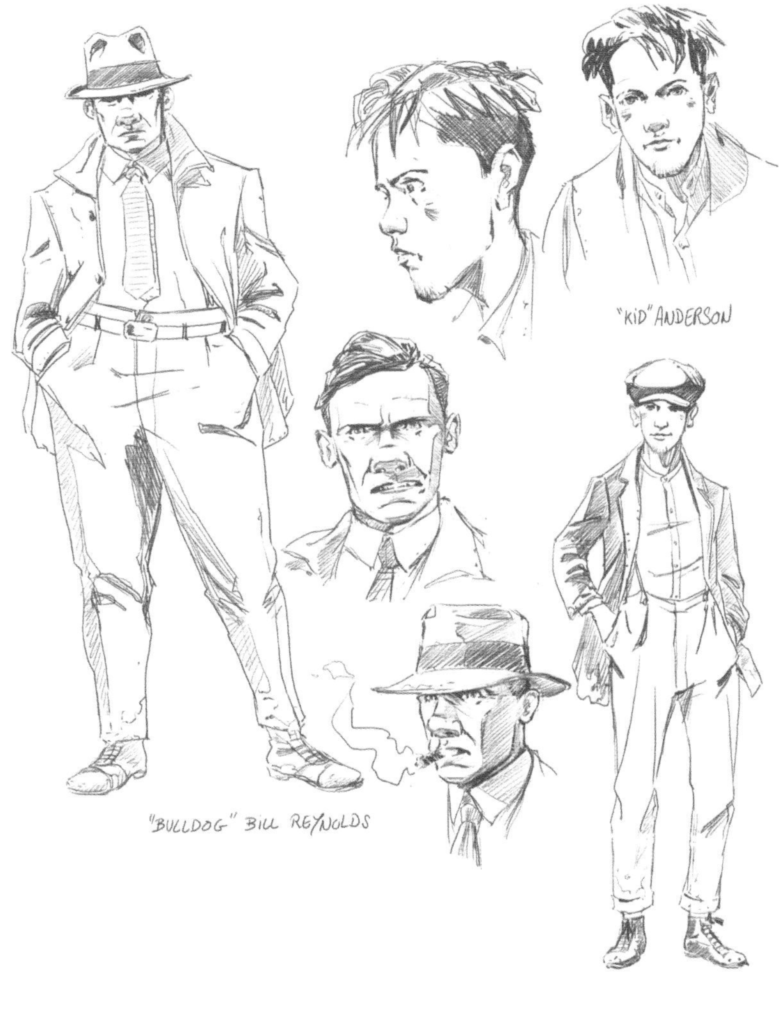
"KID" ANDERSON
"BULLDOG" BILL REYNOLDS

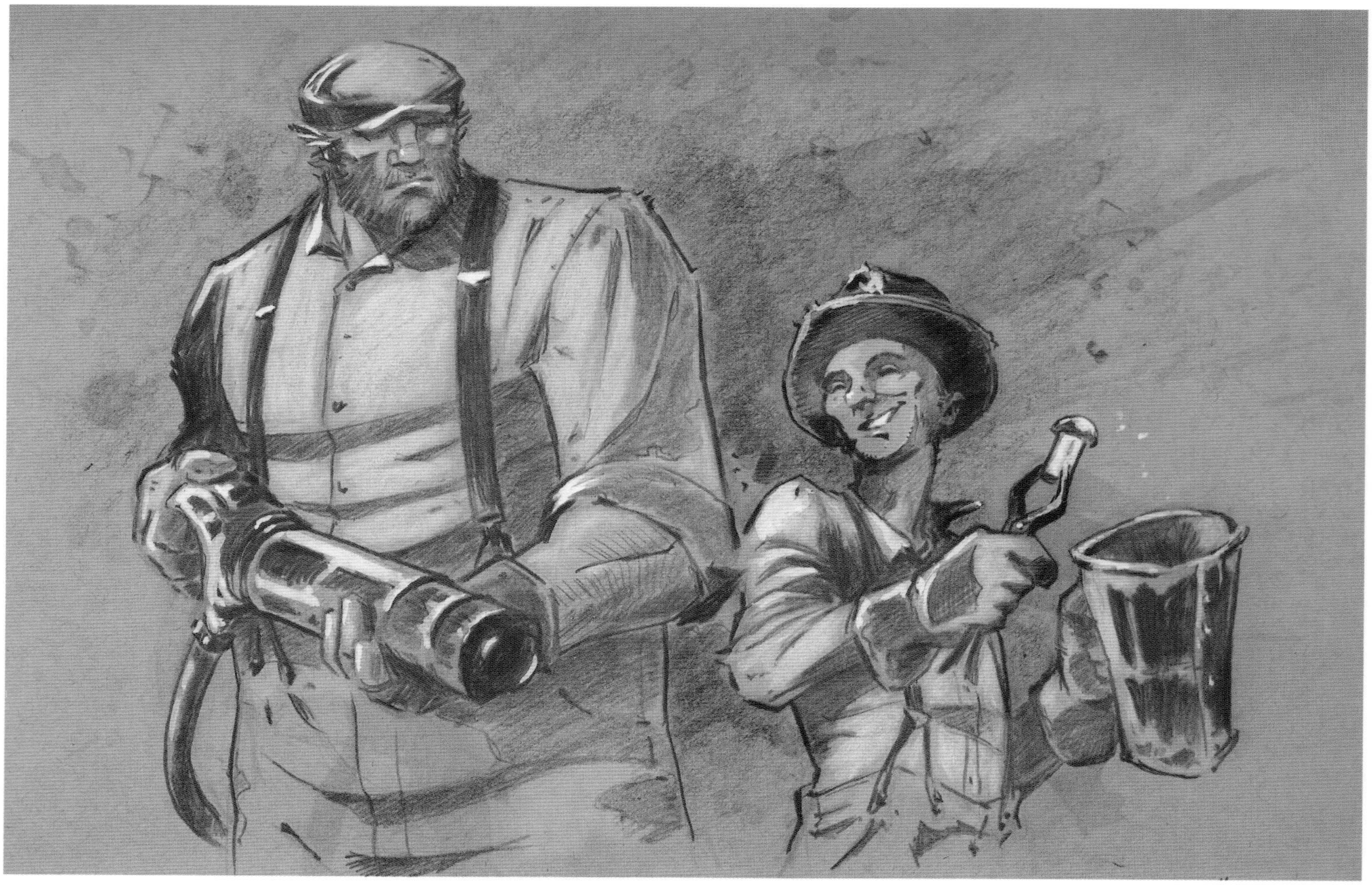
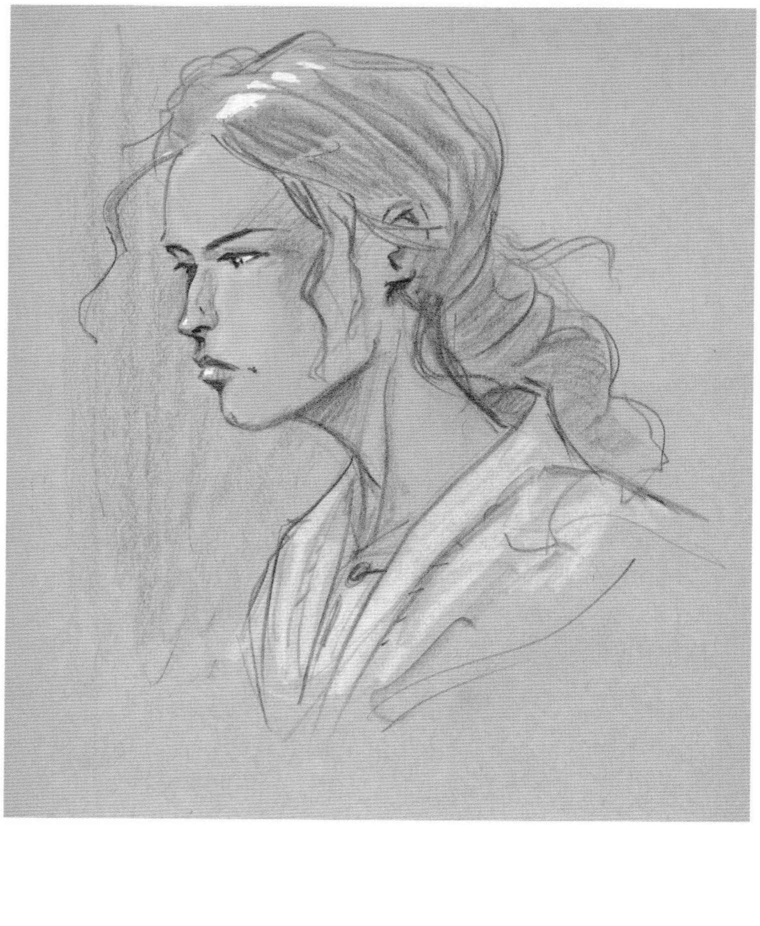
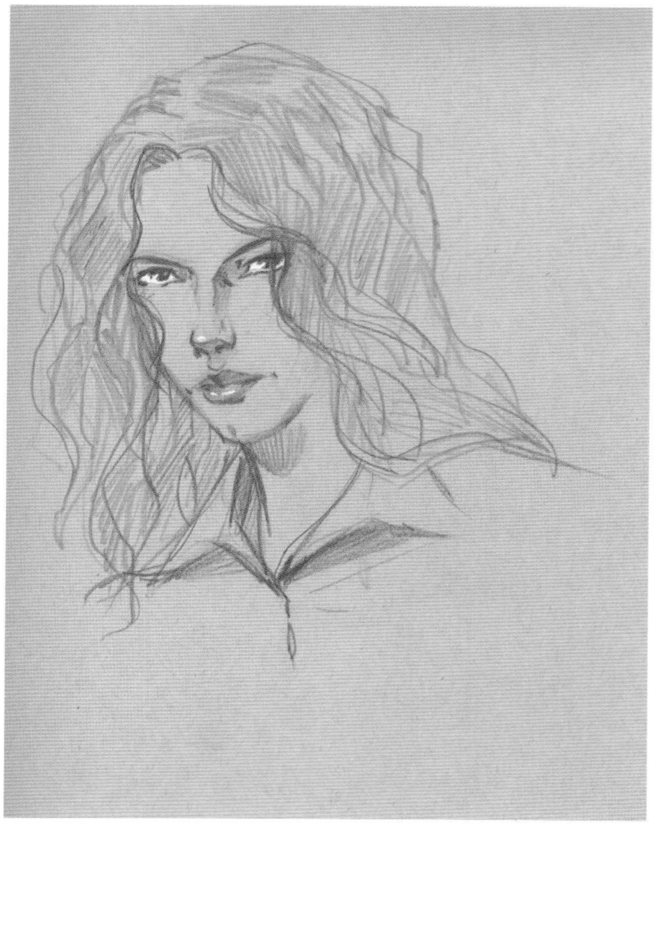

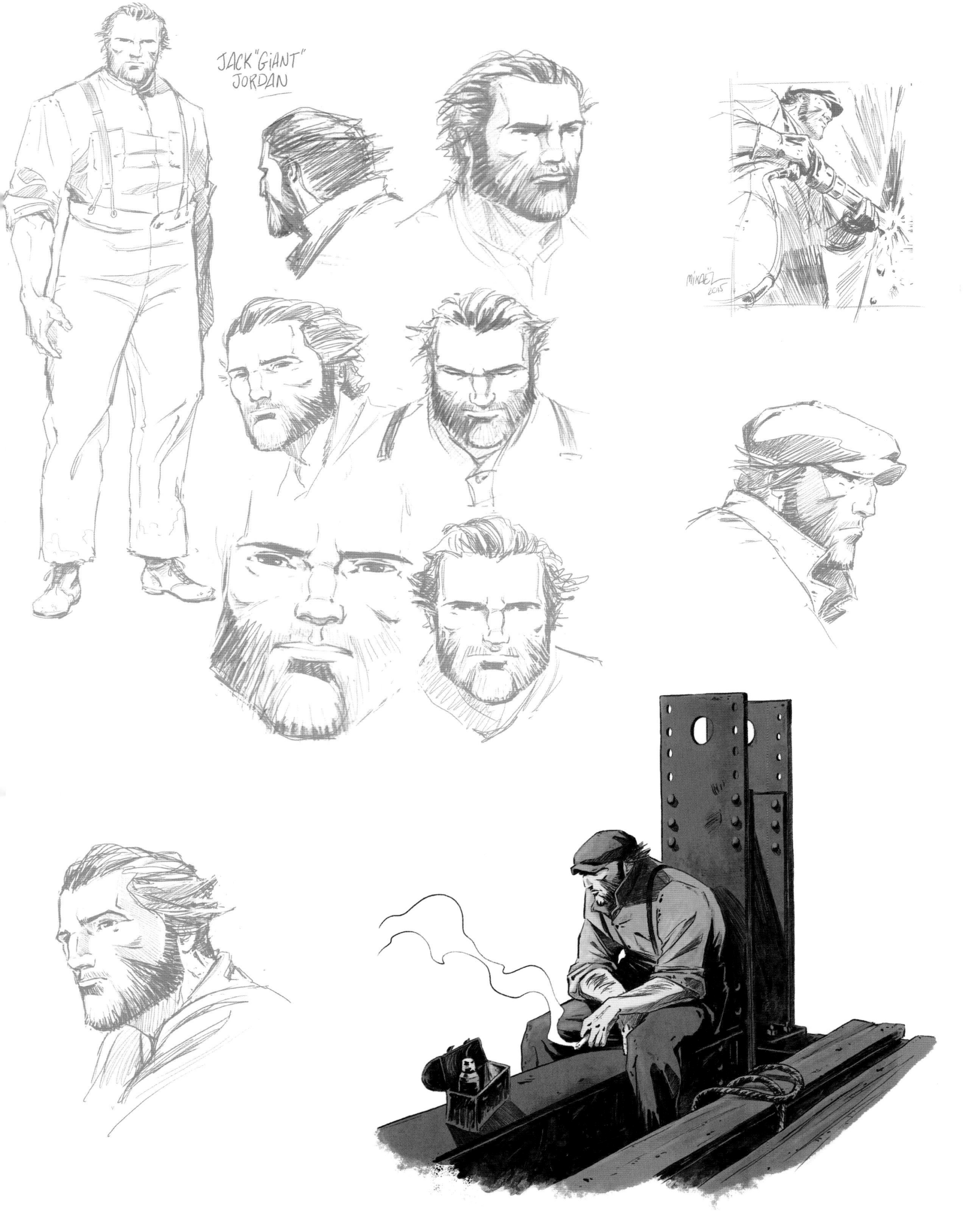
JACK "GiANT"
JORDAN
MiKAËL
2015

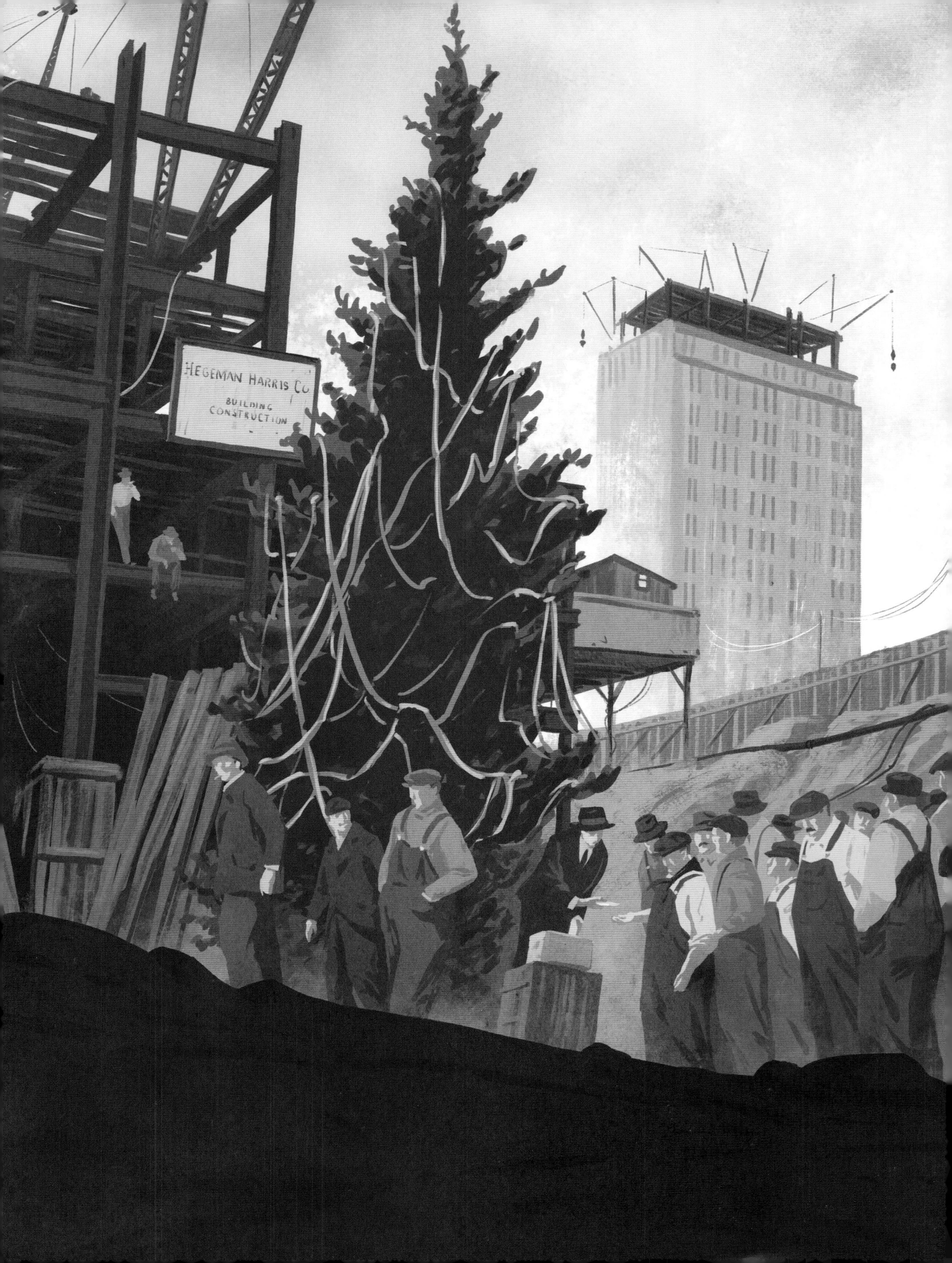
HEGEMAN HARRIS CO
BUILDING
CONSTRUCTION

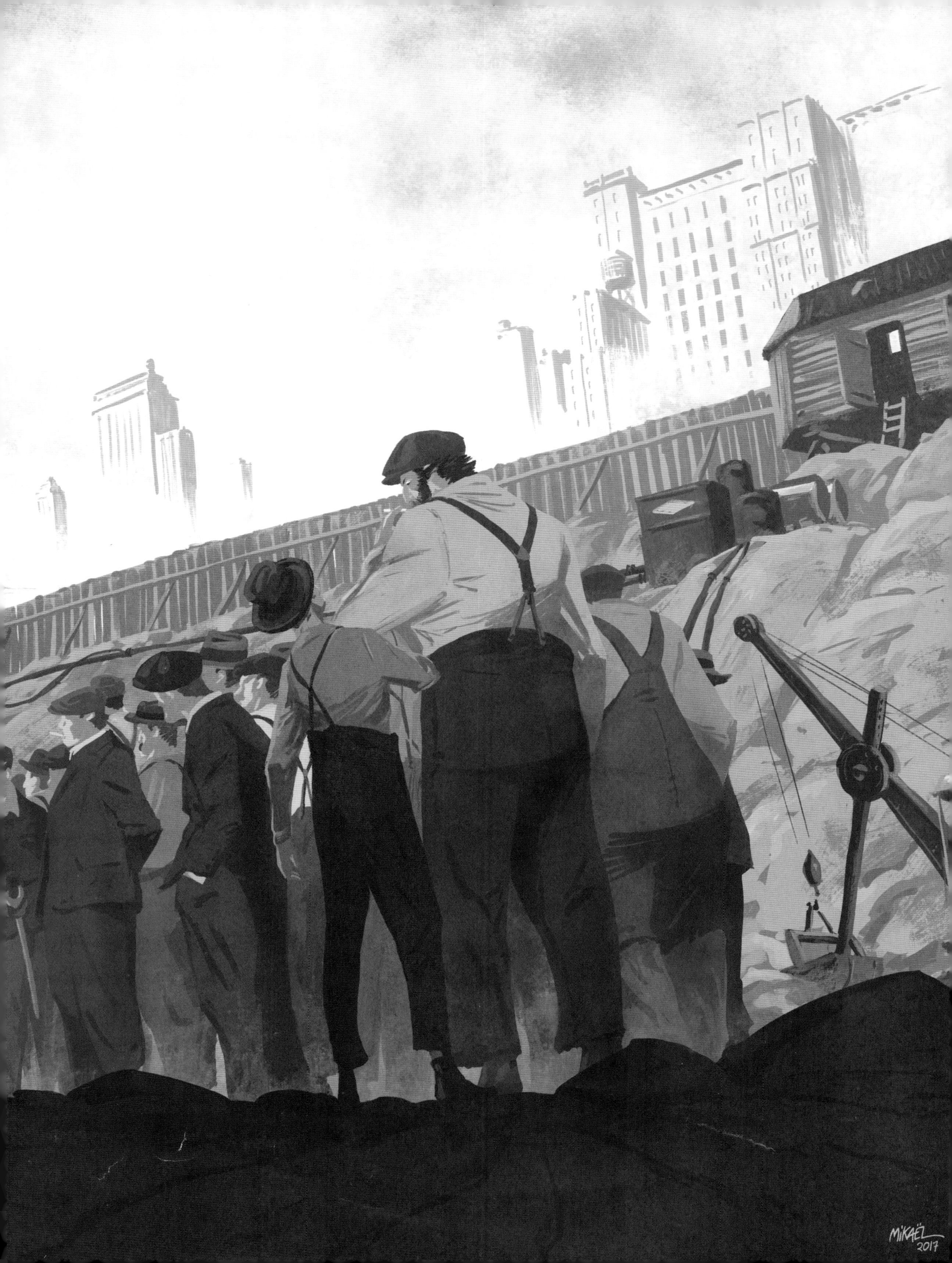
MIKAËL
2017

Teresa Radice
Stefano Turconi
THE FORBIDDEN HARBOR
nbm

750cc DOWN LINCOLN HIGHWAY
BERNARD CHAMBAZ
BARROUX
nbm

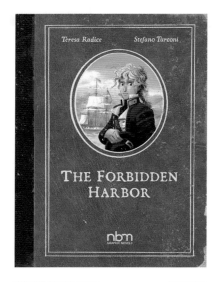